ABSOLUTE BEGINNER'S GUIDE

TO

Microsoft® Office
Access 2003

Mike Gunderloy
Susan Sales Harkins

800 East 96th Street,
Indianapolis, Indiana 46240

Absolute Beginner's Guide to Microsoft® Office Access 2003

International Standard Book Number: 0-7897-2940-7

Library of Congress Catalog Card Number: 2003102739

Printed in the United States of America

First Printing: August 2003

05   04   03   02   4   3   2   1

Trademarks

All terms mentioned in this book that are known to be trademarks or service marks have been appropriately capitalized. Que Publishing cannot attest to the accuracy of this information. Use of a term in this book should not be regarded as affecting the validity of any trademark or service mark.

Microsoft and Access 2003 are registered trademarks of Microsoft Corporation.

Warning and Disclaimer

Every effort has been made to make this book as complete and as accurate as possible, but no warranty or fitness is implied. The information provided is on an "as is" basis. The author and the publisher shall have neither liability nor responsibility to any person or entity with respect to any loss or damages arising from the information contained in this book.

Bulk Sales

Que Publishing offers excellent discounts on this book when ordered in quantity for bulk purchases or special sales. For more information, please contact:

U.S. Corporate and Government Sales
1-800-382-3419
corpsales@pearsontechgroup.com

For sales outside of the U.S., please contact:

International Sales
+1-317-581-3793
international@pearsontechgroup.com

Associate Publisher
Michael Stephens

Acquisitions Editor
Loretta Yates

Development Editor
Sean Dixon

Managing Editor
Charlotte Clapp

Project Editor
Matthew Purcell

Indexer
Ken Johnson

Proofreader
Juli Cook

Technical Editor
Mark Hall

Team Coordinator
Cindy Teeters

Interior Designer
Anne Jones

Cover Designer
Anne Jones

Page Layout
Cheryl Lynch
Michelle Mitchell
Heather Stephenson

Graphics
Tammy Graham
Laura Robbins

Contents at a Glance

Table of Contents

Index

About the Author

Mike Gunderloy is an independent developer and author who has been working with computers for 25 years. He's been using databases since the release of PC-File for DOS, and has been writing and speaking about Microsoft Access ever since version 1.1 was released in 1993. Over the last decade he's spoken about Access at conferences, written Access courseware, and contributed numerous articles about Access and other database topics to magazines including *Smart Access*, *Access-VB-SQL Advisor*, and *Microsoft Office Solutions*. He's worked closely with the Access product team in that time, and has contributed code to several versions as a member of the development team.

Mike has written or contributed to more than thirty books on Access and other database and development topics. He's currently the editor of the monthly *Developer Central* newsletter as well as Pinnacle Publishing's *Hardcore Web Services* newsletter.

Susan Sales Harkins is an independent consultant with an expertise in Access. *SQL: Access to SQL Server*, (Apress) her latest book on Access, was released in January 2002. "Mastering Dreamweaver MX Databases," by Sybex is due to be released in January 2003. Currently, Susan writes for a number of technology-based publishers and magazines including Element K Journals, builder.com, devx.com. Susan has written *Using Microsoft Access 2000*, and *Using Microsoft Access 97, 2E* for Que.

Dedication

To Digi-Comp and CARDIAC, who got me started

—Mike Gunderloy

To Orega, who quietly works behind the scenes toward all I accomplish.

—Susan Sales Harkins

Acknowledgments

One of the best things about writing a book is finishing it and getting to thank all of the other people who contributed. Authors can come up with a pile of manuscript (or, these days, computer files), but many other people are essential for producing the printed book that you're reading. So our thanks to Acquisitions Editor Loretta Yates, Development Editor Sean Dixon, Project Editor Matt Purcell, and Technical Editor Mark Hall. We'd also like to thank Stephanie McComb, who got us started on the first edition of this book. Thanks go out also to our able production staff. We couldn't have done it without you.

Access 2003 is the eighth version of Access. Although the program has come a long way in that time, an Access 1.0 developer would still recognize the version that we work with today. The original Access team and their successors did phenomenal work in coming up with this groundbreaking database, and we're pleased to build on their work. There's no way to individually thank the hundreds of developers, testers, writers, and managers at Microsoft who pulled together Access, but we are keenly aware of their contribution to this book.

Of course, we each have our own support system as well. Mike's consists of his wife Dana and his wonderful kids Adam and Kayla, who help out around the farm, appreciate home-cooked meals, play, smile, and otherwise make life worthwhile. And big thanks to Susan for being such a great writing partner.

Susan thanks Mike Gunderloy for agreeing to take on the project at the last minute and to Stephanie McComb at Que for contacting me about the book. Thanks to The Cobb Group for changing the focus of my career. Mostly, I thank my family for helping me to work from home in my socks and sweatshirt.

We Want to Hear from You!

As the reader of this book, *you* are our most important critic and commentator. We value your opinion and want to know what we're doing right, what we could do better, what areas you'd like to see us publish in, and any other words of wisdom you're willing to pass our way.

As an associate publisher for Que Publishing, I welcome your comments. You can email or write me directly to let me know what you did or didn't like about this book—as well as what we can do to make our books better.

Please note that I cannot help you with technical problems related to the *topic* of this book. We do have a User Services group, however, where I will forward specific technical questions related to the book.

When you write, please be sure to include this book's title and author as well as your name, email address, and phone number. I will carefully review your comments and share them with the author and editors who worked on the book.

Email: feedback@quepublishing.com

Mail: Michael Stephens
             Que Publishing
             800 East 96th Street
             Indianapolis, IN 46240 USA

For more information about this book or another Que title, visit our Web site at www.quepublishing.com. Type the ISBN (excluding hyphens) or the title of a book in the Search field to find the page you're looking for.

Introduction

Maybe you picked this book up because you already know you want to learn about Access, Microsoft's user-friendly database for the Windows operating system. Or perhaps you know that you're drowning in a sea of information and vaguely think that Access might be the answer. Then again, maybe you just liked the cover. Whatever the reason, welcome! We think you've come to the right place.

As we said, Access is a *database*. What does that mean? You'll learn more in this book, but for now, think of Access as a handy place to store and organize things. You can store almost anything you please in an Access database:

- Your recipe collection
- Pictures of your pets
- The inventory records for your home-based business
- Birthdays and addresses of friends and relatives
- The author and title of every book you own
- Just about anything else you can think of

Databases are used by everyone from grandmothers to major corporations. If you've never used a database before, don't worry. Access is the friendliest and easiest-to-use database on the market today. If you can click a mouse and type, you can use Access.

Some Key Terms

Access runs on the Windows operating system. We'll be using Microsoft Office Access 2003 (which we'll just call "Access 2003" in the rest of this book), which runs on Windows 95 or any later version of Windows. We assume that you already know how to start Windows, log in, and use the mouse; from there, we'll teach you everything else that you need to know to get started.

There are some key terms you should know. Understanding the distinctions between these various actions will help you follow the numerous step-by-step examples in this book on your own computer.

- Press—By itself, usually refers to a key on the keyboard. When we tell you to press F11, it means to press and release the F11 key on the top row of the keyboard. To press Alt-F, hold down the Alt key and press and release the F key before letting go of the Alt key.

- Point—Move the mouse on the desk to move the pointer onscreen. The tip of the arrow should be on the item to which you are pointing. To open a menu or an icon, you point to the item you want.

- Click—Press and release the primary mouse button once. Usually this will be the left mouse button, though if you're a leftie you may have changed this. You use click to select commands and toolbar buttons, as well as perform other Windows tasks.

- Double-click—Press and release the primary mouse button twice in rapid succession. Double-clicking opens an icon or launches an action.

- Right-click—Press and release the right mouse button once. You often right-click to display a shortcut menu.

- Drag—Hold down the mouse button and drag the pointer across the screen. Release the mouse button. Dragging is most often used for selecting text.

- Drag and Drop—Point to the item that you want to drag and hold down the primary mouse button. Now you can move the mouse to drag the item around the screen. When you've dragged the item to the location where you'd like to drop it, release the mouse button.

Some Things to Keep in Mind

You can personalize many features of Windows so that it is set up the way you like to work. That's one of the benefits of Windows. For consistency, though, this book makes some assumptions about how you use your computer. When working through steps and especially when viewing the figures in this book, keep in mind the following distinctions:

- Access provides many ways to perform the same action. For instance, for many commands, you can select a command from a menu, use a shortcut key, use a toolbar button, or use a shortcut menu. Throughout the book, we'll try to show you the variety of different ways that you can do things in Access. Sometimes we'll tell you where to find an action on a menu; other times we might have you use the toolbar to perform the same action. As you try things out in Access, you'll find the methods that work best for you.

- Your particular Windows setup may not look identical to the one used in the figures in this book. For instance, you might have a different desktop background than the one we used in the book, or be using a different color scheme. Don't let these differences distract you; Windows may look different, but it works the same way.

■ Your computer setup is most likely different from the one used in the book. Therefore, you will see different programs listed on your Start menu, different folders and documents, and so on. Again, don't be distracted by the differences.

■ You might even be using a different version of Windows. We used Windows XP throughout this book. If you're using a different version of Windows, there will be minor differences in appearance, but Access will still function exactly the same way.

The Basic Structure of This Book

This book is divided into five parts, each centered around a certain theme. The book builds on the skills you need, starting with the basics and then moving to more complex topics such as customizing databases or working with other applications. You can read the book straight-through, look up topics when you have a question, or browse through the contents, reading information that intrigues you. We've also included many references between chapters to help you find more information.

This section provides a quick breakdown of the parts.

Part I, "Getting to Know Access," guides you through an exploration of the Access user interface. This part of the book will help you to recognize all the things that you see on screen when Access is running, and to understand what you'll see in a database. This part covers the use of databases in general (Chapter 1), the Access user interface (Chapter 2), and the Database Window, which is the central starting point of your Access databases (Chapter 3).

Part II, "Building and Using a Database," contains four chapters. If you read through this part, you'll learn enough to actually build your own database and to use it for data storage. Topics include planning a database (Chapter 4), creating tables to hold your data (Chapter 5), connecting tables to each other (Chapter 6), and writing queries to extract information from the database (Chapter 7).

Part III, "Putting a Friendly Face on Your Data," helps you design the user interface for your database. Here you'll learn about data entry forms (Chapter 8), printed reports (Chapter 9), and Web-based pages (Chapter 10). By the time you reach the end of Chapter 10, you'll be familiar with all of the major objects that an Access database can contain, and you'll know how to build each one.

Part IV, "Making Access Work Your Way," shows you how to fine-tune the objects you've already built. You'll learn about more techniques for tables (Chapter 11), queries (Chapter 12), forms (Chapter 13), and reports (Chapter 14). You might not need this part until you've worked with Access for a few weeks or months, but skimming through it might give you some ideas.

Finally, Part V, "Letting Access Do Your Work for You," covers two topics that will help point the way for further explorations in Access. Chapter 15 discusses automating your Access databases so that the program does repetitive tasks for you. Chapter 16 shows you how to exchange data between Access and a variety of other programs, so that you can make the most of Microsoft Office. In Chapter 17, you'll learn how to use Office features inside Access.

We hope you'll learn to enjoy Access as much as we do!

Conventions Used in This Book

There are cautions, tips, and notes throughout this book.

caution

A *caution* will tell you to beware of a potentially dangerous act or situation. In some cases, ignoring a caution could cause you significant problems—so pay particular attention to them!

note

A *note* is designed to provide information that is generally useful, but not necessarily essential for what you're doing at the moment. Some are like extended tips—interesting, but not essential.

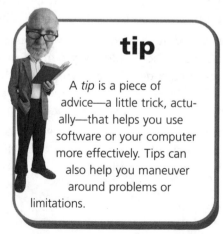

tip

A *tip* is a piece of advice—a little trick, actually—that helps you use software or your computer more effectively. Tips can also help you maneuver around problems or limitations.

Contacting the Authors

One of the best things about writing a book is the opportunity to hear from readers. We can't write your databases for you, but we'd be happy to hear from you if something's not clear, or if you just want to tell us how much you liked the book. You can email Susan at `harkins@iglou.com`, or Mike at `MikeG1@larkfarm.com`.

PART

1

GETTING TO KNOW ACCESS

IN THIS CHAPTER

- Why you need a database
- What databases can do for you that spreadsheets can't
- How to launch Microsoft Access
- A quick test drive of an Access database

1

WELCOME TO DATABASES

Perhaps you've been looking at the Microsoft Access icon on your Start menu and wondering what you can use it for. Or perhaps you already have a database project in mind and don't quite know how to get started. Either way, you've come to the right place! Microsoft Access combines a friendly and easy-to-use interface with many powerful and professional features to produce a database anyone can use. As you work with Access, you'll discover new ways to view your data and turn that data into meaningful information. In this book, we'll help you go from that Start menu icon to a full working Access application.

But maybe you're not yet sure that you want to build a database. Can't you just stick with the spreadsheet interface of Microsoft Excel? In this chapter, we'll answer those questions and then give you a quick look at some of the useful and friendly features of Access.

What Can You Do with a Database?

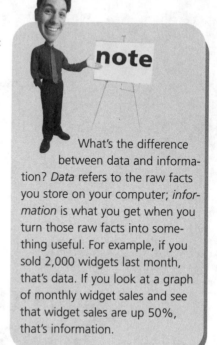

Perhaps the better question would be the following: What *can't* you do with a database?

The most basic feature of databases is that they provide unified storage for all the data related to a particular topic. Rather than scatter information through a series of Word documents, Excel spreadsheets, text files, email messages, and sticky notes, you can bring it all together in a database. A database can hold something as simple as the list of guests for your wedding or something as complex as every customer who has ever visited your e-commerce Web site and every order they've ever placed.

But a database can do much more than just store reams of data for you. Here are some of the other capabilities of Microsoft Access that you'll learn about in this book:

> **note**
>
> What's the difference between data and information? *Data* refers to the raw facts you store on your computer; *information* is what you get when you turn those raw facts into something useful. For example, if you sold 2,000 widgets last month, that's data. If you look at a graph of monthly widget sales and see that widget sales are up 50%, that's information.

- Present an easy-to-use interface for entering new data
- Find related data quickly (for example, find all books by a particular author)
- Display your data as a chart, graph, or Web page
- Provide easy-to-understand reports that can be printed or displayed onscreen
- Export data to Microsoft Word or Microsoft Excel
- Protect your data from errors
- Automate common operations to cut down on typing

The more you work with Access, the more you'll want to work with it. This book will get you up and running quickly. Then the sky's the limit!

Why Not Just Use Excel?

Many people learn to use spreadsheets at the very start of their computer experience. Of course, Microsoft Excel is the premiere spreadsheet today, offering fabulous flexibility and ease of use. So, why not just keep all your data in Excel? The spreadsheet in Figure 1.1 shows just a few of the problems that crop up when you try to use a spreadsheet like a database.

FIGURE 1.1

Data stored in an Excel spreadsheet.

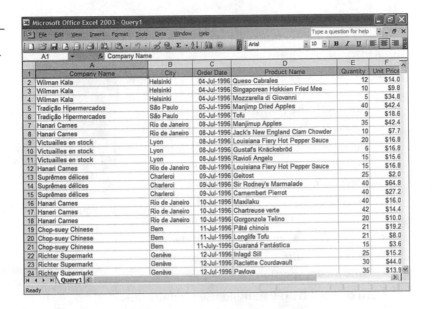

Even though it looks like this spreadsheet is doing a good job of tracking customers and orders, there are four problems with it:

■ In cell A17 (that is, the cell in the first column of row 17), the customer's name is spelled "Haneri Carnes." Everywhere else, the customer's name is spelled "Hanari Carnes."

■ In cell C21, July is spelled out. This is inconsistent with the other cells, where it's abbreviated.

■ In cell D5, the product name is "Manjimp Dried Applies." In cell D7, the product name is "Manjimup Apples." Which one is right? Or are these two different products?

■ To see the fourth problem, put yourself in the shoes of the person maintaining this spreadsheet. Each time an order comes in, you need to type the company name, over and over again, along with the city and any other information (such as a telephone number or address) that you're tracking for customers. No wonder there are typos in the customer name!

The basic problem is that Excel does not have good facilities for checking data integrity. If you type a name incorrectly or enter a date that isn't really a date, Excel won't tell you. The problem is more than just cosmetic. You might have heard the expression "garbage in, garbage out." Suppose your boss asks you to find out how many products have been ordered by Hanari Carnes. If you search the spreadsheet for that customer name, you'll miss the row in which the name is spelled incorrectly.

Without going into any depth, we can tell you right now that Access has solutions for all these problems:

- Access stores each piece of data (such as a customer name) in just one place. You can't type the name the wrong way because you're not constantly retyping it.

- Access can force some pieces of data to match particular patterns. For example, you can make sure that only valid dates are entered as order dates and that the same format is used for every date.

- Access can easily check a set of data to find all the different values it contains. This makes spotting typos easier.

- Access can help you build user-friendly data entry interfaces (called *forms* in Access). Instead of typing the customer name for every order, you can just select the name from a list onscreen.

There's another reason Access is a better choice than Excel for many business uses. If you've ever tried to share an Excel spreadsheet with another user, you know that only one person can edit an Excel spreadsheet at a time. If two people want to use the same spreadsheet, they have to wait and take turns. Not so with Access! Access is designed for multiuser scenarios. If you need to type in inventory information while another user edits product names in the same database, there's no problem. More than one user can even access the same types of data at the same time. If a user happens to request a record that's already in use, he might have to wait a second or two until the first user is done. For the most part, many users can happily work with the data at the same time.

tip

What happens if you want to store your data in Access and work with it in Excel? No problem! When you want to take advantage of one of Excel's features (such as its flexible charting interface), you can export Access data to Excel. You'll learn how to do this in Chapter 16, "Sharing Data."

note

Access is an example of a desktop database designed for one user, a workgroup, or a small department. In theory, an Access database can accommodate 255 users simultaneously. In practice, you'll probably find acceptable performance until you get up to around 50 users.

A Sample Database: Northwind Traders

Rather than tell you any more about the features of Microsoft Access, we're going to show you. Figure 1.2 shows the opening form of the Northwind Traders sample database in Access 2003. (Northwind will first display a splash screen until you check the Don't show this screen again option.) This sample database ships with Access 2003, and it demonstrates many of the features of Access. (If you can't find Northwind, you might need to install it from the Office CD.)

note

You'll learn how to launch Access and how to open a database in Chapter 2, "Take a Quick Tour of Access." For now, just sit back and enjoy the ride.

The Main Switchboard is the starting point of this particular database. When the user opens the database, it automatically displays the Access form in Figure 1.2. You can see a hint of the complexity of Access behind the Main Switchboard, in the area called the Database window. But don't worry—you'll learn about that complexity in easy pieces throughout this book.

FIGURE 1.2

The Main Switchboard in the Northwind sample database.

The Main Switchboard is really just a specialized form that serves as a guide from task to task. The user doesn't have to know a thing about the actual objects in the database—she simply clicks the appropriate button to open the form or report that's needed to complete the task at hand. You'll learn more about creating and working with switchboards in Chapter 15, "Automating Your Database."

Clicking the Categories button on the Main Switchboard opens another form, shown in Figure 1.3.

FIGURE 1.3

Looking at product information in Categories.

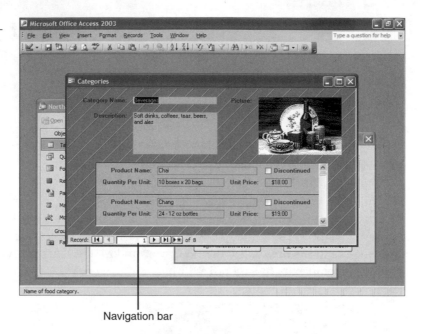

Navigation bar

Here you can see that Access is capable of constructing all sorts of graphical interfaces. The striped background and the picture on the form are both stored as part of the database. Figure 1.3 shows the Beverages category. It also shows you a couple of the products (Chai and Chang) that are part of this category.

The set of arrows at the bottom of the form is called the *navigation bar*. The navigation bar lets you move easily to other parts of the data. You'll learn more about it in Chapter 5, "Building Your First Tables."

Forms can have many looks and functions. Figure 1.4 shows another form from the Northwind sample database. This Customer Phone List form includes a set of push buttons along the bottom. When you push a button, the form shows only the customers whose names start with the selected letter. You can see how this makes working with the data simpler: Instead of wading through a long list of customers, you can jump directly to the customer you want.

Figure 1.5 shows another example of a flexible user interface that you can create with Access. When the user clicks the Print Sales Reports button on the Main Switchboard, this form pops up to prompt the user for further details. After he selects a report in the Report to Print section, he can click the Preview button to see the report onscreen or click the Print button to send it directly to the printer.

FIGURE 1.4

A form that helps you select specific information.

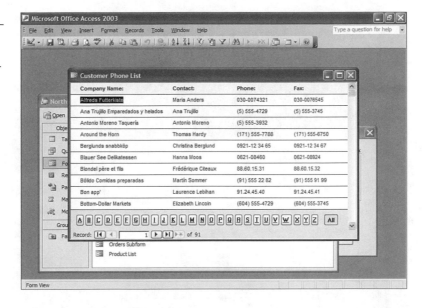

FIGURE 1.5

Guiding the user through a complex process.

Radio buttons

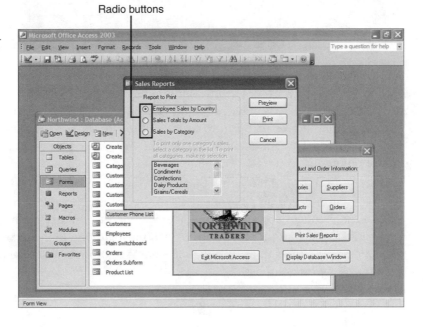

Figure 1.6 shows one of the reports from the Sales Reports form open in preview mode. As you can see, the reports can summarize information. In this case, the report has summed the sales for each product in the Beverages category and displayed these totals both numerically and on a graph. We've clicked the OfficeLinks toolbar button to give you a hint as to how easily you could send this same view of the data to Word or Excel.

The other toolbar buttons let you control how many pages of the report are displayed, as well as how magnified the view should be. You'll learn more about these options in Chapter 9, "Printing Information with Reports."

FIGURE 1.6

Access reports offer an attractive way to extract information from your data.

Access also offers flexible tools for designing and formatting reports. Figure 1.7 shows a different report—the Northwind product catalog. You could print this and use it to hand out to customers, without needing to use a desktop publishing program or a word processor. Business cards, mailing labels, employee records—Access reports can handle them all. Note the magnifying glass cursor that lets you zoom in on the report onscreen.

Want to publish your data on the Internet? With Access, that's no problem. Figure 1.8 shows an Access data page open in the Internet Explorer Web browser. This page takes data about employees from the Access database and displays it for the Web. Hyperlinks at the bottom of the page let you move around to the records for other employees. You can even edit the data in your Web browser and save the changes back to the Access database!

Magnifying Glass cursor

FIGURE 1.7
The Product
Catalog report is
suitable for
handing out at
trade shows.

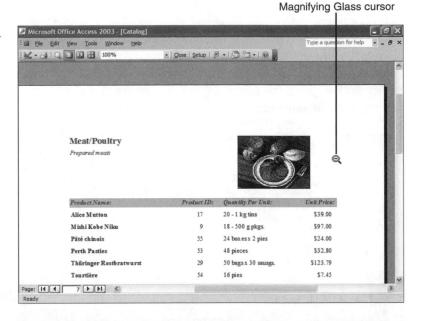

FIGURE 1.8
Data from an
Access database
can be displayed
and even edited
in a Web
browser.

After seeing the various ways in which your data can be presented (forms, reports, and pages), you might be wondering where the data is stored. The answer is that Access doesn't store data in any of these objects! Instead, it keeps its data in tables. A table, as you can see in Figure 1.9, resembles a spreadsheet; it holds rows and columns of your data. But in most Access databases, you won't work directly in the tables. Rather, you'll use forms, reports, and pages to make life simpler and more attractive at the same time.

FIGURE 1.9

An Access table provides a view of the raw data in your database.

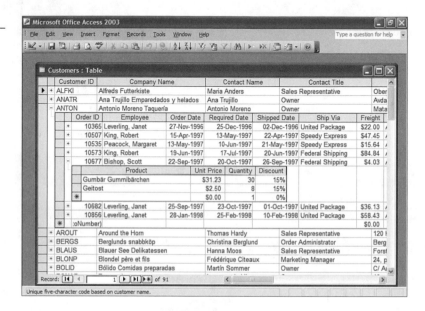

By now, hopefully we've convinced you that an Access database can be a friendly and useful place to work with your data. Whether it's the sales records for your business, your recipe collection, or the contacts for your high school class reunion, you can trust Access to store and organize your data.

What's next? In Chapter 2, you'll learn more about the Access features you've seen in this chapter. You'll see how to launch Access and open a database, and you'll start to become familiar with the toolbars, menus, task panes, and other features of Access itself. Follow along, and you'll be entering data before you know it!

THE ABSOLUTE MINIMUM

In this chapter, you got your first glimpse of Microsoft's desktop database, Access.

You also saw some of the main user interface features of Access:

- Access is Microsoft's desktop database, designed for personal use or small businesses.
- Databases such as Access can protect your data from accidental errors and speed up data entry.
- Access forms offer an easy way to enter and display data.
- Access reports turn your data into attractive printed output.
- Access data pages let you move your data to the Internet.

IN THIS CHAPTER

- Decide whether to begin from scratch or use a template
- Learn how to launch Access and how to create, open, and exit a database
- Become familiar with the application window

2

TAKE A QUICK TOUR OF ACCESS

Getting started might be your biggest hurdle in learning Access. If you've worked with spreadsheets and word processors in the past but never looked at Access, you might be unsure about what a database does and how to get started with it. Access is called a *relational database management system (RDBMS)* because it stores data and provides tools with which you can manipulate that data. Fortunately, Microsoft has gone a long way toward making Access an easy-to-use product, even for the novice.

In this chapter you'll learn where to start. Specifically, we'll show you how to launch Access and how to create, open, and exit a database. We'll also introduce you to the application toolbar, menu bar, and task pane. We recommend that you take the time to learn these basics. Once you're ready to learn Access's more complicated features, you'll be glad you did.

Launching Access

Launching Access couldn't be simpler, especially if you're familiar with other Office products. If you can open one Office product, you can open them all. The following are the two menu options in the Administrator window for launching Access:

■ **Click Start in the Windows taskbar**—If you use Access often, it will appear on the Start menu, as shown in Figure 2.1.

■ **If Access isn't listed in the Start menu, select All Programs and then select Microsoft Office and then Microsoft Office Access 2003 from the resulting submenus**—This is also shown in Figure 2.1. After opening Access, Windows adds it to the Start menu. After you launch Access, Windows displays a small representative button on its taskbar, which is circled in Figure 2.2.

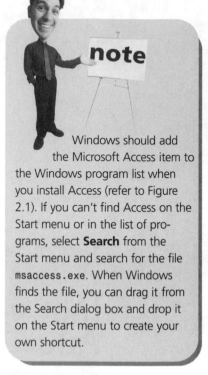

note

Windows should add the Microsoft Access item to the Windows program list when you install Access (refer to Figure 2.1). If you can't find Access on the Start menu or in the list of programs, select **Search** from the Start menu and search for the file `msaccess.exe`. When Windows finds the file, you can drag it from the Search dialog box and drop it on the Start menu to create your own shortcut.

Access on the Start menu

FIGURE 2.1
You can launch Microsoft Access from the Start menu or the All Programs menu.

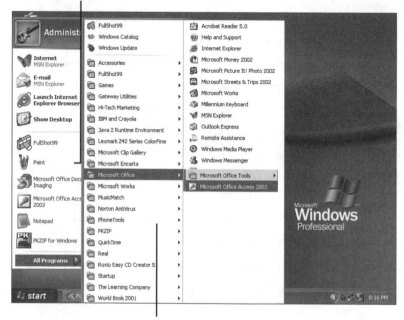

Access on the All Programs Menu

New button

File menu

Task pane

FIGURE 2.2

Look for the Access button on the Windows taskbar when Access is displayed and running on the desktop.

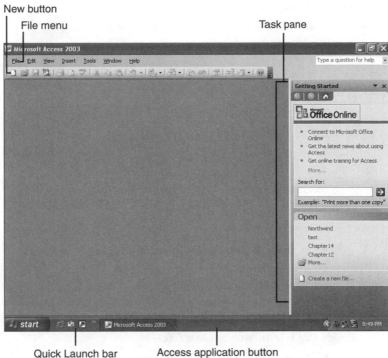

Quick Launch bar

Access application button

Figure 2.2 also shows you the parts of Access you'll most likely work with first. The File menu and the New button let you open or create databases. The task pane provides handy shortcuts to common tasks you might want to perform.

Opening a Database

After you're inside Access the adventure begins (refer to Figure 2.2). Right now, there's no active file, so let's explore the various methods for creating and opening a database:

- Beginning with a blank file
- Basing a new database on an existing database
- Renaming a database
- Using a template

tip

The Windows Quick Launch bar (to the right of the Start button) displays small representative icons for programs. Instead of browsing through all the programs on the Start menu, you can simply click the icon on the Quick Launch bar.

To add Access to the Quick Launch bar, drag the Access icon from the Start menu to the Quick Launch portion of the taskbar. That's all there is to it! If your Quick Launch bar isn't visible, right-click an empty area on the taskbar and select **Toolbars, Quick Launch**.

As you work through these tasks, you'll learn how to use some of the basic parts of the Access interface, including the New button on the database toolbar and the task pane.

Beginning with a Blank File

There are several ways to create a database, but most of the time, you'll probably just start with a blank database that contains no data or any of the other objects you learned about in Chapter 1, "Welcome to Databases." You'll be expected to build your application from the ground up.

Here's how to create a new, blank database:

1. Click the **Blank Database** link under New in the task pane to display the File New Database dialog box. If the task pane isn't open, do one of the following: Click the **New** button on the Database toolbar, select **New** from the **File** menu, or press **Ctrl+N**.

2. In the Save In list box at the top of the dialog box, select **My Documents** (the default).

3. In the File Name text box, enter a name for the database—we entered **MyDatabase**.

4. Don't change the Save As Type option, which defaults to Microsoft Office Access Databases (*.mdb). You'd change this option to create a workgroup file (.mdw), but don't do so now. At this point, your dialog box should resemble the one shown in Figure 2.3. Keep in mind that your system's file hierarchy won't be the same as ours.

5. Click **Create**, and Access displays a blank Database window similar to the one shown in Figure 2.4. The Database window appears within the overall Access window. You'll learn more about the Database window in Chapter 3, "Exploring the Database Window."

note

Remember, we're using Windows XP in this book. If you have a different version of Windows, things will look different—but Access will still work fine! Access 2003 runs on Windows 2000, Windows XP, or Windows 2003 Server only.

caution

Access security is an advanced topic that we don't cover in this book. We recommend you not create an MDW file until you're very familiar with Access security because you could inadvertently disable your databases.

FIGURE 2.3

Use these settings to save a new database named `MyDatabase` in the `My Documents` folder.

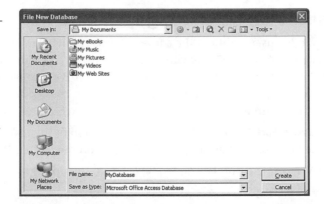

FIGURE 2.4

The Database window displays the name of your new database in its title bar.

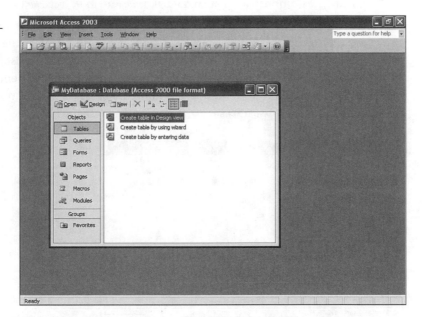

In the previous exercise, you saved a new database in the `My Documents` folder, which is the system's default folder. If you don't use this folder or if you save files more frequently to another folder, you can change the default. To do so, follow these steps:

1. Select **Options** from the **Tools** menu.

2. Click the **General** tab.

3. Enter the full path of the folder you want the File New Database dialog box to default to in the **Default Database Folder** text box at the bottom of the page.

4. Click **OK** to return to the Database window, or click **Apply** to save the change without closing the dialog box.

Basing a New Database on an Existing Database

It's not uncommon for users to share the same database structure without sharing the data. For instance, suppose one of your friends has created a database to keep track of her DVD collection. If you want to track your own DVD collection, you might want to start with a copy of that database and then customize it for your own use. To create a copy of an existing database from inside Access, follow these steps:

1. Click the **From Existing File** link in the New section of the task pane. You can display the task pane by clicking the New button on the toolbar if necessary.

2. In the New From Existing File dialog box, locate the appropriate folder in the Look In list.

3. Locate the database we just created, MyDatabase, in My Documents (see Figure 2.5).

4. Double-click **MyDatabase**, and Access creates a copy of it. If you receive a security warning, click yes. Access assigns a default name to the new database and opens a copy in Access. The default name will consist of the original file's name and the value 1, or the most appropriate sequential value. For instance, if the original database is named MyDatabase, Access names the new copied database MyDatabase1.

FIGURE 2.5

Locate the original file in the New from Existing File dialog box.

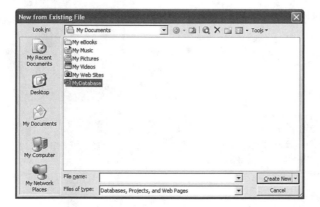

Renaming an Access Database

You'll probably want to rename any database that Access names for you. First, if you're working in a multiuser environment (in a networked copy), make sure all users have closed the database. Although Access will let multiple users work with data in a database at the same time, you must have exclusive access to rename the database. Then, from inside Access, do the following:

1. Click the **Open** button on the Database toolbar to display the Open dialog box.

2. Locate the appropriate database file using the Look In list.

3. Right-click the file in the list.

4. Select **Rename** from the resulting submenu, as shown in Figure 2.6.

5. Access highlights the file in Edit mode. At this point, enter the new name. Be sure to retain the .mdb extension.

6. Press **Enter** to complete the change. However, Access will return an error because you can't change the name of an open database file. We don't really need to change the name, we just wanted to walk you through the process and experience the error. Close MyDatabase1 by clicking the Windows **Close** button (**X**) in the Database window's title bar.

FIGURE 2.6

Right-click the database file in the Open dialog box to display a submenu of options.

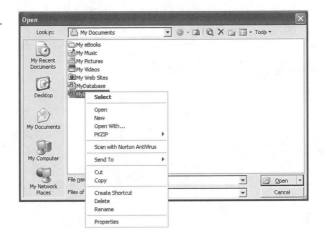

Using a Template

Access uses the Database Wizard to base a new database on a template file. Fortunately, several templates are available from which to choose and the process is simple. In fact, we won't even walk you through the wizard process because it's so straightforward. However, we will help you get started.

Templates contain tables, forms, reports, and other objects Access uses to tie the database together. Templates provide a convenient way for you to get started with a full-blown database with very little effort. To create a file from a template, follow these steps:

1. Open the task pane (press **Ctrl+N**), and then click the **On my computer** link in the Templates section in the task pane.

2. Click the **Databases** tab (if necessary) to display the available templates in the Templates dialog box.

3. Double-click any of the template files shown in Figure 2.7. Or, alternatively, click the file and click **OK**. We chose the Asset Tracking template.

4. In the resulting File New Database dialog box, Access has assigned a default name for the new file in the File Name combo box at the bottom of the dialog box. Accept this name or enter a new one, which we've done in Figure 2.8.

5. Click **Create**. At this point, Access launches the Database Wizard, which walks you through the process of adding objects to your new database. Feel free to experiment with the wizard, or click **Cancel** to abandon the task. If you choose to explore the wizard, you'll be able to customize the tables in the new database by choosing what information they should contain. (You'll learn more about customizing tables in Chapter 5, "Building Your First Tables.") Then, you'll specify a display style for forms and reports or accept the template's defaults. You might want to read a few more chapters before tackling any of these changes! Finally, you'll determine the database's title. At any time, you can click Finish to accept all the template defaults and skip most of the wizard's questions.

FIGURE 2.7

Select a template on which to base the new database.

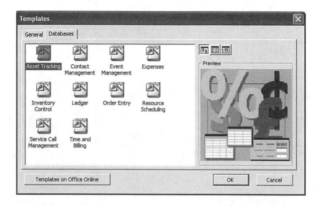

FIGURE 2.8

Enter a name for the new database.

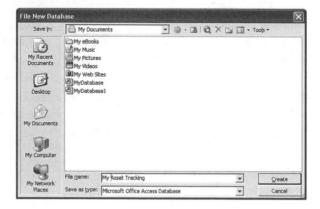

Opening an Existing File

After you've created an Access database, whether from scratch, from an existing database, or from a template, you'll probably need to open it occasionally to modify the data or perform maintenance tasks. To open an existing database, do the following:

1. Click the **Open** button on the Database toolbar to open the Open dialog box.

2. Locate the appropriate folder in the Look In list, and then double-click the .mdb file in the list. We selected MyDatabase in the My Documents folder.

3. Select **Open** to see its drop-down list, as shown in Figure 2.9. As you can see, opening a database isn't as simple as it first appears. Select one of the options, which we've explained in Table 2.1, and then click **Open**.

FIGURE 2.9
Four different modes exist in which you can open a database.

TABLE 2.1 Open Options

Option	Explanation
Open (the default)	Opens the database and allows others to also open the database in a multiuser environment.
Open Read-Only	You can view everything, but you can't edit anything.
Open Exclusive	Opens the database exclusively in a multiuser environment. In other words, no one else can open the database while you have it open in this mode.
Open Exclusive Read-Only	Combines the two previous options, opening the database exclusively but not letting you edit anything.

Access automatically updates the recently used files list on the File menu as you open files. If the file appears in that list, simply click the link to quickly open that database and thereby skip the Open dialog box.

Converting

Like Access 2002, Access 2003 defaults to the Access 2000 file format, supposedly for backward-compatibility. To change the default format for the open database, select **Tools, Database Utilities, Convert Database**; then select the appropriate file format from the last submenu (see Figure 2.10). Access prompts you to give the converted database a new name—enter one and click **Save**. Keep in mind that anytime you convert a database to an earlier version, Access might have to remove database features that aren't supported in that version.

FIGURE 2.10

Select a file format for the database.

You can change the format default permanently. Select **Tools, Options**. Next, click the **Advanced** tab and select **Access 2002-2003** from the Default File Format option shown in Figure 2.11. (You must have an open database to alter settings in the Options dialog box.) If you'll never need to share your databases with someone who's using a version of Access older than Access 2002, you should make this change. That's the easiest way to ensure that you can use Access 2003 to its fullest potential.

FIGURE 2.11

Permanently modify Access's file format.

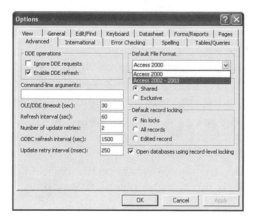

Opening Databases from Earlier Versions

When you open a database that was saved in an earlier format, Access displays the Convert/Open Database dialog box shown in Figure 2.12. The default option is Convert Database, which converts the earlier format to the default format (see the previous section).

FIGURE 2.12

Choose to convert or open without converting.

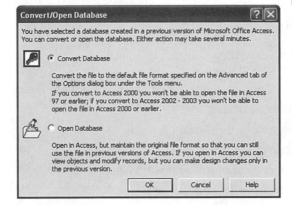

> **caution**
>
> Be especially careful when you choose to convert an earlier file version when opening that file in Access. After you convert the file, you won't be able to open it in the original version. In other words, if you convert an Access 97 or Access 2000 file to Access 2003, you will no longer be able to open that file in Access 97 or Access 2000, respectively.

On the other hand, the Open Database option enables you to view the database without changing the file's format. While in this mode, you can modify data, but you can't make design changes. For example, you can't change the color of a form or the caption on a report in this mode.

Exploring the Access User Interface

Earlier, in Figure 2.2 we showed you the Access application window with its default interface tools and no open database. By default, Access displays the Database toolbar, menu bar, and task pane when you launch the program. In the next sections, you'll learn more about these tools.

The Database Toolbar

First, let's review all the tools on the Database toolbar, which is active before a database is open and when the Database window is current. Even with an open database, many of these tools are disabled, as they are in Figure 2.13. In addition, this toolbar automatically updates its available tools as you move from object to object. Table 2.2 defines each tool, from left to right.

FIGURE 2.13

This is the Access Database toolbar, with many disabled tools, just as they are in the application window.

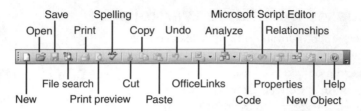

TABLE 2.2 Toolbar Tools

Tool	Purpose
New	Displays the task pane.
Open	Displays the Open dialog box and opens a database file.
Save	Saves a database object.
File Search	Searches for text or files within Access.
Print	Prints the current object.
Print Preview	Previews the current object as it will print.
Spelling	Runs the Office Spell-Check feature.
Cut	Deletes the current object.
Copy	Copies the current object.
Paste	Copies the current contents of the Clipboard in the active object.
Undo	Voids the last action.
OfficeLinks	Provides a quick way to merge data with or publish data in Word or analyze data in Excel. You'll learn about these in Chapter 16, "Sharing Data."
Analyze	Launches one of three utilities: Analyze Table, Analyze Performance, and Documenter.
Code	Allows you to edit programming code associated with an object. You won't need to do this in your first databases.
Microsoft Script Editor	Allows you to edit HTML code in Data Access Pages. You'll learn more about pages in Chapter 10, "Take Your Data to the Web with Pages."
Properties	Displays the current object's properties in the Properties window.
Relationships	Shows a graphic representation of the existing relationships. You can also create new relationships and modify existing ones in this window. (Chapter 6, "Tapping the Power of Relationships," covers more about relationships.)
New Object	A quick way to create database objects. (For a more thorough discussion of database objects, see Chapter 3.)
Help	Displays the Office Assistant or the Help window if the Office Assistant is disabled. (We'll discuss the Office Assistant in Chapter 17, "Using Common Office Features.")

We could write a whole chapter just on toolbars and the menu bar, but instead we'll offer a few tidbits here to get you started. First, to display other toolbars, right-click any open toolbar or menu bar and select the appropriate toolbar or select **Customize** from the resulting submenu. You can select Customize to display a number of options for customizing a toolbar or the menu bar. You can also add or delete tools, change the size of the icons, and much more. To reset a toolbar or the menu bar to its default settings, simply click the **Reset** button on the Toolbars tab of the Customize dialog box.

You can move almost any toolbar by grabbing the handle at the left margin (refer to Figure 2.13) and dragging it to a new position. If you drag a floating toolbar too close to the edge of the application window, Access automatically docks it. In other words, Access attaches the floating toolbar to the window's edge or another toolbar. To quickly redock an undocked toolbar, just double-click the toolbar's title bar. An undocked toolbar is known as a *floating toolbar*.

The Menu Bar

Unlike Access toolbars, there's only one menu bar, although it changes commands according to the current environment. This section reviews the application menu bar, which is displayed at the top of the Access window as soon as you open it. The following are several tasks you can perform via a menu command:

- You can manipulate database files.
- You can create and modify database objects.
- You can share data with other Office applications.
- You can customize the Access environment.

As you select commands from each open menu, note the icons to the left of some of the commands, as shown in Figure 2.14. These icons denote duplicated efforts between a tool (toolbar) and the menu command. In addition, keystroke combinations are listed to the right of some commands—press those keys to quickly execute the corresponding command in lieu of using the mouse.

tip

Notice that some of the characters in the menus are underscored, which indicates a hotkey. That means you can press that key to initiate the command. For instance, to display the File menu, you'd press **Alt+F**. After the menu itself is open, you press just the underscored key. For instance, the letter O in the Open command (File menu) is underscored. After the File menu is displayed, you press just **O** to display the Open dialog box.

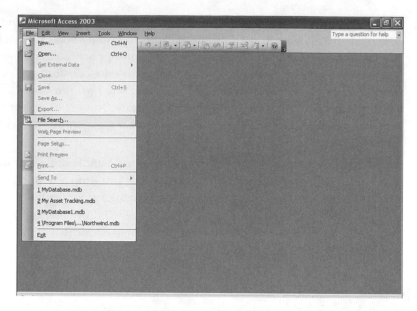

The Personal Touch—Understanding IntelliMenus

Office introduced personalized menus in Office 2000. These menus (and submenus)
adapt to the way you work, displaying the commands you use most often and hid-
ing those you never or seldom use.

You can tell when Access has personalized a menu by the small double arrow at the
bottom of the menu. We've highlighted one in Figure 2.15. Simply click the double
arrow to display all the commands for that particular menu.

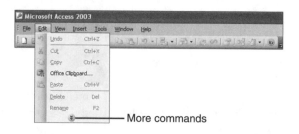

Many people find personalized menus annoying, especially when they're trying to
learn a new program. Fortunately, you can easily disable this feature. To do so, follow
these steps:

1. Select **Toolbars** from the View menu.
2. Select **Customize**.
3. Click the **Options** tab.
4. Select the **Always Show Full Menus** option in the Personalized Menus and Toolbars section, as shown in Figure 2.16.
5. Click **Close**.

FIGURE 2.16

Disable the personalized menus feature.

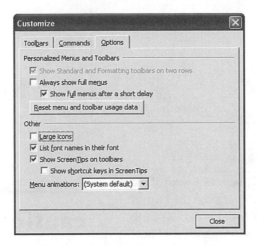

Disabling the Task Pane

Earlier, we showed you how to use the links in the task pane to open or create files. Access displays the task pane by default when you launch it. You'll find shortcuts for opening and creating a database or an Access project. If you don't want to see the task pane, follow these steps:

1. Select **Options** from the Tools menu.
2. Click the **View** tab.
3. Clear the **Startup Task Pane** option in the Show section, as we've done in Figure 2.17.
4. Click **OK** to return to the application window.

You must have a database open to change this option.

FIGURE 2.17

Disable the task
pane.

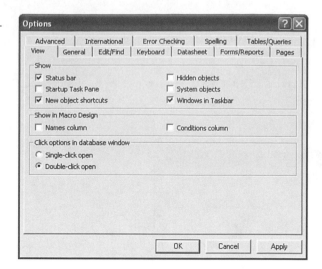

Making a Grand Exit

After you finish your work, be sure to exit the database and Access properly. First, close the current database by clicking the **Close** button (**X**) in the right corner of the Database window's title bar. Or, alternatively, select **File, Close**.

To close Access, click the **Close** button in the right corner of the application window's title bar. Or, select **File, Exit**. It's all right to close Access with an open database using one of these methods—Access will close both the open database and itself.

caution

Turning off your system without properly closing your database (and Access) could result in a corrupted file and unrecoverable data.

THE ABSOLUTE MINIMUM

After reading this chapter, you should be familiar with Access's application window, Database toolbar, menu bar, and task pane. You'll be seeing a lot of these tools in the remaining chapters. In this chapter you mastered the following:

- Launching Access
- Opening and creating database files
- The many application window interface tools

3

EXPLORING THE DATABASE WINDOW

In Chapter 2, "Take a Quick Tour of Access," you learned about some of the Access user interfaces. So far, you've learned about the edges of the screen—the task panes, toolbars, and menus. Now it's time to tackle the core of Access itself: the Database window. As you'll learn in this chapter, the Database window is the place where you can find everything you'll need in Access—data, forms, reports, and other objects. You'll learn how to navigate in this window and see how to start customizing objects for your own use.

What's in the Database Window?

The easiest way to learn what's in the Database window is to open an Access database and explore. Fortunately, Access comes with several sample databases you can use for just this purpose. You don't have to worry about breaking anything because you can always reinstall the samples if a problem occurs. Now that you know how to launch Access (refer to Chapter 2 if you need a refresher), here's how to open the sample database called Northwind Traders:

1. Launch Access.

2. Select **Help, Sample Databases, Northwind Sample Database**.

note

If you didn't install the samples when you installed Access, you'll be prompted to insert your Office CD-ROM the first time you try to open one of the sample databases.

Depending on how your computer is configured, you might need to respond to two separate warnings after selecting the first database to load. First, you may see a warning that states "Security Warning: Unsafe expressions are not blocked." This is Access's way of informing you that there's a potential bug in the Microsoft Jet database engine, which is used by Access. To be safe from this bug, you need to install Service Pack 7 (or a later version, when one comes out) for Jet 4.0. The easiest way to do this is to visit the Windows Update Web site at http://windowsupdate. microsoft.com, where Jet 4.0 SP7 will be one of your choices to download and install.

Installing SP7 will keep this warning from appearing in the future. In the mean time, it's safe to click the Yes button to open the Northwind sample database, because it comes from a trusted source. But beware of blindly clicking Yes for every database, especially if you're not sure where it came from or who created it.

After you deal with the first security warning (if it appears), you'll get a second security warning. This one will tell you "This file may not be safe if it contains code that was intended to harm your computer." The issue here is that Access databases can contain code, and if a nasty person wrote that code, it could be designed to destroy or damage the files on your computer. Because the Northwind file is from a trusted source, it's safe to click Open here. But once again, be cautious: A database that was just emailed to you or downloaded from a Web site could contain malicious code. It's up to you to decide whether to trust the sender.

When the Northwind database loads, you are presented with the splash screen shown in Figure 3.1. If you've seen this screen often enough, you can check the check box to make it go away. For now, just click the **OK** button and it will vanish. A *splash screen* is really just a programming trick that displays information about the application that's loading. It keeps you from getting bored while Access loads the database.

After you dismiss the splash screen, your Access window contains two things, as shown in Figure 3.2. In the front is the Main Switchboard, which is actually an Access form designed to let you perform various functions in this sample database. You'll learn a bit about creating your own switchboard forms in Chapter 15, "Automating Your Database." For now, click the **Close** button (the **X** in the upper-right corner of the Main Switchboard) to make it go away. Behind the Main Switchboard is the Database window for this database.

FIGURE 3.1

The Northwind database splash screen.

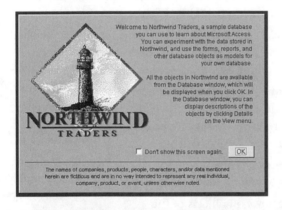

FIGURE 3.2

The Northwind database Main Switchboard and Database window.

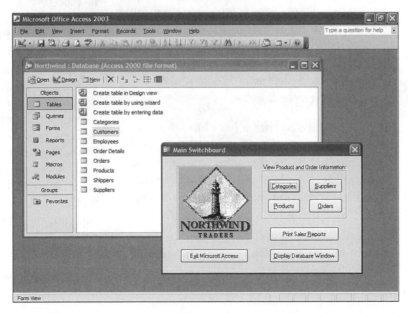

Close the Main Switchboard form, and you're left with only the Database window. But there's a lot going on in this window! Here's a rundown of the parts of the Database window (Figure 3.3 shows where these items are located):

- **Shortcut buttons**—Give you one-click access to common operations. The exact shortcut buttons available change depending on the type of object selected in the database.

- **Delete button**—Deletes the object highlighted in the object list. Fortunately, it asks you to confirm before it actually deletes anything.

- **View buttons**—Let you choose between large icon, small icon, list, and detail view in the object list.

- **Objects button**—Opens the list of object types in the object bar at the left side of the window.

- **Shortcuts**—Select the type of object to display in the object list. For example, in Figure 3.3, the Tables shortcut is selected, so the objects showing in the object list are all tables.

- **Groups button**—Opens the list of groups in the object bar at the left side of the window. You'll learn more about groups later in this chapter.

- **Design shortcuts**—Gives you easy access to ways to create new objects.

- **Object list**—Shows all objects of the selected type. For example, with the Tables shortcut selected, you can see that the Northwind sample database contains a table named Categories, a table named Customers, and so on. Each of these is called a *table object*.

Take a moment and click a few of the shortcuts in the Northwind sample database. You'll see that dozens of objects of various types appear in this database. But you'll recall that when you make a new database, you're prompted to save only a single file. What's going on here?

The answer is that Access acts like its own little directory of files. When you look at an Access

caution

Because a database stores all your data in one place, you need to be especially cautious with database files. Access stores all your data in a single file with the extension .mdb. You therefore should make a backup copy of this file on a regular basis by copying it to a disk, a CD-ROM, or another computer. Access 2003 provides a new feature for backing up the current database. Choose Back Up Database from the File menu. Then, tell Access where to save the backup if other than the current folder, and click Save. By default, Access will add the backup date to the backup file's name.

database in Windows Explorer, you can't see into it; it's just one big file. But when you open that database in Access itself, Access knows how to extract all the little files and display them by name in the Database window. Compared to some older databases, this is immensely convenient. To give someone an Access database, you just have to copy the one file, instead of rounding up dozens of little files (and probably missing some).

Before digging into the actual objects—the tables, queries, forms, reports, and so on—you might want to change slightly the way things look in the Database window. If you increase the size of the window vertically (click the cursor on the bottom border of the window and drag down), it will eventually be tall enough to show all the shortcuts simultaneously. Click the **Details** view button to get more information on each object in the object list (although you'll see fewer objects at one time). Figure 3.4 shows the resized and restyled Database window.

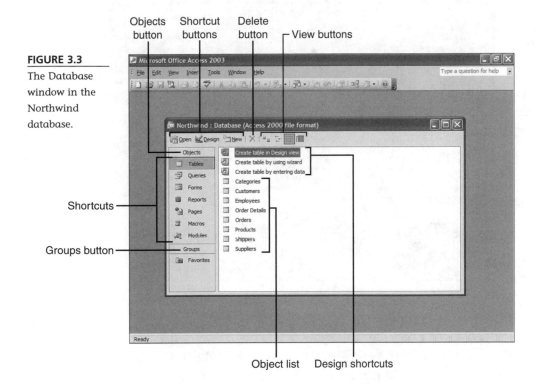

FIGURE 3.3

The Database window in the Northwind database.

Any Access database can contain seven types of objects (although it's possible that any of these types contain no objects):

- Tables
- Queries
- Forms
- Reports
- Pages
- Macros
- Modules

Next, let's take a quick look at each of these objects. Don't worry, you'll learn about each one in more detail later in the book. For now, just concentrate on getting an overview of what the database contains.

FIGURE 3.4

Another view of the Database window in the Northwind database.

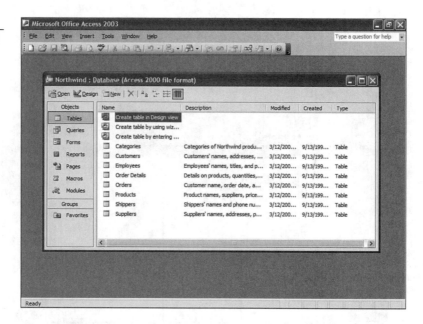

Tables

Tables are where the data in a database is actually stored. The Northwind sample database has tables named Categories, Customers, Employees, and so on.

The Northwind sample database uses *natural* naming. That is, objects have names that identify what they contain or do. Some database designers advocate a more formal, program-like style for naming objects. You can view one such naming convention at http://msdn.microsoft.com/archive/en-us/dnaraccgen/html/ msdn_20naming.asp. For your own databases, feel free to name objects in any way you feel comfortable with.

To see the data in a table, just double-click the table in the Database window. For example, Figure 3.5 shows the data in the Orders table (you can see it identified in the caption area of the window displaying the data). Click the **Close** button at the upper-right of the table window (not the main Access window!) to exit the table when you're done inspecting it.

If you right-click a table item in the Database window, you'll get a shortcut menu of things you can do with the table. This shortcut menu varies depending on which type of object you've clicked, but some choices are the same. Right-click and select **Properties** to open the Properties dialog box for the table. Here you can type a description that will appear in the Database window when you're displaying objects in detail view.

You'll learn more about tables starting in Chapter 5, "Building Your First Tables."

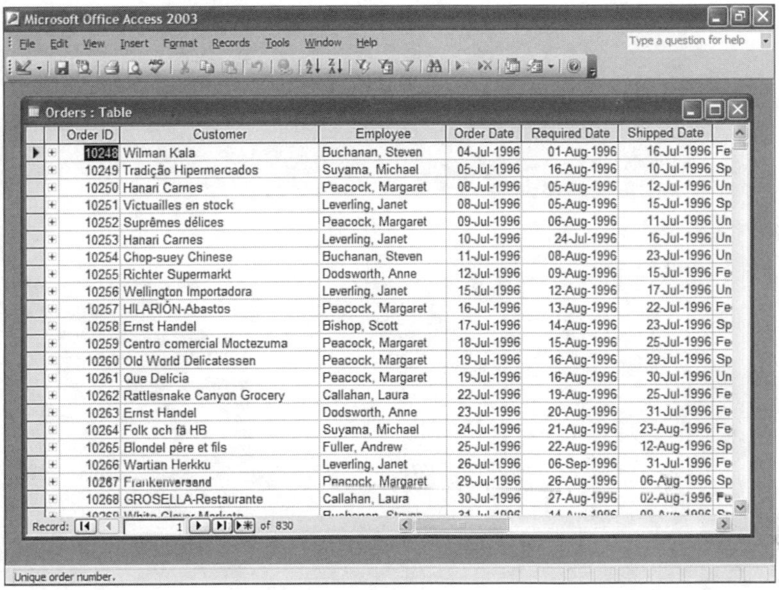

FIGURE 3.5

A table opened from the Database window.

Queries

Click the **Queries** object type (also known as a *shortcut*) button to see a list of queries in the Database window. Of course, you know that in plain English, queries are questions. But in the world of Access, it's easier to think of queries as the *answers* to questions.

For example, the Northwind sample database contains information on a fictional food importing company. The tables contain data on the customers of the company, the products the company sells, the employees who sell the products, the orders that customers have placed, and so on. You might think of the tables as a gargantuan filing cabinet filled with sales receipts, employee time cards, and so on.

Faced with this mass of data, you might want to ask some questions, such as, "What were the total sales of all our beverage products in 1997?" If you had the sales slips and a calculator, you could work this out. But in Access, you can use a query to find the answer quickly. Locate the query named `Category Sales for 1997` in the Database window and double-click it. You'll see the answers in the form of a datasheet (similar to a table), as shown in Figure 3.6. Close the query window by clicking its **Close** button when you're done inspecting its contents.

Even though queries look like tables when you open them, there's a difference. You enter data into the database through tables, and then retrieve it (possibly rearranged and summarized) through queries. You'll learn more about queries starting in Chapter 7, "Retrieving Data with Queries."

FIGURE 3.6

A query opened from the Database window.

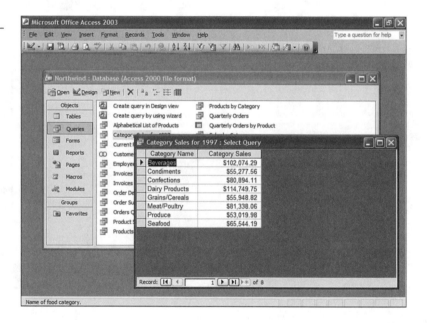

Forms

Click the **Forms** shortcut to see a list of forms in the Database window. Real life is full of forms: tax forms, medical insurance forms, rebate forms, and so on. Access forms share some of this fill-in-the-blank aspect, but they also offer additional flexibility that you'll never find in a paper form.

Just like tables and queries, you can open a form by double-clicking it in the Database window. For example, double-click the Employees form in the Database window to open it, as shown in Figure 3.7.

This particular form displays some information about Scott Bishop, a sales representative for Northwind Traders. You can click the Company Info and Personal Info tabs to see two different sets of information.

But this form holds more than just information on Scott Bishop. The set of controls at the bottom of the form is called the *navigation bar*. These controls let you select different sets of information to display. Click the right-facing arrow on the navigation bar (just to the right of the box containing the numeral 1), and the form shows Andrew Fuller's information. Keep clicking here and you can see every employee in the database. Close the form by clicking its **Close** button when you're done. In this particular case, the form is drawing its information from the Employees table, which you saw when you clicked the Tables shortcut. But forms need not display any data at all; they can also be a home for Windows controls such as push buttons and list boxes. For example, the Splash Screen (which you saw in Figure 3.1) and the Main Switchboard (which you saw in Figure 3.2) in the Northwind sample database are both forms.

Tabs

FIGURE 3.7

A form opened from the Database window.

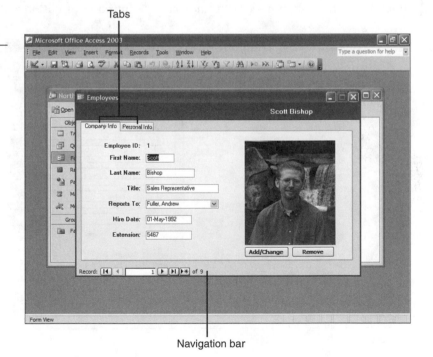

Navigation bar

You'll learn more about forms in Chapter 8, "Creating and Using Data Entry Forms."

Reports

Click the **Reports** shortcut to see a list of reports in the database. Reports provide a different way to display the data contained in tables. Reports are designed to be attractive when they're actually printed, although you can also view them onscreen. For example, locate and double-click the Summary of Sales by Quarter report. The report opens onscreen, as shown in Figure 3.8. If you move your cursor over the report, the cursor turns into a magnifying glass; click the report to see it with larger type.

If you look at the information in this report, you'll see that it consists of summary sales and orders numbers. Once again, Access has compiled this information by aggregating the raw data contained in the tables in the database.

If you have a printer, you can click the Print button on the Print Preview toolbar to get a paper copy of the report. You'll find that the onscreen rendition is almost indistinguishable from the printed version. Use the Close button on the preview window to close the report when you're done investigating it.

You'll learn more about reports in Chapter 9, "Printing Information with Reports."

FIGURE 3.8

A report opened from the Database window.

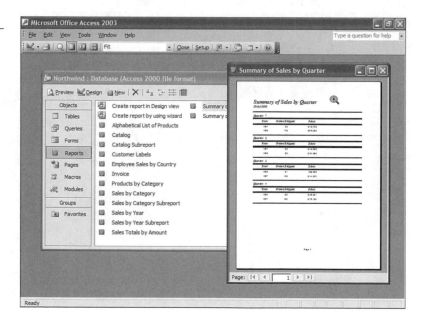

Pages

Click the **Pages** shortcut to see a list of pages in the database. Pages are very similar to forms, but there's a twist: They can be displayed in a Web browser as well as in Access itself.

Right-click the Employees page in the Database window and select **Web Page Preview**. This launches your default Web browser (most likely Internet Explorer) and loads the Employees page. As you can see in Figure 3.9, the page is very similar to the Employees form you saw in Figure 3.7.

Select **File, Close** in the Web browser to close the page.

> **tip**
>
> If you have a Web site, you can post Access pages to the Internet. Just ask the Office Assistant "How do I publish pages?" for more information. Select **Show the Office Assistant** from the **Help** menu to display the Assistant.

Access is the first database to let you so easily move your data to a Web site. You'll learn more about pages in Chapter 10, "Take Your Data to the Web with Pages."

FIGURE 3.9

A page open in Internet Explorer.

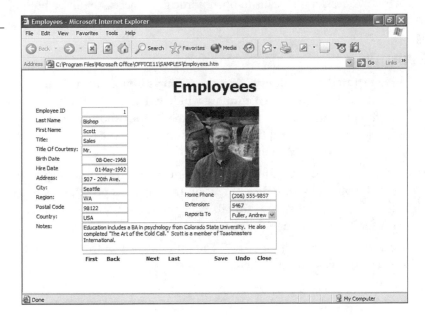

Macros

Click the **Macros** shortcut to see all the macros in the database. *Macros* are lists of commands that Access can save and execute. For example, a macro might open up a particular form or prompt the user for some information. You'll learn just a bit about macros in Chapter 15. Until then, you won't need to use this object type.

Modules

Click the **Modules** shortcut to see a list of the modules in the database. *Modules* are objects that actually contain programming code, written in a language called Visual Basic for Applications (VBA). Modules are designed to give advanced users extra power in customizing a database and its contents. We won't be using modules in this book, although you might occasionally see a database that contains a module.

Organizing Database Objects

As you've seen, an Access database can contain many objects. The Northwind sample database contains about 75 objects. A large database might contain hundreds or even thousands of objects. Given that many different objects, how can you keep track of the ones with which you want to work? Access provides you with two ways to do this. First, you can group objects together in the Database window. Second, you can create Windows desktop shortcuts to open particular objects. You'll see both of these techniques in the remainder of this chapter.

Using Groups

To get started using groups, click the **Groups** button at the bottom of the object section at the left side of the Database window. This opens the groups area and shows you the built-in Favorites group. Click the **Tables** shortcut to display the tables in the database. Now drag the Customers table from the object list and drop it on the Favorites group, as shown in Figure 3.10.

Now click the **Forms** shortcut and repeat the process, dragging the Customers form from the object list and dropping it on the Favorites group, which is an object group Access supplies to get you started. Switch to the list of reports and repeat the process with the Customer Labels report.

Click the **Favorites** group itself. The list of objects in the group will be just those objects that you dropped there:

- The Customers table
- The Customers form (which Access renames to Customers1, so that it has a different name from the table)
- The Customer Labels report

FIGURE 3.10

Dragging an object to a group.

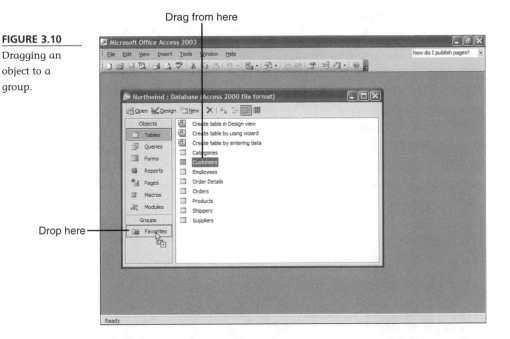

Drag from here

Drop here

You can double-click any of these objects to open them, or you can right-click them to get a shortcut menu.

You're not limited to the built-in Favorites group. To create a new group, follow these directions:

1. Right-click the **Favorites** group and select **New Group**.

2. Access opens the New Group dialog box.

3. Accept the default group name (Group1), or enter a group name of your own.

4. Click **OK**.

The new group shows up in the Groups section, below the Favorites group.

tip

When you drag an object to a group, it creates a shortcut to the object, not a copy of the object. If you change the original object, the shortcut in the group automatically opens the new version.

To change the name of a group, right-click the group and select **Rename Group**. To delete a group, right-click the group and select **Delete Group**. You can create as many groups as you need to keep database objects grouped together. You can also place individual objects in more than one group if you want; just drag and drop them to each group in turn.

Using Desktop Shortcuts

Groups give you a way to organize objects within a database. There's one more way to easily get to a database object: Create a desktop shortcut for the object. To see how this works, follow these steps to create a desktop shortcut to the Customers form:

1. Click the **Restore Down** button in the Access window, so that Access doesn't take up the entire desktop.

2. Click the **Forms** shortcut to see a list of forms in the database.

3. Drag the Customers form from the Database window, out of Access, and drop it on the Windows desktop, as shown in Figure 3.11.

note

You can't rename or delete the built-in Favorites group. Don't be alarmed when you see that the Rename and Delete menu items are grayed out when you right-click that group.

FIGURE 3.11
Creating a desktop shortcut.

4. Access will create a desktop shortcut where you dropped the form.

5. Select **File, Exit** within Access to close the Access window.

6. Double-click the shortcut you just created on the desktop. Windows launches Access and then opens the Customers form (the splash screen and Main Switchboard also open).

You can create a desktop shortcut to any object in Access by dragging the object and dropping it on the Windows desktop. This gives you an easy way to have frequently used objects close at hand without needing to launch Access first.

THE ABSOLUTE MINIMUM

In this chapter, you got to know the Database window and the objects it contains. An Access database can contain many objects, and all these objects are stored in a single file. The Database window in Access lets you view and manipulate Access objects. You also learned the following:

- Table objects hold your raw data.
- Query objects provide answers to questions about the data.
- Forms provide a data-entry and display interface.
- Reports enable you to make attractive printed versions of your data.
- Pages help you publish your data to the Web.
- Macros and modules enable advanced programming operations in a database.
- Groups in the Database window let you create subsets of your objects for easy reference.
- Desktop shortcuts let you launch Access and open a particular object, such as a form or a report, directly from the Windows desktop.

PART

BUILDING AND USING A DATABASE

IN THIS CHAPTER

- Planning a database
- Organizing your data
- Designing your first tables

4

PLANNING A DATABASE

In the simplest terms, a *database* is a collection of persistent (or related) data. For instance, you might store information about your household goods and assets in a paper notebook. Or, you might collect personal information about your relatives and friends, such as addresses, birth dates, and so on, in an address book or day planner. Both collections are really just simplified databases. Both systems have a specific structure, and you follow a routine to store and retrieve information. Even a pile of little scraps of paper, Post-it Notes, and napkins with ideas for that great American novel you mean to write could be considered a database—if you're willing to stretch your imagination a bit.

Most of us are satisfied with our paper notebooks, day planners, and even our little piles of notes. In the business world they can prove haphazard— lose the little scrap of paper with a huge order from your company's most important client and you might find yourself in the unemployment line. Even in your personal life, losing track of things can be a severe annoyance.

Was that check due this week or next week? Do you remember when the tomatoes were planted? In this chapter, we'll show you how to turn data into an effective database that works for you.

The Goal

Access is simply a tool, like a hammer or screwdriver. Used correctly, the end result will make your life easier; ignore the tool's purpose, and you might just bang your thumb. Just remember that your goal is personal in terms of what the database can do for you. For your own purposes, a database can help you become more efficient or more productive.

note

You can download the `Chapter 4.mdb` sample file for this chapter from `http://www.quepublishing.com/`.

But there's more to a database than just storing data. A well-designed database helps protect the validity of your data and is also easy to use, flexible, and efficient. If you design your database properly, it will help you store exactly the data you need.

Determining the Database's Purpose

Designing a database can be the hardest part of the whole process, and it's one many users try to skip, to their own regret. Few developers are so smart and so in tune with the data that they can skip this task and still build a successful database application. If you learn nothing else from this chapter, remember this—do not skimp when designing your database.

After you've decided that you need to design your database, rather than just throwing things together, write a short mission statement on the purpose of your database. Don't sweat over this part; the statement can be a simple sentence if that's all that's required. "Store and analyze wooly worm sightings for predicting subsequent winter conditions" says quite a lot. By the end of the process, you might need to update your mission statement, but that's the whole point of the design process.

For the purposes of this book, we'll create a database that stores gardening information. Specifically, we'll track flowers, plants, and vegetables. Using the previous sentence as our mission statement, we'll get started. We'll use this database for the rest of the book—but don't be surprised as we modify and enhance the database in later chapters. Most of the time, you'll need to change your initial database design as you work with the database and understand new requirements.

The Discovery Process—Finding the Data

At this stage of the process, it isn't important to know all that much about the database program you'll be using, which in this case is Access. Concentrate on the data you'll be storing. There's simply no substitute for knowing your data. Fortunately, when you build a database for yourself, you probably have a pretty good idea of the things you want to keep track of.

Creating a Paper Trail

Get ready to learn the job your database will be expected to perform, step by step. When you're done, you should be on very intimate terms with the data and everything you do with that data.

You can't build a database without knowing what you want to store in the database. That might seem obvious, but if you're used to just jotting down things on scraps of paper or tossing them all in an Excel spreadsheet, you might not have thought about keeping just one type of information separate. To build the gardening database, we need to define just what it is about gardening we want to keep track of.

In preparation for creating the gardening database we'll design in this chapter, you could gather your favorite gardening books, magazines, and seed catalogs and have them ready for inspiration and actual data. Or perhaps you already have a list of catalogs, such as the one in Figure 4.1. Now, get ready to design!

FIGURE 4.1

Not a database—but it's a start!

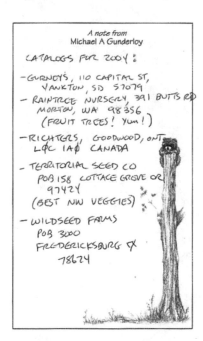

The First Data List

Whether you're working from printed forms, personal notes, or gardening books, this is the time to list the actual data the database will store and process. Don't worry about the order, and don't try to categorize the items—simply create one long list. Let's do that now with our gardening database:

- Common name
- Latin name
- Decorative, edible, or medicinal
- General notes—problems, future plans, and so on
- Picture of the plant
- Names and addresses of favorite seed catalogs

Don't limit the list or your expectations. It doesn't matter how short or long the list is. The point is to just get started. Maybe you already have a paper gardening journal, such as the one in Figure 4.2, or a list of plants to start from. Great! That will make the process much easier because so much of the discovery work is already done. However, don't make the mistake of just listing the things you're already tracking in written form—you could omit important data. This is your chance to take a fresh look at the data and decide what's really important. For example, digital camera pictures, such as the one in Figure 4.3, can also be in your database.

FIGURE 4.2

Your existing gardening journal can serve as a source of inspiration for a database.

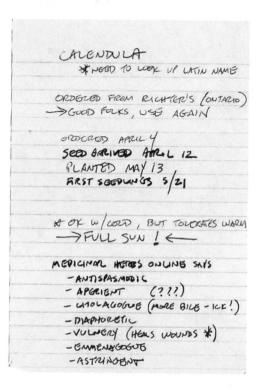

FIGURE 4.3

Pictures can also
be stored in an
Access database.

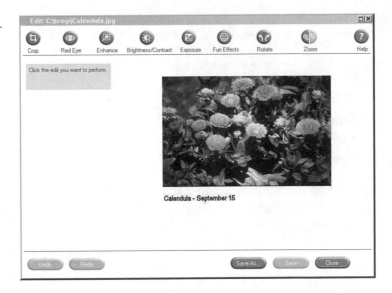

Calendula - September 15

Identifying Tables

Resist the urge to throw all your data into one big table and hope for the best. That
isn't the way a relational database works. A *table* is a collection of related data
stored in rows and columns. In a *relational* database, the data is stored in multiple,
but related, tables.

Each table stores data for an *entity*, a conceptual
collection of one type of data. In other words, for
each entity type, you'll need one table. (It's actually a bit more complicated, but for now, that
description satisfies our purposes.)

We said that a table consists of columns and
rows. In database terms, the column houses a
field, the smallest unit of data in the database.
Each field in the table defines the table's entity.
Together, the fields create a record, and one
record stores the data for one entity.

That's all clear as mud, right? Don't worry, it'll
make more sense as we continue. Let's apply all
these new terms to our gardening database by
identifying the entities from our earlier list.

tip

Don't assume that your
tables will mirror your existing paper records exactly.
You'll see as we proceed that
the information in Figure 4.2
gets split up among several
tables.

Initially, we seem to have two entities—individual plant information and catalog data. That means we'll need at least two representative lists:

Plants	Catalogs
Common Name	Name
Latin Name	Address
Type	Specialty
Notes	
Picture	

Remember, we're not actually working with Access yet. We're just making lists of potential tables and fields. You'll learn how to actually create an Access table in Chapter 5, "Building Your First Tables."

Congratulations! You just took your first step toward organizing your data. An entire field of study is devoted to figuring out how to split data into tables that make sense—it's called *normalization*. But you don't have to worry about that. You've taken the first step based on common sense, and as we continue, you'll see that the rest of database design is largely common sense as well.

caution

Don't get too attached to your original design. As you think more deeply about your data, you should be prepared to rearrange it for the best results.

Rather than deal with technical definitions for database design, here are the common-sense rules you can use when designing your own databases:

- **Rule One**—Split up your data into the smallest pieces that make sense.
- **Rule Two**—Don't try to store two things in one place.
- **Rule Three**—Make sure you can tell things apart.

Applying Rule One

Rule one says that each unit of data (field) should be as small as possible. Right now, we've followed that rule in designing our potential table of plants. We can't say the same for the catalog table, however. Storing the entire address in one field is a bad idea and breaks the first rule.

As you know, an address has several components: a street address, a city, a state, a ZIP code or regional code, and sometimes even the country. That means the address field could contain up to five (or even more) pieces of data.

You're probably wondering why you should bother to split this up. It's very difficult to work with multiple pieces of data stored in one field. For instance, let's suppose you want information on a catalog, but you can't remember the catalog's name. All you can remember is that the company is based in Iowa. If Iowa is stuck in the middle of a field between Sioux City and USA, you're going to have a hard time finding that record. On the other hand, if you store Iowa in its own field, all you have to do is search that field for Iowa entries. To that end, let's rethink the catalog table:

Catalogs
Name
Street Address
City
State
ZIP
Country
Specialty

Applying Rule Two

Rule two says you can't store more than one piece of data in a field. The type field identifies the plant as decorative, edible, or medicinal. But what do you do when an overlap exists? Some plants could be both decorative and medicinal, for example, but you can't enter more than one type in the same field. To resolve the conflict, you can create a new table to hold the type information. After doing so, we have two tables (not including the catalogs table):

Plants	Types
Common Name	Type
Latin Name	
Notes	
Picture	

Later, you'll see how you can link these two tables together to tell which type applies to which plant. Right now, you should still concentrate on splitting things up.

Applying Rule Three

You'll be storing information on corn, beets, petunias, and who knows what else. How do you tell one plant from another? The answer is that each plant has some unique information about it. In database terms, this unique information is referred to as a *primary key*. The third rule says that each table must contain a primary key.

Simply stated, a primary key field contains a value that uniquely identifies each record and can't be null (blank or otherwise unknown). The following are the two ways to choose a table's primary key:

- **You can rely on the stored information to uniquely identify each record—** One or more fields in the data might already be unique for each record. Developers refer to this type of primary key as a *natural key*.

- **You can insert an AutoNumber data type field—**When using this data type, Access automatically enters a consecutive value when you insert a record. For instance, the first record's primary key value would be 1, the second record's value would be 2, the third record's value would be 3, and so on. You might think of this as an *artificial primary key*, in contrast to a natural key.

note

As you become more familiar with Access, you'll find that developers disagree on whether to use artificial or natural primary keys. We'll use both, depending on which works better for a particular table.

Figure 4.4 shows the difference between the two types of keys schematically.

FIGURE 4.4

Natural and artificial keys.

| Gurney's |
| Raintree Nursery |
| Richters |
| Territorial Seed |
| Wildseed Farms |

Natural Key

1	Gurney's
2	Raintree Nursery
3	Richters
4	Territorial Seed
5	Wildseed Farms

Artificial Key

At this point, we really need to define just what we mean when we say a primary key uniquely identifies each record: That means the primary key field can't contain duplicate entries. Suppose, for example, that you chose the type of plant as the primary key for the plants table. What happens when you get two plants with the same type? If you'd made type the primary key, you couldn't put them both in the same table. Clearly, that's not a good choice of primary key.

The goal of choosing a primary key is to find data that's different for every record that you might ever store in the table. You have three basic choices:

- Use an autonumber as an artificial key.
- Choose a single field from the data.
- Choose more than one field from the data.

That third choice might require a bit more explanation. Suppose you were truly determined that type should be the primary key of the plant table. How could you make this unique for every record? Well, you might make the primary key consist of the type and something else—say, the type and the common name of the plant. Perhaps that combination is unique, even though types and common names individually could be repeated. If you need to, you can select any number of fields together to make up the primary key.

Fortunately, you don't need to get that fancy to find a good primary key for the plant table. The plant table's most likely key candidate is the Latin name field because each Latin name should be unique. What about the catalog table? It's unlikely that we'll ever run into two or more catalogs with the same name, so we'll use the name of the catalog as our primary key for that catalog table.

The type table has just one field. When you run into a table with only one field, you almost always have what's known as a *lookup* table: a table that is used to look up values for data linked to another table. In this case, the type table is a lookup table used by the plant table. You could leave the table as is (making the single field the primary key) or add an AutoNumber field. Let's do the latter for the experience, and we'll make the AutoNumber field the primary key. Our current table lists are as follows, with each table containing several fields (we've marked the primary key with the letters PK):

- **Plants**—Common Name, Latin Name (PK), Notes, Picture
- **Catalogs**—Name (PK), Street Address, City, State, ZIP, Country, Specialty
- **Types**—Type (PK), Description

At this point, you might be wondering how the plant table knows which type goes with each plant or how you know which catalog has your favorite carrot seeds. That's where relationships come into play. A *relationship* is simply an association between two tables. You might express a relationship in words by saying, "Each catalog has information about many plants," or "Every plant has a type." (You'll learn more about relationships in Chapter 6, "Tapping the Power of Relationships.")

Related tables require two keys—the primary key and what's known as a foreign key. A *foreign key* is simply another table's primary key inserted in a related table. Figure 4.5 shows this schematically.

FIGURE 4.5

Primary and foreign keys.

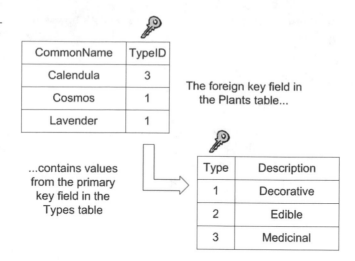

CommonName	TypeID
Calendula	3
Cosmos	1
Lavender	1

The foreign key field in the Plants table...

...contains values from the primary key field in the Types table

Type	Description
1	Decorative
2	Edible
3	Medicinal

We can best illustrate the way related tables work by adding the appropriate foreign keys to our gardening tables.

If you recall, we moved the type field from the plant table to a new table. Now, we need to relate both the plant table and the type table. To do so, we must include the primary key field from the type table in the plant table as a foreign key:

- **Plants**—Common Name, Latin Name (PK), Notes, Picture, TypeID (FK)
- **Types**—Type (PK), Description

Now, let's do the same for the plant and catalog tables, so we can quickly view the catalogs that offer our favorite seeds. In this case, we should add the primary key from the catalog table—the name field—to the plant table as a foreign key:

- **Plants**—Common Name, Latin Name (PK), Notes, Picture, TypeID (FK), Catalog Name (FK)
- **Catalogs**—Name (PK), Street Address, City, State, ZIP, Country, Specialty

Did you notice that both foreign key fields don't use their corresponding primary key fields' names? That's all right—the field names don't have to match. You can call the field "Name" in the Catalogs table and "CatalogName" in the Plants table; Access will know how to keep them linked.

tip

If you need help dividing the data, you're not alone. This task can be perplexing to even the experts. That's why Access includes the Table Analyzer—a utility that helps you correctly divide your data. We'll review this tool in Chapter 6.

At this point, our final table lists are

- **Plants**—Common Name, Latin Name (PK), Notes, Picture, TypeID (FK), Catalog Name (FK)
- **Types**—Type (PK), Description
- **Catalogs**—Name (PK), Street Address, City, State, ZIP, Country, Specialty

Identifying Possible Forms

You should have a good idea of the tables you'll be creating after you actually start building your application. The next step in designing a database is to consider other objects you might need to work with your data. A good place to start is with the forms you'll need to maintain and view that data. This early in the process, you can probably depend on needing a data entry form or two.

This is a good time to pull out all those paper forms you gathered during the discovery process and determine how efficient they were. You might want to continue to work with the original form design translated from paper to computer screen. Or, you might want to consider a more efficient or productive design. Just because you've recorded information one way for a while, doesn't mean you can't improve on it.

Remember, you're just sketching with paper and pencil right now. Don't attempt to create these forms in Access just yet. After you have tables, you can use the wizards to create your prototype forms. (Read Chapter 8, "Creating and Using Data Entry Forms," to learn more about using wizards to create forms.)

Now, let's turn to our gardening design and see which types of forms we might need. You should be able to add new catalogs and new plants, and you might even need to update the types list.

You might benefit from a form that displays fields from more than one form. In fact, you might want to use a *subform*, which is simply one form in another. For instance, wouldn't it be convenient to view catalog information and view the seeds you've purchased from each catalog? Or, you could view the catalog information and enter new seed information for plants you haven't yet listed.

caution

You should always use Access forms to enter, delete, and modify records. Although you can update the data in Datasheet view interacting directly with the table, you shouldn't. In addition, you should never allow users access to the underlying tables.

Restricting use and access to the tables is the only way you can protect the integrity of your data. Using the table, a user can bypass all the validation rules and security measures you've taken to ensure that the data is valid and that it remains valid.

You could do quite a lot with a form such as the one shown in Figure 4.6. Of course, we're cheating a bit here and using Access to design our sample forms. Until you're familiar with the tools in Access, you can use pencil and paper for this step instead.

FIGURE 4.6

You can base forms on more than one table.

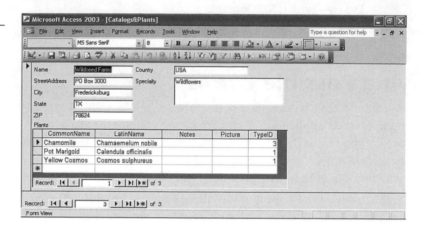

Besides the previous form, you'll probably need a simple data entry form to update the types table, such as the form shown in Figure 4.7.

FIGURE 4.7

Use a form to update the types table.

For more information on forms, read Chapter 8; to learn about subforms, read Chapter 13, "Customizing Forms."

Planning Possible Reports

Planning your reports is similar to planning the forms. The difference between forms and reports, you'll recall, is that reports are meant to be printed out on paper, rather than worked with onscreen. You might have collected reports during the discovery process; if so, get them out now because they can provide inspiration. Some applications don't even generate reports, but most have at least one or two.

Reports are usually the final product of the application and often tell the application's story. For instance, the plants database might provide reports you can store to use as records of your garden in future years.

Now, think about the types of gardening information you'd like to store on paper. You'd probably like a list of plants for general reference, or maybe you'd like to print mailing labels for seed companies. A report with pictures is always nice and can be extremely helpful during the planning stages. The possibilities are only as limited as your imagination.

Perhaps you'd like to print labels similar to the ones shown in Figure 4.8 for all your plants, sorted by their Latin names, so you can update your file folders. The report in Figure 4.9 would be useful for planning next year's garden plots. (You can learn more about reports in Chapter 9, "Printing Information with Reports," and Chapter 14, "Dressing Up Your Reports.")

FIGURE 4.8

You can use a label report for any data, not just address information.

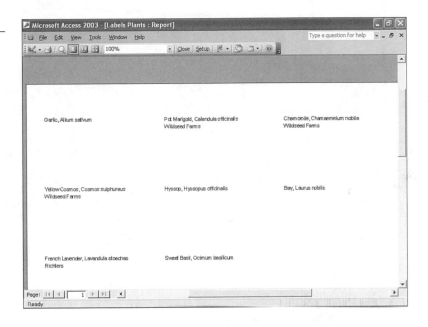

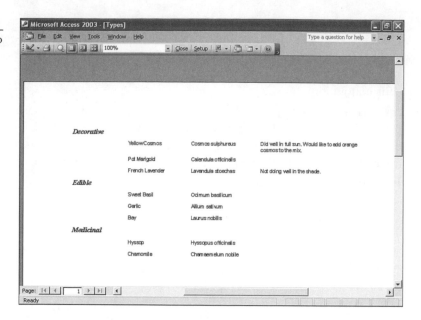

THE ABSOLUTE MINIMUM

The key point of this chapter is simple: Design your database before you build it.
Even if you're itching to get started with the software, time taken now with pencil
and paper will be repaid later with a database that's more efficient and easier
to use.

In this chapter, you learned about

■ The discovery process

■ Dividing data into multiple but related tables

■ How to see your data in terms of a database application

IN THIS CHAPTER

- Learn how to create tables by entering data, by using a wizard, or in design view

- Add smart tags to your tables

- Start storing data in your new tables

- Use formatting options to make a table look the way you want

- Use keyboard keystrokes instead of the mouse to speed up data entry

- Find the data you need when you need it

5

BUILDING YOUR FIRST TABLES

By now, you're probably more than ready to get started in Access. You've seen the product, you know what you can find there, and you've thought through the logical design of your database. The time has come to begin using Access and you'll start by building Access tables. You already know that tables contain your data. In to this chapter, you'll see how to build tables and how to enter your data into them. By the end of the chapter, you'll be ready to build tables in your own database.

What's in a Table?

You learned about some of the basic parts of a table in Chapter 4, "Planning a Database." But before you actually build a table, you should review the three basic components one more time:

- Fields
- Records
- Primary key

You can download the `Chapter 5.mdb` sample file, which is inclusive of all the examples in this chapter, from `http://www.quepublishing.com/`.

Fields

A *field* is the smallest unit of data in the database. In the plants database, some of the fields are CommonName, LatinName, StreetAddress, and City. Each thing you store in the database is described by one or more fields. As part of the process of designing tables, you'll tell Access which fields belong in each table.

Records

When you fill in the fields in a table, you're creating a *record*. A table might contain no records at all (if you haven't entered any data yet), or it might contain hundreds, thousands, or even millions of records. In the plants database, for example, each individual plant is the subject of one record. You can't enter records in a table before you have defined the fields for that table—until then, there's no place to enter the data!

Figure 5.1 shows the connection between fields, records, and tables.

FIGURE 5.1

Fields and records in a table.

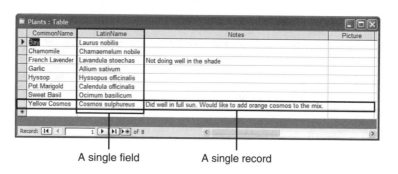

A single field   A single record

Primary Key

The other thing to keep in mind when building tables is that each table should have a primary key. A *primary key*, you'll recall, is the field (or group of fields) that uniquely identifies each record in a table. A bit later in the chapter you'll learn how to tell Access which field in your table contains the primary key.

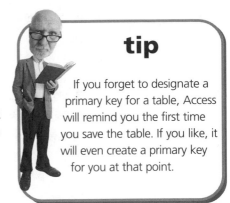

tip

If you forget to designate a primary key for a table, Access will remind you the first time you save the table. If you like, it will even create a primary key for you at that point.

How to Create a Simple Table

As you work with Access, you'll notice that there is usually more than one way to do things. The following are the three ways in which you can create a new table in Access:

■ **Start typing data into a blank table**—Access will create the fields in the table for you. If you're used to working with Microsoft Excel, this method might be the most comfortable one for you.

■ **Use the Table Wizard**—It guides you through the steps of building some common table types.

■ **Work directly in table design view**—You specify the details of each field yourself. This is the most powerful and flexible way to design a new table.

In this section, you'll learn how to use each of these techniques.

Entering Data to Create Your Table

To begin with, we'll show you how to create the Types table, just by entering data. Table 1.1 shows the data this Access table will contain.

TABLE 5.1   Data for the Type Table

TypeID	Description
1	Decorative
2	Edible
3	Medicinal

To create the Types table, follow these steps:

1. Launch Access.

2. In the New File task pane, click the **Blank Database** link. Name the new database `Plants.mdb`, and click **Create**.

3. In the Database window, click the **Tables** shortcut.

4. Double-click the **Create Table by Entering Data** shortcut in the Database window to open a blank datasheet.

5. Click the mouse in the first row of the first column of the datasheet; then type the value 1.

6. Press the **Tab** key to move to the next column, and type the value Decorative.

7. Use the mouse or arrow keys to move to the first column of the second row. Continue entering data by typing it into the table until the datasheet looks similar to Figure 5.2.

Use Tab, Enter, or Arrow
keys to move from
one field to the next

Use Arrow keys to move from
one record to the next

FIGURE 5.2

Creating a table
by entering
data.

	Field1	Field2	Field3	Field4	Field5	Field6	Field7	F
1	Decorative							
2	Edible							
3	Medicinal							

Record: 21 of 21

Enter values directly
into datasheet

8. Right-click the header for the first column, where the text Field1 appears. Select **Rename Column** (see Figure 5.3) from the shortcut menu to highlight the current name of the field. Type the new name, TypeID, and press **Enter**.

9. Here's another way to rename: Double-click the header for the second column, where the text Field2 appears. This highlights the current name of the field. Type the new name, Description, and press **Enter**.

10. Select **File, Save** to open the Save As dialog box. Enter Types and click **OK**.

11. Access displays the warning dialog box shown in Figure 5.4 because you can't specify a primary key when you create a table by typing in data. For now, just click **No**.

note

In Access, *column* and *field* mean the same thing.

Right-click the header field

FIGURE 5.3

Change a field's
name.

Change a field's name

FIGURE 5.4

Access warns you
that your table
doesn't have a
primary key.

12. The blank cells in the datasheet will vanish
(except for one blank row, which is discussed
later in the "Using Datasheets" section of the
chapter), and the caption of the table will
show its new name. Click the **Close** button
to close the new table.

Congratulations! You've just created your first
Access table.

Using the Table Wizard

> **note**
>
> The design you worked
> through in Chapter 4
> defines the TypeID field in the Types
> table as an AutoNumber primary
> key field. However, that isn't what
> actually happened because Access
> automatically assigns the Number
> data type to the TypeID field when
> the contents are numerical values.
> This small deviation from the origi-
> nal plan is insignificant at this stage.

Access also includes a Table Wizard that can
streamline the job of creating new tables. The Table
Wizard knows how to create fields for a variety of common situations. You'll use it to
create the basic structure of the Catalogs table.

To build the initial Catalogs table, follow these steps:

1. Double-click the **Create Table by Using Wizard** link in the Tables section
of the Database window. Like most wizards, this one presents information
and asks for input in a series of panes. Each pane displays and fills the entire
wizard window, and you can navigate from pane to pane by clicking Next or
Back.

2. On the first pane of the Table Wizard, select the **Business** radio button and the Mailing List sample table. (Actually, these are the default choices, so you shouldn't have to do anything, but do make sure these options are the current choices.) If you scroll down the list, you'll see that you have the choice of many sample tables here. You should start with a sample table that's relatively close to the one you want to build.

3. The next step is to move fields from the Sample Fields box to the Fields in My New Table box. You'll see this dual box interface at many places in Access. Figure 5.5 shows the functions of the four buttons between the boxes, which move items back and forth between the lists. Click the **Select One** button to select the OrganizationName, Address, City, State, PostalCode, Country/Region, and Notes fields. (Our original plan called for naming the address field, StreetAddress, but Address will do.)

FIGURE 5.5

Controls to select items in the Table Wizard.

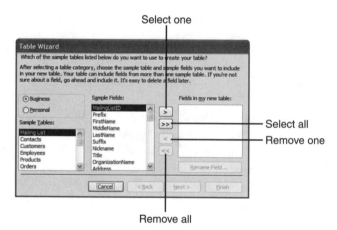

4. Select the **OrganizationName** field in the Fields in My New Table box. Then click the **Rename Field** button and enter `Name` in the Rename Field dialog box. Click **OK** to rename the field. Similarly, rename PostalCode to `ZIP`, Country/Region to `Country`, and Notes to `Specialty`. This matches the field names you designated in Chapter 4. (In Chapter 4, you worked with pen and paper lists and the table names contained spaces, which we've omitted in our actual table names.)

5. Click the **Next** button.

6. In the second pane of the Table Wizard, name the new table `Catalogs`. Click the radio button labeled **No, I'll Set the Primary Key**, as shown in Figure 5.6. Click **Next**.

FIGURE 5.6

Creating a table
in the Table
Wizard.

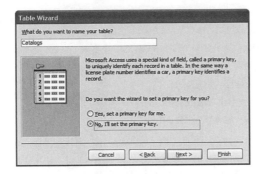

7. In the third pane of the Table Wizard, specify the Name field as the field that will hold unique data. Select the radio button for **Numbers and/or Letters I Enter When I Add New Records** and click **Next**.

8. The fourth pane of the Table Wizard asks how this table is related to the Types table you already created. You'll learn more about relationships in Chapter 6, "Tapping the Power of Relationships." For now, just accept the default (no relationship) and click **Next**.

9. Select the **Enter Data Directly into the Table** radio button and click **Finish**. This creates the table and opens it as a datasheet. Now you can type the data for the Catalogs table directly into the datasheet, as shown in Figure 5.7.

FIGURE 5.7

Entering data in
a new table from
the Table
Wizard.

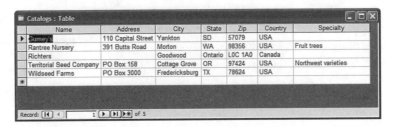

When you're dealing with common tables, the Table Wizard can provide a fast way to get started. But sometimes your database needs a table that doesn't resemble any of the choices from the wizard. Those are the times when you'll need to use table design view.

Working in Design View

Design view gives you a way to look at all the nuts and bolts of a table and its fields. You can change anything about a table in design view: the names and numbers of the fields, the type of data they can hold, the primary key of the table, and more. This section introduces you to table design view, and you'll learn more about this view in Chapter 11, "Customizing Your Tables."

The plants table in the database isn't really like any of the sample data in the Table Wizard. So, in this section, you'll use table design view to create this table. To build the plants table, follow these steps:

1. Double-click the **Create Table in Design View** link in the Tables section of the Database window to open the design view of a new table.

2. Type `CommonName` in the first row of the Field Name column. Access automatically assigns Text as the data type for the field, as shown in Figure 5.8. You'll learn more about data types in a few pages.

3. Type `LatinName` in the second row of the Field Name column to create another field. Accept the default Text data type.

4. Type `Notes` in the third row of the Field Name column to create another field. For this field, click the drop-down arrow next to the Text data type and select **Memo** as the data type for this field.

5. Similarly, add three more fields to the table: `Picture` (data type should be OLE Object), `TypeID` (data type should be Number), and `CatalogName` (data type should be Text).

tip

Although Access lets you include spaces in field names, we recommend that you avoid this. Using spaces makes working with some other parts of the product, such as queries, more difficult.

In steps 4 and 5 of the accompanying exercise, you must select a data type other than the default, from the Data Type column's drop-down list. If you prefer to designate a data type from your keyboard, enter the first letter of the data type's name and Access will automatically fill in the rest of the entry for you. For instance, when selecting Memo in step 4, just type **m**, and Access will do the rest.

FIGURE 5.8

Creating a new table in design view.

Field Name	Data Type	Description
CommonName	Text	

Field Properties

General | Lookup

Field Size	50
Format	
Input Mask	
Caption	
Default Value	
Validation Rule	
Validation Text	
Required	No
Allow Zero Length	Yes
Indexed	No
Unicode Compression	Yes
IME Mode	No Control
IME Sentence Mode	None
Smart Tags	

The data type determines the kind of values that users can store in the field. Press F1 for help on data types.

6. Right-click the **CommonName** field and select **Primary Key**. Access places a small key icon next to this field's name to indicate that it is the primary key.

7. Select **File, Save** and name the new table `Plants`. Figure 5.9 shows the completed table in design view.

FIGURE 5.9

A newly saved table in design view.

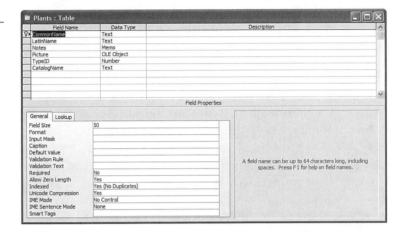

8. Click the **Close** button to close the newly created table.

You might have noticed the Field Properties area at the bottom of design view as you worked through the previous steps. As you select different fields, this area shows more information about each field. For example, the first property for the CommonName field is Field Size, and it has a default value of 50. This tells Access that the CommonName field can hold up to 50 characters, but no more. Field properties are an important part of ensuring that only reasonable data is saved in your database. You'll learn more about field properties in Chapter 12, "Getting Down to Business with Queries."

Modifying an Existing Table

You can also use table design view to modify an existing table. For example, you'll recall that you didn't create a primary key for the Types table. You can use table design view to correct this oversight by following these steps:

1. Click the **Types** table in the Database window.

2. Click the **Design** button at the top of the Database window, in what's known as the Database Window toolbar, to open the table in design view.

3. Click the **TypeID** field to select it. You'll see a black triangle to the left of the field name when you do.

4. Click the **Primary Key** button on the Access toolbar, as shown in Figure 5.10, to set this field as the primary key of the table (another case of Access providing more than one way to do something).

5. Select **File, Save** to save your changes. Alternately, you can click the Save tool on the Table Design toolbar.

6. Click the **Close** button to close the table.

You can change almost anything about a table in design view. In fact, you can change things you probably shouldn't. For example, what happens if you click in the data type column for the Description field and change the data type of the field from Text to Number? Well, the existing data isn't numbers, so if you save this change, Access will just throw your data away! Fortunately, it gives you a warning, as shown in Figure 5.11, before saving any such potentially disastrous changes. Be sure to click **No** if you followed along with this example.

FIGURE 5.11

Access warns you if you try to do something that will cause a loss of data.

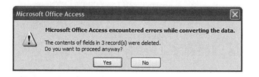

Adding a Smart Tag

 Right now, we'd like to introduce you to a table property that's new to Access 2003—smart tag. (Chapter 11 discusses common table properties in depth.) Smart tags are one of those features that you'll love or totally ignore, but they're certainly not critical to any application. They are useful in the right circumstances.

If you use Excel 2002 (or later), you've probably seen a smart tag or two. Excel uses smart tags to flag spreadsheet errors and offer possible solutions. A *smart tag* is an icon that reacts dynamically to a predefined term when clicked. For instance, a smart icon might access information on the Internet or perform a specific data task. For the most part, you'll use them to automate tasks that require input from another program. Smart tags are provided by Microsoft and other vendors, and so far, most of them are free. You can also create your own.

You'll apply a smart tag at the field level and forms inherit the property. When you move the mouse over a form control that has a smart tag setting, Access will display a small icon to the right of the control. Clicking the icon will activate the smart tag link and download the appropriate information or perform the appropriate task automatically.

In this short example, we'll grab local weather information using a smart tag provided by MSNBC. It's free, but you must download it from `http://www.msnbc.com/tools/newstools/d/smart_tags.asp`. Follow the instructions on that page to install the smart tag on your computer, and learning whether today will be a good day to work in your garden will be just a click away. You can also work with any of the smart tags that come with Access 2003. In that case, you don't have to download a thing. Doing so will allow you to walk through this next example, but of course, the tag you choose won't respond the same as the one in our example.

Now, let's add that smart tag to the Catalogs table:

1. Click the **Tables** shortcut in the Database window, select **Catalogs**, and then click the **Design** button on the Database Window toolbar to open Catalogs in design view.

2. Select the Name field row (it should be selected by default) because we're adding the smart tag to that field.

3. Find the Smart Tags property. It's the last property field in the Field Properties section. Click in the field to display the builder button (three little dots). Click the builder button to open the Smart Tags dialog box.

4. Check the weather smart tag. In this case, that's **Local News on MSNBC.com**, as shown in Figure 5.12. If that tag's not available and you don't want to download it, select an available tag. Click **OK** to continue.

FIGURE 5.12

Choose a smart tag file.

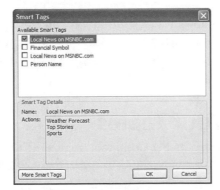

5. Access adds the appropriate tag reference in the Smart Tags property, as shown in Figure 5.13. Click **Save** and close the table.

FIGURE 5.13

Access updates the Smart Tag property setting.

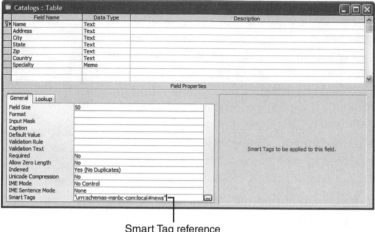

Smart Tag reference

Click **View** on the Table Design toolbar to see how adding the smart tag changes your sheet. Each field in the Name field now contains a small black triangle in the bottom-right corner. That triangle is your visual clue that the field has a smart tag. Hover over any triangle and Access will display a smart tag icon. Click the icon to display that tag's options, shown in Figure 5.14.

FIGURE 5.14

A form based on the Catalogs table displays a smart tag icon.

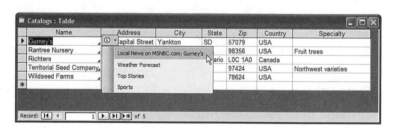

Clicking the icon displays a drop-down list of information you can download. Choosing **Weather Forecast** will launch your browser and link to a site that displays a local forecast. (If you're not connected to the Internet, the smart tag will prompt you to connect.)

Working with Data in Your Tables

Now that you know about designing and creating tables, it's time to think about using data in these tables. In this section you'll learn how to enter data in tables, how to move around in a table datasheet, and how to use the AutoCorrect functionality that's built into all the Microsoft Office products.

Using Datasheets

Access supplies multiple views of each object that you can find in the Database window. In the case of tables, you've already seen both views. Design view is useful when you want to manipulate the structure of a table: its fields or its primary key, for example. But to actually work with data, you need to use the other view of a table, datasheet view.

You've already seen datasheet view in this chapter several times, beginning with the steps where you created the Types table. Now it's time to look at a datasheet in more detail. Figure 5.15 shows the Catalogs table in datasheet view, with the important parts of the datasheet labeled.

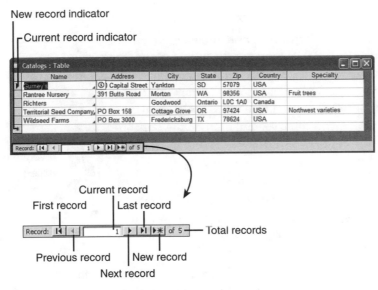

FIGURE 5.15

The parts of a datasheet.

To open a table in datasheet view, just double-click the table in the Database window. Alternatively, you can click the table once and then click the Open button, or right-click the table and select Open from its shortcut menu.

To enter or edit data in a datasheet, just click in the cell you want to change and type the value. You can press the Insert key on your keyboard to toggle between inserting new characters and overwriting the characters that are already there.

If you make a mistake typing, don't panic! You can press **Ctrl+Z** (hold down the Control key on the keyboard and press Z) or **Esc** to undo your most recent change. You can also press **Ctrl+Z** twice to undo all the changes you've made to the current record. Access doesn't save changes until you move to another row in the datasheet.

To add a new record to the table, click in the row marked with the asterisk, which is called the *new record indicator*. Then type the values you want to save in the new record. Click in any other row of the table to save your data. You can also save the new data by pressing **Shift+Enter** or by selecting **Records**, and then **Save Record**.

You can use the buttons in the navigation bar area at the bottom of the datasheet to move between records in the table. These buttons offer quick access to the first record, the previous record (the one just before the current record), the next record (the one just after the current record), the last record, and the new record row. You can also click in the current record box and type a number to move directly to that row of the table.

Access also allows you considerable latitude to customize a datasheet. For example, you can click and hold the mouse on the vertical line between field names at the top of the table and drag it from side to side to resize the columns. Similarly, you can click and drag on the horizontal line between records in the record indicator area to resize the rows of the datasheet.

You can even rearrange the columns in the datasheet. Click the column header (the area with the field name) and drag it to a new location. Then release the mouse to put the column in that location.

note

When you resize a column, it affects only that column. When you resize a row, the new size applies to all the rows in the table.

tip

Any changes you make to the format of a datasheet apply only to that datasheet. If you make any changes, Access asks you whether to save those changes.

You can select **Format, Datasheet** to dress up your datasheets even more. This opens the Datasheet Formatting dialog box shown in Figure 5.16. Here you can choose to apply a 3D effect to the cells in the datasheet; decide whether to show gridlines; and select the background color, gridline color, and border styles. You can also choose whether text in the datasheet should read right-to-left instead of left-to-right (generally this is useful only for languages such as Arabic or Hebrew).

FIGURE 5.16

Formatting the look of a datasheet.

Datasheet Navigation Tips

Access supports a rich set of keystrokes for working in a datasheet. Table 5.2 shows you some of the ways you can work with a datasheet from the keyboard. You probably won't memorize all these shortcuts unless you're doing lots of data entry, but it's good to know they are available.

TABLE 5.2 Datasheet Keyboard Shortcuts

Keystroke	Effect
F5	Moves to the record number box to allow you to easily jump to an arbitrary record.
Ctrl+;	Inserts the current date.
Ctrl+:	Inserts the current time.
Ctrl+'	Copies the value in the current field from the previous record.
Ctrl++	Adds a new record to the table
F2	Switches between edit mode and navigation mode. Keystrokes for moving between fields and records work only in navigation mode.
Tab	Moves to the next field.
Right arrow	Moves to the next field.
Shift+Tab	Moves to the previous field.
Left arrow	Moves to the previous field.
Home	Moves to the first field.
End	Moves to the last field.
Down arrow	Moves to the current field in the next record.
Up arrow	Moves to the current field in the previous record.

TABLE 5.2 (continued)

Keystroke	Effect
Ctrl+Up Arrow	Moves to the first row in the current field.
Ctrl+Down Arrow	Moves to the last row in the current field.
Ctrl+Home	Moves to the first field in the first record.
Ctrl+End	Moves to the last field in the last record.
Page Down	Scrolls down one screen of records.
Page Up	Scrolls up one screen of records.
Shift+F2	Opens the Zoom box, which allows you to edit the current field in a more spacious area.

How to Find Information

So far, you've dealt with only comparatively small amounts of information in your database. When you're looking over a list of five seed companies, you can easily find the one you want. But what happens when you have thousands of rows of data in one of your tables and need to find something? Fortunately, Access offers several ways to find data. We'll introduce a few of these ways in this chapter, and you'll see more later in the book:

- Sorting datasheets
- Using Filter by Selection
- Using the Find dialog box

(Chapter 8, "Creating and Using Data Entry Forms," shows you how to search for data in a form.)

Sorting in a Datasheet

Sometimes, you can find information just by scanning down a list, provided that the list is sorted in the correct order. Access enables you to sort a datasheet according to the data in any column. Follow these steps to see how datasheet sorting works in Access:

1. Open the Catalogs table in datasheet view. By default, the records will be sorted by their primary keys, in alphabetical order.

2. Click anywhere in the **Address** column, and then click the **Sort Ascending** button on the Access toolbar (it's the one with the A above the Z and a down arrow next to them). Now the records are sorted by address. Note that all the other columns are rearranged at the same time as the address column; Access doesn't sort just one column because this would break up records.

3. Click anywhere in the **City** column and select **Records, Sort, Sort Ascending** to sort the records by city.

4. Right-click in the **State** column and select **Sort Descending** to sort the records in descending order by state.

5. Click the **Close** button to close the table. Access asks whether to save changes to the design of the table. If you click Yes, the last sort you applied will be reused the next time you open the table. Click **No** this time.

As you can see, this is another area where Access offers you multiple ways to perform the same task.

Using Filter by Selection

Sometimes, the easiest way to find what you're looking for is to narrow the search. Access provides a feature called Filter by Selection for those times. Here's how it works:

1. Open the Catalogs table in datasheet view.

2. Click in the **Country** field, on one of the rows whose country is USA.

3. Right-click and select **Filter by Selection**. The datasheet changes to show only records whose country is USA. The navigation bar shows the text Filtered in the navigational toolbar to let you know that some records might be missing (see Figure 5.17).

FIGURE 5.17

A filtered datasheet.

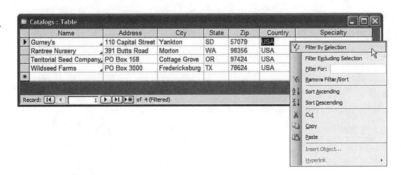

4. Right-click in the field again and select **Remove Filter/Sort** to see all the records in the datasheet.

5. Right-click in the field again and select **Filter Excluding Selection**. This time, the datasheet shows only records that do *not* match the selected value.

6. Remove the filter and close the datasheet.

You can also invoke Filter by Selection from the Records, Filter menu or from buttons on the table datasheet toolbar.

Using the Find Dialog Box

For maximum flexibility in locating data, Access also supports a standard Find and Replace dialog box. To invoke this dialog box, shown in Figure 5.18, open a datasheet, select any cell in the field you want to search and then press **Ctrl+F**.

> **tip**
>
> Access also supports an even more flexible filtering mode called Filter by Form, in which you can select the values by which to filter without needing to find them first. You'll learn about Filter by Form in Chapter 8.

FIGURE 5.18

The Find and Replace dialog box.

Type the data you want to find in the **Find What** combo box. If you've recently searched for something, you can repeat the search by selecting the data from the drop-down list in this combo box.

The Look In box gives you the choice between searching the field in which the cursor is positioned (in this case, Name) or the entire table.

The Match box lets you choose whether the data you've entered needs to match the whole field, any part of the field, or characters at the start of the field to be considered a match.

The Search box lets you choose whether to search up from the current cursor position, down from the current cursor position, or through the entire table.

You can also use the check boxes to make the search case sensitive or to search the data as it's presented rather than as it's stored. Access has the capability to format data onscreen differently from how it stores it in the table (see Chapter 11 for more details).

> **tip**
>
> To change the data after you find it, select the **Replace** tab in the Find and Replace dialog box and enter the new value in the control that appears. Access prompts you before making any data changes.

When you've entered all your options, click the **Find Next** button (or press **Alt+F**). Access finds the next matching data in the table and either highlights it onscreen for you or displays an error message if it was unable to find any matching data.

THE ABSOLUTE MINIMUM

In this chapter you learned the following:

- You can create Access tables by typing data in a datasheet, by using the Table Wizard, or by working in table design view.

- How to add smart tags at the table level.

- You can enter data by typing it in the datasheet. Access offers a rich set of controls for formatting and moving around in datasheets.

- You can use the Sorting, Filter by Selection, or Find and Replace capabilities of Access to quickly find data, even in very large tables.

IN THIS CHAPTER

- Learn how to add lookup fields to your tables
- Run the Table Analyzer to get hints on making your design more efficient
- Create and modify relationships between tables
- Use referential integrity to protect your data

6

TAPPING THE POWER OF RELATIONSHIPS

The average person might define the term *relationship* as a connection of blood or marriage. In the relational database world, the term *relationship* simply refers to an association between two records. That's the good news—you don't have to send your Access database flowers when you mess up. The bad news is that you might find Access relationships just as frustrating as your blood relations. An irate mother-in-law has nothing on an Access relationship run amuck.

The truth is that relationships are like everything else in Access. If you learn the basics and apply them correctly, they will serve you, your data, and your users well. In fact, they're the foundation on which the entire database stands. After you have the hang of it, you'll see that creating the correct relationship between two tables is rather intuitive.

You can think of a relationship as a connection between fields in two related tables where the two fields share common values. By matching the values, Access can combine records from those related tables to display related data. That's the real power behind relationships—the capability to display just the data you need when you need it. For example, if you're storing catalogs in one table and plants in another, you can use a relationship to tell Access how to figure out which plants came from which catalog.

note

You can download the `Chapter 6.mdb` sample file, which is inclusive of all the examples in this chapter, from `http://www.quepublishing.com/`. If you want to follow along with our examples, download `Chapter 5.mdb`.

You've already completed the hardest section of this book—you learned about primary and foreign keys (in Chapter 4, "Planning a Database") and created the tables (in Chapter 5, "Building Your First Tables"). In this chapter, we'll show you how to create relationships between those tables. The result will be that you can quickly learn from which catalog you ordered your last batch of cosmos seeds. Or, you can list all the edible plants you're currently growing and so on.

Using the Lookup Wizard

In Chapter 5, you created the three tables in the sample database. You also entered three type records and a few catalog addresses, as shown in Figure 6.1. At this point, you should be ready to enter a few plant records.

FIGURE 6.1

You created these three tables in Chapter 5.

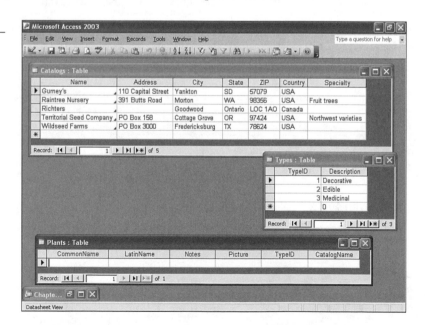

Let's open the empty Plants table and enter records for a few of the latest season's new plants, which are listed in Table 6.1.

TABLE 6.1 Plant Records

Common Name	Latin Name	Catalog	Type
Yarrow	Achillea millefolium	*Wildseed Farms*	Decorative
Purple Coneflower	Echinacea purpurea	*Wildseed Farms*	Medicinal
Cosmos	Cosmos bipinnatus	*Gurney's*	Decorative
Black-eyed Susan	Rudbeckia hirta	*Wildseed Farms*	Decorative
Rocket Larkspur	Delphinium ajacis	*Wildseed Farms*	Decorative
German Chamomile	Matricaria recutita	*Gurney's*	Medicinal
Calendula	Calendula officinalis	*Richters*	Decorative

Just to refresh your memory, we'll help you enter the first record:

1. Select the first field in the first row and enter `Yarrow`.

2. Press the right arrow key and enter `Achillea millefolium`.

3. Skip the next two fields and enter the TypeID value for decorative. This is where data entry becomes a bit challenging. You probably don't have these values memorized, so open the Types table. After viewing the table, you can clearly see that the TypeID value for decorative type is 1.

4. Return to the Plants table and enter 1 in the TypeID field for yarrow.

> **note**
>
> In Chapter 4 we advised you not to enter data directly into a table. During the design and development stage, it's common to play with a few records, just so you can test your design. Later, you'll create data entry forms that you'll use when you actually put the application to work.

Repeat steps 1–4 to enter the record for Purple Coneflower, which we've planted for its medicinal value. Even though you just looked at the Types table, you'll have to return to that table to learn the value for medicinal plants. To do so, find the Types table on the Windows taskbar and browse the records. This time, the appropriate value is 3, so return to the Plants table and enter 3 in the Purple Coneflower's TypeID field.

This routine could quickly become annoying, not to mention that it's horribly inefficient. If working with related tables is so efficient, why are you working so hard just to enter the few records shown in Figure 6.2?

FIGURE 6.2

Remembering
the appropriate
type value for
each record is
difficult.

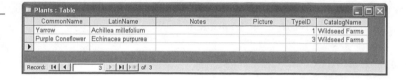

One way to solve this problem is to create what's known as a *lookup field* in the plant
table. A lookup field refers to a field that displays one value but stores another. The
best part is that a wizard is available that will help you create the lookup field.

As is, the TypeID values are meaningless, and remembering which value to enter is
difficult. If your table had hundreds of records, it would be impossible, so let's convert the plant table's TypeID field to a lookup field. To do so, follow these steps:

1. Open the plant table in Design view by selecting it in the Database window
   and then clicking **Design** on the Database Window toolbar.

2. Currently, the TypeID data type is Number. Click the right side of the TypeID
   field's Data Type column to display its drop-down list.

3. Select **Lookup Wizard**, as shown in Figure 6.3.

FIGURE 6.3

Select Lookup
Wizard from the
Data Type col-
umn's drop-
down list.

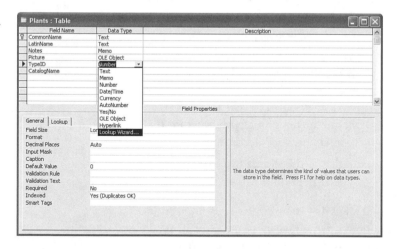

4. The wizard's first panel lets you choose between displaying existing values
   from a table (or query) and entering a list of items. You want to display the
   descriptive entries from the Types table, so accept **I Want the Lookup
   Column to Look Up the Values in a Table or Query**, which is the
   default option. Then click **Next**.

5. When you want to display existing values, the wizard displays a list of tables.
   The values you want to display are in the Types table, so select **Table: Types**.

Notice the View panel at the bottom of the wizard window. If you want to choose values from a query, select the **Queries** option to update the wizard's list. Or, you can display both tables and queries by clicking the **Both** option. Click **Next** to continue.

6. The next panel displays all the fields in the table or query you selected in the previous window. Generally, you should select the field that is the primary key of the lookup table and the field that contains the values you want to display. In the case of our example, click the double arrow button to move both fields to the Selected Fields list, as shown in Figure 6.4. TypeID is the primary key of the table, and Description is the field whose values you want to display to the user. Click **Next** when you're ready to continue.

FIGURE 6.4

Move both fields to the Selected Fields list.

7. The next panel allows you to decide which fields should be used to sort the list of data. In this case, the default sort order is fine, so click **Next**.

8. The panel shown in Figure 6.5 displays the values the lookup field will display. Notice that the Hide Key Column option is checked by default; that means Access won't display the primary key values (refer to Figure 6.2). Instead, the list will display only the descriptive values shown in the current list. If you need to, adjust the width of the column so you can completely see each entry. To continue, click **Next**.

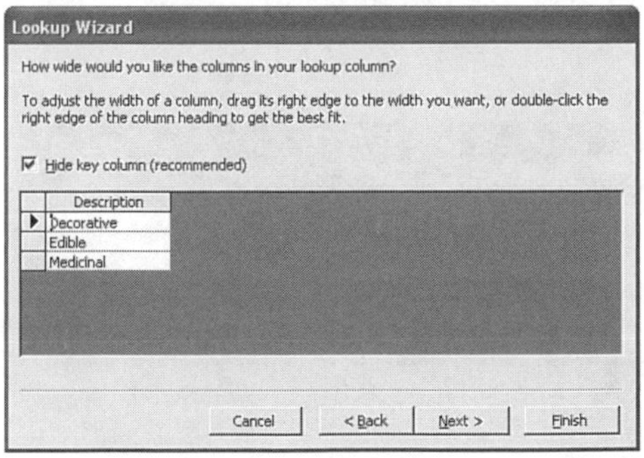

FIGURE 6.5

Adjust the width of the column if necessary.

9. Finally, the wizard borrows the field's name for the new lookup field. Accept the wizard's suggested name and click **Finish**.

10. When prompted to save the table, click **Yes**. If you click No, the wizard will discard the lookup field properties you just created.

To see the new lookup field, view the table in Datasheet view by clicking **View** on the Table Design toolbar. You might recall that the original TypeID field contained numeric values (refer to Figure 6.2). Now that field displays descriptive text instead. Specifically, the lookup field automatically displays the appropriate description for any existing records instead of the value it's actually storing.

The new lookup field also lets you easily enter the foreign key values for each record in the plant table. Refer to Table 6.1 to enter the next record, the one for cosmos. When you get to the TypeID field, click the arrow to open the new lookup field's drop-down list, as we've done in Figure 6.6.

You can use the list to enter a type value for a new record by simply clicking the value in the list. Select **Decorative** to finish the record for cosmos and enter the remaining records in Table 6.1. When you're done, your table should resemble the one shown in Figure 6.7. (Close and reopen the table to see your records sorted as shown.)

Open the Plants table in Design view so you can examine the lookup field properties. (Click the **View** button on the Table Datasheet toolbar.) Next, select any field in the TypeID field row and click the **Lookup** tab in the Field Properties pane.

note

Did you notice that Access sorted the records after you added the lookup field? The sort really has nothing to do with the lookup field; it just appears that way because the sort showed up after you added the lookup field, which is just a coincidence. Access is actually sorting the records by the primary key values. Because the primary key field is a text field (CommonName), Access sorts the records alphabetically by the values of that field.

It might not matter to you right now, but forms and reports inherit a table's lookup fields. That means any forms or reports bound to the Plants table will use a combo box—not a text box control, which is the default control—to display the TypeID field's contents. This will make more sense to you in Chapter 8.

FIGURE 6.6

Open the lookup field's drop-down list to see the data items you can enter.

CommonName	LatinName	Notes	Picture	TypeID	CatalogName
Purple Coneflower	Echinacea purpurea			Medicinal	Wildseed Farms
Yarrow	Achillea millefolium			Decorative	Wildseed Farms
Cosmos	Cosmos bipinnatus				

Plants : Table

Decorative
Edible
Medicinal

Record: 3 of 3

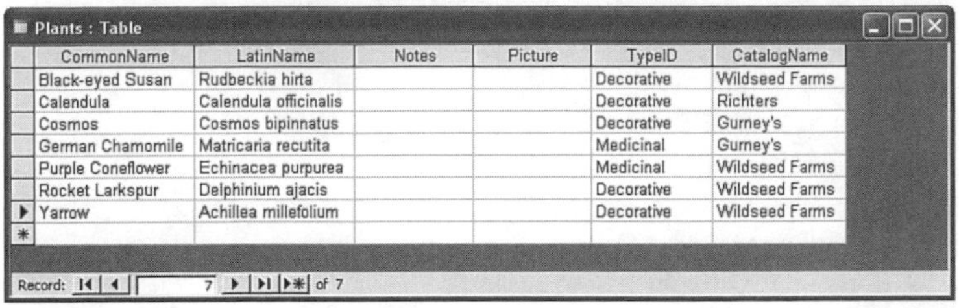

FIGURE 6.7

FIGURE 6.7

Seven plants
now appear in
the plant table.

CommonName	LatinName	Notes	Picture	TypeID	CatalogName
Black-eyed Susan	Rudbeckia hirta			Decorative	Wildseed Farms
Calendula	Calendula officinalis			Decorative	Richters
Cosmos	Cosmos bipinnatus			Decorative	Gurney's
German Chamomile	Matricaria recutita			Medicinal	Gurney's
Purple Coneflower	Echinacea purpurea			Medicinal	Wildseed Farms
Rocket Larkspur	Delphinium ajacis			Decorative	Wildseed Farms
Yarrow	Achillea millefolium			Decorative	Wildseed Farms

Record: 7 of 7

Notice that the Display Control is a combo box control. You haven't been introduced
to controls yet, but a *combo box* is a complex control with a text box for entering data
and a list. You can enter data directly into the text box component, or you can select
an item from the control's drop-down list. You'll learn more about creating and using
the various controls that Access offers in Chapter 8, "Creating and Using Data Entry
Forms," and Chapter 13, "Customizing Forms."

Deleting a Lookup Field

To delete the lookup field, select **Text Box** from the
Display Control property field's drop-down list, as
shown in Figure 6.8. But don't do so right now—
you need to keep the lookup field you just added to
the TypeID field. Close the plant table without
making any changes to the lookup field.

Wouldn't it be much easier to just select an item
from a drop-down list than type the entire entry
yourself? Not only is it easier and more efficient, a
drop-down list is a more reliable data-entry solution
because it eliminates typos and other human errors.
We recommend you limit the choices a user can
enter in this manner as often as possible.

note

You don't realize it
now, but the wizard cre-
ated your first relationship. Later in
this chapter, you'll get a closer
look at that relationship.

While you were entering records into the Plants
table in the last section, did you think that it might
be nice to also add a lookup table to the CatalogName field? It certainly would be
more efficient, and it would also eliminate typos. You probably had to correct at
least an entry or two. (Stay tuned because we'll use another method for displaying
items in a drop-down list in Chapter 13.)

To delete the
lookup field,
select Text Box
from the Display
Control property.

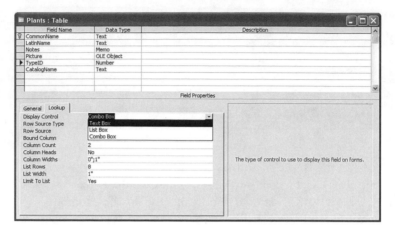

Using the Table Analyzer to Create Relationships

At this point, are you completely satisfied with the design? Let's see whether the
Table Analyzer agrees with you. This utility reviews current entries and makes suggestions on improving the design.

In a nutshell, the utility looks for repeated data and helps you copy that data to a
new and related table. Not every table will need changes, but it doesn't hurt to run
the analyzer just to see what it proposes. In addition, until you're more familiar with
design rules, you can rely on the Table Analyzer to help you through the process of
creating properly normalized tables. (Refer to Chapter 4 for a definition of normalization.) To analyze the Plants table, follow these steps:

1. Select **Analyze** from the Tools menu and select **Table** from the resulting submenu.

2. The first pane in the wizard offers to show you a sample problem that you
   might experience with duplicate data. Feel free to review the example. Click
   Next when you're ready to continue.

3. The next pane offers to explain, by example, how the analyzer will split a
   table. View the example, and when you're ready to continue, click **Next**.

4. Select the table you want to analyze—we selected Plants. Click **Next** when
   you're ready to continue to the next step.

5. While learning, you'll probably want to let the wizard do as much work as
   possible. Let the wizard choose which fields to split into a new table by
   accepting the default option **(Yes, Let the Wizard Decide)**. Click **Next** to
   continue. We won't even look at the other option; if you knew how to split
   the table, you wouldn't need the wizard!

6. The next pane, shown in Figure 6.9, displays the wizard's suggestions for splitting the table. Does the solution look familiar? It might because this is exactly the route you took in Chapter 4, when you designed the database. Right now, there's no relationship between the Catalogs and Plants tables, so the wizard has no way of knowing that you already have a catalog table.

FIGURE 6.9

The wizard offers its solution.

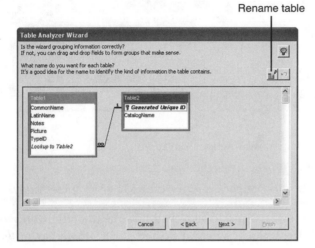

At this point, you could abandon your task, but let's continue because you're probably unfamiliar with how this utility works. Just remember: You had the right design; all you're lacking is the relationship between the two tables.

7. Select **Table1** and click the **Rename Table** button to the right of the window (refer to Figure 6.9). Enter the name `PlantsNew`, and then click **OK**.

8. Repeat step 7 and rename Table2 `CatalogsNew`. Then click **Next** to continue.

9. The next pane enables you to reset the suggested primary key. The wizard suggests adding an AutoNumber data type field to the CatalogsNew table and using it as the primary key. However, the wizard doesn't define a primary key for PlantsNew, so you must do so. Select the **CommonName** field in the **PlantsNew** list and click the **Set Unique Identifier** button. In response, the wizard displays a primary key icon next to that field. Click **Next** to continue.

10. In the final pane, the wizard offers to create a query. You're not ready for queries yet, so select the **No, Don't Create the Query** option. You'll probably want to deselect the Display Help on Working with the New Tables or Queries options. Otherwise, you'll just have an additional window to close. Click **Finish** to complete the changes.

The two new tables, PlantsNew and CatalogsNew, are for the most part, just like Plants and Catalogs. The two fields in CatalogsNew are transposed, but that doesn't matter. In addition, PlantsNew has a second lookup field. Select any value in the CatalogName field to display that field's new lookup field, as shown in Figure 6.10. The Table Analyzer created it automatically.

FIGURE 6.10

The Table Analyzer has added a second lookup field to the Plants table.

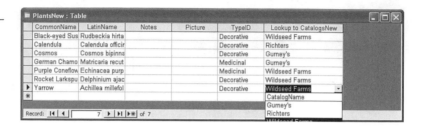

At this point, you have two relationships in your database:

- Between the TypeID fields in Plants and Types
- Between ID and CatalogsNew_ID (created by the Table Analyzer)

We completed this exercise just to show you how the analyzer works. Now you'll know what to expect when you need it. For now, delete both PlantsNew and CatalogsNew. To delete a table, simply select it in the Database window and then press the **Delete** key. After deleting the two tables the Table Analyzer created, just one relationship exists—the one between the Plants and Types table the Lookup Wizard created in the first section. It's okay to leave the new tables in the database if you want to study them later. They won't interfere with other objects.

Using the Relationships Window

It's fine to use the Lookup Wizard or the Table Analyzer, but you can create relationships yourself. First, open the Relationships window shown in Figure 6.11 by clicking the **Relationships** button on the Database toolbar. If that button is not visible, press **F11** to give focus to the Database window. Then, the button should be available.

The window contains two field lists, one for Plants and one for Types. (If your window is empty, click the **Show All Relationships** button on the Relationship toolbar.) In addition, there's a line between the two tables, which is known as a *join line*. When you created the lookup field for the TypeID field in the Plants table, the wizard created this relationship.

When you need to create a relationship, drag a field from one list to another. In almost all cases, you'll drag the primary key field to its counterpart in the related table. If you look closely at the existing join line, you'll see that it connects the two TypeID fields in both tables.

FIGURE 6.11
Open the Relationships window.

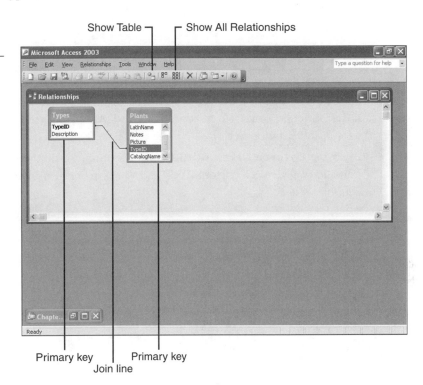

You can easily find the primary key fields in both tables because Access displays the primary key fields in bold text. Most of the time, you'll rely on the Relationships window to create permanent relationships between tables.

You still have a relationship you need to create—the one between the Catalogs and Plants tables. So, let's get started:

1. Click the **Show Table** button on the Relationship toolbar.

2. In the resulting Show Table dialog box, select **Catalogs**, and then click **Add**. Alternatively, you could double-click **Catalogs**.

3. Close the Show Table dialog box by clicking **Close**.

4. Select the **Name** field in the Catalogs list, but don't release the mouse. Access will display the field pointer shown in Figure 6.12.

Field pointer

FIGURE 6.12

FIGURE 6.12

Access displays
the field pointer
when you drag a
field from one
list to another.

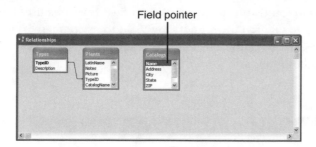

5. Still holding down the mouse, drag the Name field to the CatalogName field
   in the Plants list and then release the mouse. Access displays the Edit
   Relationships dialog box.

6. Check the **Enforce Referential Integrity** option, as shown in Figure 6.13;
   then click the **Create** button. (We'll introduce referential integrity in the next
   section.)

Primary Key table   Foreign Key table

FIGURE 6.13

Specify relation-
ship properties
in the Edit
Relationships
dialog box.

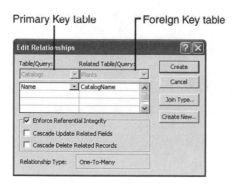

Figure 6.14 shows the new relationship between the two tables. Notice that the join
line is very different from the one connecting the Plants and Types tables:

- **The 1 next to the Catalogs list defines the primary key table, or the
  one side of the relationship**—Only one matching record exists in this
  table, which makes sense because the relationship is based on the primary
  key value, which as you've already learned, must be a unique value.

- **The infinity symbol next to the Plants list indicates the many sides
  of this relationship**—Many related records might exist in the Plants table
  that match any given record in the Catalogs table.

The One table

FIGURE 6.14

The join line reflects the relationship you just created.

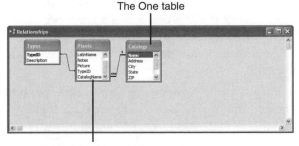

The Related Many table

The Many Sides to Relationships

We just introduced you to a new concept—a *one-to-many* relationship between the Plants and Catalog tables. There are three types of relationships. A thorough discussion of the relationship types is beyond the scope of this book, but you should be familiar with the terms:

- **One-to-one**—Has only one matching record in both tables. You won't see these relationships very often.

- **One-to-many**—The most common relationship. Each record in the primary key table can have many records in the related table. For instance, each catalog can match many records in the actual Plants table, but each plant matches only one catalog.

- **Many-to-many**—Both tables can have many records in this relationship. For instance, you could add a table of colors to describe the bloom on each plant. Each color could refer to many plants, and each plant could consist of more than one color.

Don't spend too much time thinking about the types of relationships right now. Fortunately, Access does a good job of interpreting the relationships between tables.

Modifying a Relationship

Now that you know how to create a relationship, let's modify one. Specifically, let's turn on *referential integrity* for the relationship between the Plants and Types tables. Referential integrity refers to a set of rules that protects data from changes that don't make sense. For example, think about the relationship between plants and types. What would happen if you deleted the first row from the Types table? You'd no longer be able to look up the descriptions of plants with a TypeID of 1. That's the sort of problem referential integrity prevents. We'll demonstrate how this works after adding referential integrity to the relationship.

To display the Edit Relationships dialog box for the relationship between the Plants and Types tables, double-click the join line between those two tables. In the resulting dialog box, check the **Enforce Referential Integrity** option. Then click **OK**, which is a little different from the last time when you clicked Create when you were done (refer to Figure 6.13).

After you modify the relationship between the Plants and Types tables, Access updates the join line accordingly, as shown in Figure 6.15. It's easy to see that the relationship between the two tables enforces referential integrity in a one-to-many relationship.

The Modified Join line

FIGURE 6.15

Access updates
the join line
between the
Plants and Types
tables.

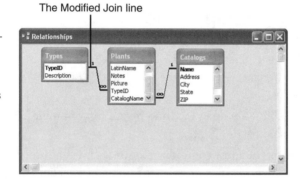

You probably noticed that several other buttons are available in the Edit Relationship dialog box (refer to Figure 6.13). Let's take a brief look at the remaining edit possibilities:

- **Table/Query**—Always lists the primary key side of a relationship. Specifies the appropriate key field(s) in the cells just below this control. Access usually defaults to the correct fields.

- **Related Table/Query**—Always lists the foreign key side of a relationship. Specifies the appropriate key field(s) in the cells just below this control. Access usually defaults to the correct fields.

- **Join type**—Displays another dialog box that lets you modify the type of join. This is an advanced operation that you won't need in this book.

- **Create New**—Offers more field possibilities for multiple field keys. (See Chapter 4 to learn more about primary and foreign keys.)

- **Cascade Update Related Fields**—A referential integrity feature that's available only when the Enforce Referential Integrity option is selected. This option automatically updates any related foreign key values when you change the value of a primary key. We recommend you not use this option unless you have a specific reason to do so.

- **Cascade Delete Related Fields**—A referential integrity feature that's available only when the Enforce Referential Integrity option is selected. This option automatically deletes any related foreign key records when you delete a primary key record. We recommend you not use this option unless you have a specific reason to do so.
- **Relationship Type**—Lists the type of relationship between the tables.

Close the Relationships window. When Access prompts you to save changes, click **Yes**.

Using Referential Integrity

Previously, we told you to select the Enforce Referential Integrity option in the Edit Relationships dialog box (refer to Figure 6.13). Referential integrity is simply a set of rules that protects your data because Access restricts the records you can add and delete. With referential integrity turned on

- You can't change a primary key value if a related record exists in another table.
- You can't enter a foreign key value if that value doesn't already exist as a primary key in the related table.

These rules will make more sense if you see them in action, so let's return to your tables and make a few changes. First, open the Catalog table and try to delete the first record. When you do, Access displays the warning message shown in Figure 6.16. Click **OK** to clear the message.

> **note**
>
> With the Enforce Referential Integrity option turned off, Access enables you to update any value or add and delete any records as long as you don't violate any data type or validation rules (which you'll learn about in Chapter 11, "Customizing Your Tables"). You must turn on referential integrity to use it. We recommend you not use either of the cascading options unless you have a specific reason to do so, and then we suggest you never turn them on permanently.

FIGURE 6.16

Referential integrity won't allow you to delete the record for *Gurney's* catalog.

You can't delete the record for *Gurney's* catalog because two plants, cosmos and German Chamomile, are related to that catalog. As long as even one of those records is there, Access won't let you delete the record for the *Gurney's* catalog.

Deleting that record would create what's known as an *orphan*—related records where the foreign key value (in this case, Gurney's) doesn't match a record in the related table. In other words, if you deleted the record for the *Gurney's* catalog, there would be no way to know from which catalog you purchased chamomile and cosmos seeds. This doesn't seem too terribly important, but can you imagine not knowing which customer placed a particular order? That would be a much more serious problem.

Now, let's see what happens when you try to modify a primary key value. In the Catalogs table, try to change `Gurney's` to `Gurneys` (delete the apostrophe character). You'll have to move the insertion point to another row to complete the action. When you do, Access displays another warning message: `The record cannot be deleted or changed because table 'Plants' includes related records`. Click **OK** to clear the message and then press **Esc** to clear the change. The problem is the same as before. Changing `Gurney's` to any other value would strand orphans—cosmos and German Chamomile—in the Plants table.

Subdatasheets—A Product of Relationships

Did you notice the plus signs (+) to the left of each record in the Catalogs table as you worked with it? Access displays those signs in the primary key table when a relationship exists between two tables. If you open all three tables, as we've done in Figure 6.17, you'll see that the Types and Catalogs tables both have a column of plus signs, but the Plants table doesn't.

FIGURE 6.17

The plus signs in a table indicate that Access has related records available.

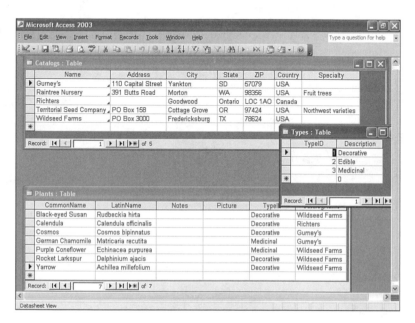

The plus sign means that the corresponding record has at least one related record in another table. If a relationship exists between two tables but no related record exists for a particular primary key value, Access displays a minus sign (–) instead of the plus sign.

Click the plus sign to the left of Gurney's in the Catalogs table. The result is shown in Figure 6.18. Specifically, a subdatasheet displays the records for cosmos and German Chamomile. A *subdatasheet* displays related values via an embedded datasheet (table).

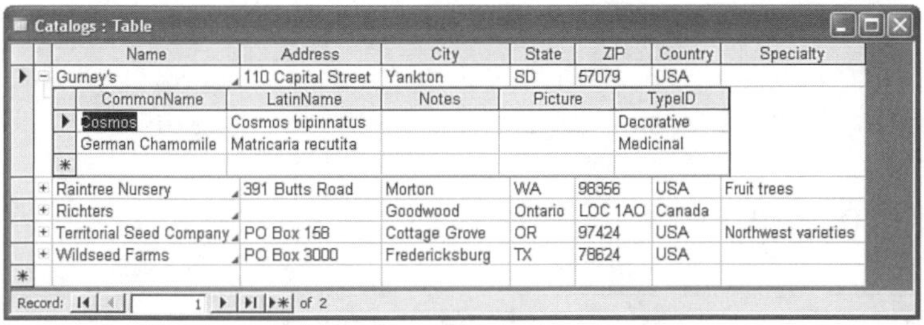
Catalogs : Table

Name	Address	City	State	ZIP	Country	Specialty
Gurney's	110 Capital Street	Yankton	SD	57079	USA	
Raintree Nursery	391 Butts Road	Morton	WA	98356	USA	Fruit trees
Richters		Goodwood	Ontario	LOC 1AO	Canada	
Territorial Seed Company	PO Box 158	Cottage Grove	OR	97424	USA	Northwest varieties
Wildseed Farms	PO Box 3000	Fredericksburg	TX	78624	USA	

CommonName	LatinName	Notes	Picture	TypeID
Cosmos	Cosmos bipinnatus			Decorative
German Chamomile	Matricaria recutita			Medicinal

Record: 1 of 2

FIGURE 6.18
Click a record's plus sign to display related records.

You can disable this feature if you like. To do so, follow these steps:

1. Open the table in Design view (click the **View** button on the Table Datasheet toolbar).
2. Click the **Properties** button on the Table Design toolbar.
3. In the resulting dialog box, select **[None]** from the Subdatasheet Name property's drop-down list. The default option is [Auto], which automatically displays one-to-many related records.

If you know the table has related records, but the plus signs aren't visible, you can update the table's properties to display subdatasheets. For instance, the Plants table doesn't display subdatsheets by default because the primary key values have no related records. All the relationships are between that table's foreign key values and the other two tables. To display subdatasheets in the Plants table, do the following:

1. Open the **Plants table** in Table Datasheet view.
2. Select **Subdatasheet** from the Insert menu to display the Insert Subdatasheet dialog box.
3. Select **Catalogs** in the Tables tab.
4. Select **Name** from the Link Child Fields control.
5. Select **CatalogName** from the Link Master Fields control, and click **OK**.

The result of this change is shown in Figure 6.19. Click any plus sign to display that record's corresponding catalog information. You don't want to display subdatasheets in the Plants table, so close the table without saving the change you just made. (Click **No** when Access prompts you to save your changes.)

FIGURE 6.19

The Plants table now displays related records in sub-datasheets.

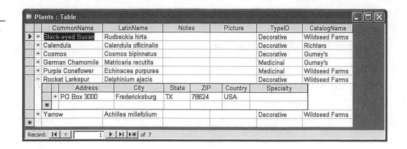

With all the extra records and fields displayed, navigating can be a bit awkward. Refer to Table 6.2 for shortcut keys for working with and navigating subdatasheets.

TABLE 6.2 Shortcut Keys

Press	Result
Ctrl+Shift+Down Arrow	Expands a record's subdatasheet
Ctrl+Shift+Up Arrow	Collapses a subdatasheet
Tab	Enters the subdatasheet from the last field of the previous record in the datasheet
Shift+Tab	Enters the subdatasheet from the first field of the following record in the datasheet
Ctrl+Tab	Exits the subdatasheet and moves to the first field of the next record in the datasheet
Ctrl+Shift+Tab	Exits the subdatasheet and moves to the last field of the previous record in the datasheet
Tab	Enters the next field in the datasheet from the last field in the subdatasheet

THE ABSOLUTE MINIMUM

The relationships between tables are the cornerstones on which all relationship database systems thrive. As you saw in this chapter, relationships can help you find related data from one table to another. Coupled with referential integrity, they can also help protect your data from accidental changes or deletions. In this chapter, you learned how to

- Create a lookup field and run the Table Analyzer
- Create a relationship between two tables
- Enforce referential integrity and why you should
- Display subdatasheets for browsing related records

IN THIS CHAPTER

- Using the Query Wizard
- Working with data in queries
- Building queries in design view

7

RETRIEVING DATA WITH QUERIES

By now, you should be comfortable with putting your data into Access tables. You know how to create a table and how to work with the data directly in a table. You've seen, too, how you can use relationships to tell Access how the data in more than one table is linked together.

But tables and relationships are just the first steps in building a truly useful Access database. You can think of these objects as the foundation of your database. They're essential, and you have to put them in place before anything else. But after the foundation is in place, you can build atop it. In this chapter, you'll start building the superstructure of your Access database to make it easier to use and more attractive. The first step in this construction process is to build queries.

How to Create Simple Queries

Access queries allow you to ask questions about your database—and, even better, to get the answers back. More generally, you might think of queries as a way to request particular bits of information from your database. Here are some examples of the types of information you can get from a query:

- What are all the plants in the database, sorted in alphabetical order?
- Which medicinal plants are in the database?
- Which catalogs have I purchased plants from?
- How many plants have I purchased from each catalog?

You can download the Chapter 7.mdb sample file, which is inclusive of all the examples in this chapter, from http://www.quepublishing.com/. If you want to follow along with our examples, download Chapter 6.mdb.

As you might guess, some of these queries are more complex than others. In this chapter, you'll learn how to construct simple queries, starting with using the aptly named Simple Query Wizard. You'll learn about more complex queries in Chapter 12, "Getting Down to Business with Queries."

Using the Simple Query Wizard

You've already seen some of the helpful wizards Access supplies to guide you through tasks as you get started with a database. Queries are no exception to this rule: The easiest way to get started with queries is by using the Simple Query Wizard. Here's how:

1. Launch Access and load the Plants database.
2. Select the **Queries** shortcut in the Database window.
3. Double-click the shortcut icon labeled **Create Query By Using Wizard**. This opens the Simple Query Wizard, as shown in Figure 7.1.
4. The drop-down list under the diagram lists all the tables and queries in your database. Right now you don't have any queries, so it shows only the three tables in the database. Select the **Plants** table from the list. You'll see that the Available Fields list changes to show the fields that are in the Plants table.

FIGURE 7.1

The Simple
Query Wizard.

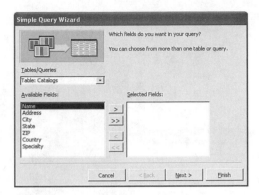

5. Select the **CommonName** field in the Available Fields list and click the **>** button to move it to the Selected Fields list.

6. Double-click the **LatinName** field in the Available Fields list. This also moves the field to the Selected Fields list.

7. Click the **Next** button to move to the second panel of the wizard.

8. Type the name `PlantNames` as the title for your new query. Select the **Open the Query to View Information** radio button, as shown in Figure 7.2.

FIGURE 7.2

Completing the
Simple Query
Wizard.

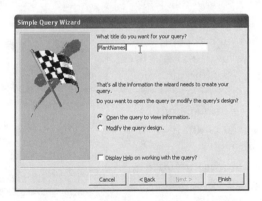

9. Click the **Finish** button to create the query and open it in datasheet view, as shown in Figure 7.3.

FIGURE 7.3

A new query open in datasheet view.

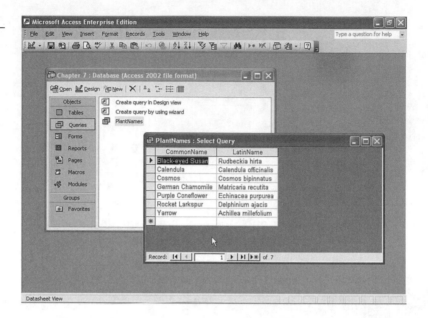

Although the query datasheet looks very similar to a table datasheet, there are some important differences:

- **A query doesn't show exactly the data from a table**—In this particular case, the query shows only two fields from the underlying table, even though you know that a lot more information exists in the table. As you'll see throughout this chapter, a query does not have to show all the rows from a table either.

- **The query doesn't actually contain any data**—The data it displays comes from the table, and any changes you make to the data are written back to the table.

> **caution**
>
> Keep in mind that if you delete data from a query, you're deleting it from the tables behind the query as well. Be sure you don't accidentally delete important data.

Later in the "Working with the Query Datasheet" section in this chapter, you'll learn more about working with data in a query datasheet. For now, just click the **Close** button to close the datasheet.

Building a Query on a Query

The PlantNames query is based directly on the Plants table. But you can also build a query that draws its data from another query. Here's an example:

1. Launch the Simple Query Wizard from the Queries tab of the Database window.

2. In the Tables/Queries drop-down list, select the **PlantNames** query. You'll see that only the fields in the query are listed in the Available Fields list box.

3. Double-click the **CommonName** field to move it to the SelectedFields list box.

4. Click **Next**.

5. Name the new query `PlantCommonNames`.

6. Click **Finish**, and Access creates the new query and opens its datasheet, which is shown in Figure 7.4.

FIGURE 7.4
A query based
on a query.

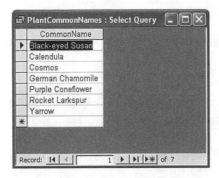

If you want, you can base a query on a query that's based on a query, and so on. You can stack them up as high as you want. No matter how many queries are in the list, though, at the bottom level the data is always stored in the tables, and any edits you make (usually) flow back to the tables.

Using More Than One Table

You might have noticed the instructions at the top of the Simple Query Wizard that state "You can choose from more than one table or query." Here's how this aspect of the Simple Query Wizard works:

1. Launch the Simple Query Wizard from the Queries tab of the Database window.

2. Select the **Plants** table from the Tables/Queries drop-down list.

3. Move the **CommonName** and **LatinName** fields from the Available Fields list to the Selected Fields list.

4. Select the **Types** table from the Tables/Queries drop-down list. Note that the fields you've already selected remain in the Selected Fields list, but the Available Fields list now shows the fields from the Types table (see Figure 7.5).

FIGURE 7.5

Creating a query with fields from more than one table.

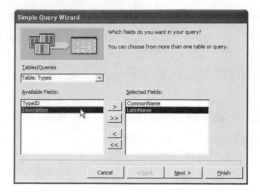

5. Move the **Description** field from the Available Fields list to the Selected Fields list.

6. Click **Next**.

7. Name the new query `PlantsWithTypes` and click **Finish**. Figure 7.6 shows the datasheet view of this query.

FIGURE 7.6

A query with fields from more than one table.

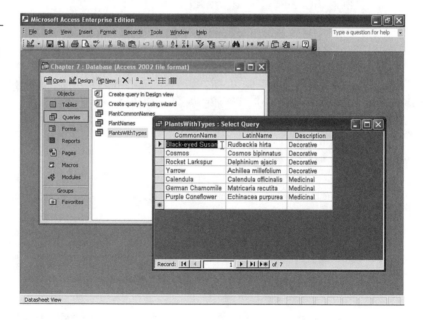

Look at all that repeating data in the Description field! You learned in Chapter 6, "Tapping the Power of Relationships," that repeating data is a bad thing, so what's going on here?

This is one of the areas where you need to care-fully distinguish between tables and queries. Repeating data in tables is indeed a bad thing; that's why you split repeating data off into sepa-rate tables when you're designing a database. By storing each piece of data in a single location, you can make your database more efficient and help prevent data entry errors.

tip

Design your tables to store data efficiently; then design your queries to present the data any way you want.

But you'll recall that storing data in relational tables does have disadvantages. The result is that the data in a table can be cryptic to human beings. Recall the difficulties in entering a TypeID for plants before you set up the lookup field.

Queries work together with tables to give you the best of both worlds. By using a query, you can store your data in an efficient, relational form while still presenting it to human beings in a more natural form, complete with repeating data if it makes sense to look at things that way. The data in a query is calculated at runtime by referring to the underlying tables; it's never stored, so there's no violation of the rule to store data in only one place.

Working with the Query Datasheet

Query datasheets not only look the same as table datasheets, but also behave the same way. All the keystroke shortcuts you learned in Chapter 5, "Building Your First Tables," apply equally well to query datasheets. You can also edit data in query datasheets, just as you can in table datasheets. Here's how:

1. Double-click the **PlantNames** query in the Database window to open it in datasheet view.

2. Click in the last cell in the CommonName column of the datasheet, where the data is currently Yarrow.

3. Change the value to Common Yarrow, as shown in Figure 7.7. Note the little pen-cil icon that appears to the left of the row while you do this. It's an indication that you've made changes that are not yet saved.

4. Click in any other row of the datasheet to save your change to the database.

5. Close the datasheet.

6. Select the **Tables** shortcut of the Database window.

7. Right-click the **Plants** table and select **Open**. You'll see that your new data appears in the table, even though you made your edit in the query.

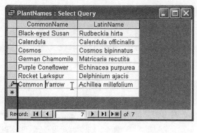

Pencil icon

8. Click in the Common Yarrow name and change it back to just `Yarrow`.

9. Close the table datasheet.

If you had any doubts that you're really editing table data when you work with a query datasheet, that set of steps should remove them.

But what happens when a query contains data from two different tables? The answer is that you can still edit the data, although sometimes the results might not be what you expect. Try these steps for an example:

1. Click the **PlantsWithTypes** query in the Database window. Then click the **Open** button on the Database Window toolbar.

2. Click in the cell containing the text `Black-Eyed Susan` and change it to `Blue-Eyed Susan`.

3. Press the **Tab** key twice to move the highlight to the last column of the first row of the datasheet, which currently reads Decorative.

4. Type `Ornamental` over `Decorative`.

5. Press **Tab** again. Your datasheet now appears similar to Figure 7.8. Note that `Decorative` has been replaced with `Ornamental` everywhere that it appears.

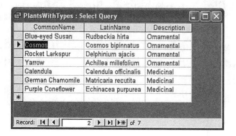

6. Click back into the original row and reverse your changes, so that the data is back to its original values.

Possibly you found the results of step 5, where four rows changed at once, rather surprising. But if you think about how the query works, you should be able to tell what's going on. The query draws its data from both the Plants table and the Types table, and each row of the query corresponds to one row in the Plants table. The CommonName and LatinName each come directly from the Plants table.

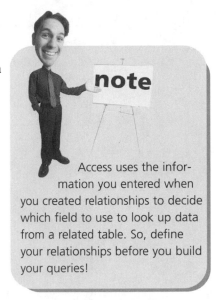

note

Access uses the information you entered when you created relationships to decide which field to use to look up data from a related table. So, define your relationships before you build your queries!

But what about the Description? That comes from the Types table. When the query needs to display the Description field, it first retrieves the TypeID value from the Plants table. That value tells the query which row of the Types table should be matched to the current row of the Plants table.

So, even though `Decorative` appears four times in the original datasheet, it's stored only once in the database. The query looks up the value for each row and thus displays it four times.

Now, what happens when you change the value? The query knows which row in the Types table it used to retrieve the original value, and it updates that row in the table. But then it reconsiders all the other rows, and it updates the value to the new value everywhere that it used that row. The net effect is that changing one row of data can affect many rows in a query that displays data from multiple tables. This feature of Access is called *row fixup*, and it prevents you from seeing data in a query that no longer exists in the underlying tables.

Using Query Design View

The Simple Query Wizard is adequate for building some queries, but it barely taps the power of Access queries. To go further with queries, you need to become familiar with query design view. Recall that you saw two views of tables in Chapter 5: datasheet view, which shows the data in a table, and design view, which shows the structure of a table. Similarly, queries have both datasheet and design views. When you look at a query in design view, you can make changes to its structure that will be represented in the datasheet view. You can use design view to alter existing queries or to build entirely new queries. In this section, you'll learn how to use design view to build new queries from scratch.

Adding Tables and Queries

The first task in building a new query in design view is to specify the table or query that contains the data you want to start with. Here's how to get started:

1. Select the **Queries** shortcut in the Database window.

2. Double-click the **Create Query in Design View** shortcut. This opens a new query in design view, along with the Show Table dialog box, as shown in Figure 7.9.

FIGURE 7.9

Creating a new query in design view.

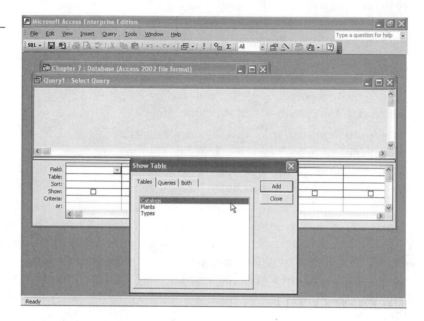

3. Select **Plants** on the Tables tab of the Show Table dialog box and click the **Add** button. This adds the table to the query.

4. Click the **Close** button to view the query in design view, as shown in Figure 7.10. The upper pane of this view shows the tables that supply data to the query, and the lower pane shows the fields that will appear in the query.

Adding tables is the first step in creating a query, but it's not sufficient. Select **View, Datasheet View** from the Access menus at this point, and you'll get the following error message: Query must have at least one destination field. Access displays this message because you haven't yet told the query which fields to display. You'll see how to do this next.

tip

If you like, you can change the font that Access uses in query design view. Select Tools, Options, and then select the Tables/Queries tab. You'll find a section labeled Query Design Font.

FIGURE 7.10

The query design grid.

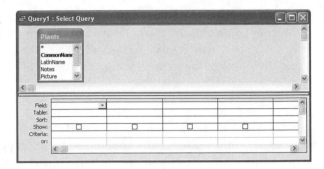

Adding Fields

To retrieve data via a query, you need to tell the query where that data is. So far, you've specified a table. Now you need to specify the individual fields, by following these steps:

1. Double-click the **CommonName** field in the Plants table in the upper pane of the query design window. This adds CommonName as the first field for the query, as shown in the first column of the lower pane of the query design window.

2. Click the **LatinName** field in the Plants table in the upper pane of the query. Now drag the field down and drop it in the second column of the lower pane of the query design window.

3. Click in the first row of the third column of the lower pane of the query design window to reveal a drop-down arrow. Click the drop-down arrow to see a list of all the available fields. Select the **CatalogName** field. Figure 7.11 shows the query in design view with three fields selected.

4. Select **View, Datasheet View** to see the data retrieved by the query.

FIGURE 7.11

Specifying fields in query design view.

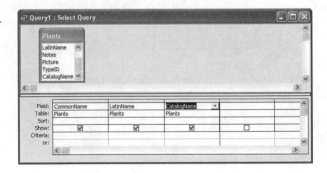

As you can see, there are several ways to specify the fields for a query. In addition to the three methods mentioned previously, you can also simply type the field name into the lower pane of the query design view. As you add fields, the grid shows the name of the field and the name of the table that contains the field.

Sorting the Results

So far, everything you've done in design view can also be done in the Simple Query Wizard. But design view has many additional capabilities. For example, you might have noticed that the results of the query you just built are sorted in alphabetical order by common name. What if you'd like to sort them in alphabetical order by Latin name instead? Query design view lets you sort the results by any field or combination of fields in the query. To do so, follow these steps:

1. Select **View, Design View** to return to query design view.

2. Click in the third row of the second column in the lower pane of the query design grid. This is the row labeled Sort under the LatinName column. When you click in the cell, a drop-down arrow appears.

3. Click the drop-down arrow and select **Ascending** from the list.

4. Click the **View** button at the left end of the Access toolbar and select **Datasheet View**, as shown in Figure 7.12.

FIGURE 7.12
Specifying the sort for a query.

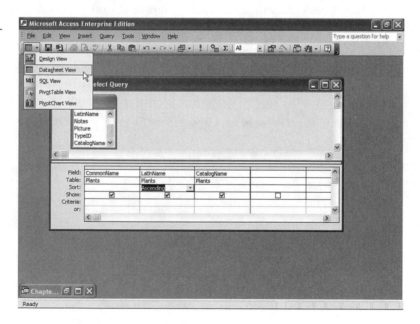

5. The query retrieves the same data that it did before, but now that data is sorted by Latin name. Use the drop-down view button to switch back to design view.

6. Remove the sort from the LatinName column by clicking in the cell and selecting **(not sorted)** from the drop-down list.

7. Move your cursor to the top of the CatalogName column and move it up slightly until it becomes a downward-pointing arrow. Click the cursor to select the entire column.

8. Click and drag the **CatalogName** column to the left until it becomes the first column in the query.

9. Set the sort for the CatalogName column to **Descending**.

10. Set the sort for the CommonName column to **Ascending**.

11. Switch the query to datasheet view. You'll see that the results are sorted in reverse alphabetical order by catalog name. Within each catalog, the results are sorted in alphabetical order by common name, as shown in Figure 7.13.

FIGURE 7.13

Sorting a query by two columns.

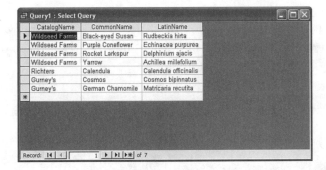

Sorting in queries is very flexible. You can sort by any field, or by any combination of fields, in either ascending or descending order. When you save a query, the sort is saved as part of the query design, so you don't need to reapply it when you open the query again. Sorts are applied in the order in which columns are displayed in the design view. As you saw previously, you can use drag and drop to change the order of columns.

note

If you don't specify a sort in a query, Access decides how to sort the results for you. Usually this is according to the first field of the first table in the query.

Filtering the Results

Query design view also enables you to specify a *filter* for query results. Filters are a very powerful concept for sorting through large masses of data. When you apply a filter, you specify some characteristics of the data that you actually want to see, and Access shows you only the matching rows. Here's how to do this:

1. Switch back to query design view.

2. Type **Wildseed Farms** in the criteria row of the first column of the query, as shown in Figure 7.14.

FIGURE 7.14

Adding a filter to a query.

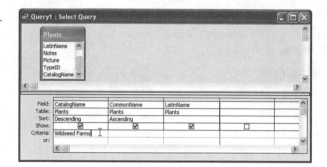

3. Switch to the datasheet view of the query. You'll see that it now displays only rows in which the CatalogName field contains Wildseed Farms, as shown in Figure 7.15.

FIGURE 7.15

Results of filtering a query.

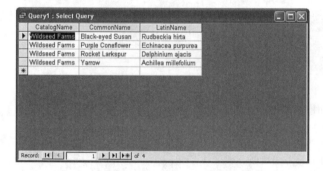

4. Switch back to design view. Type **Richters** on the next row of the design grid in the first column, directly beneath the existing filter.

5. Switch to datasheet view. You'll see that the datasheet now displays rows for both Wildseed Farms and Richters. When you enter multiple criteria on different rows in the query grid, a row is shown if it matches any of the criteria.

6. Switch to design view and remove the Richters value by highlighting it and pressing **Delete**.

7. Enter **Yarrow** as a criteria value in the first criteria row under CommonName, directly to the right of the Wildseed Farms entry.

8. Switch to datasheet view, and the query displays a single row, showing Yarrow plants from Wildseed Farms. When you enter multiple filters on the same row in the design grid, a row is shown only if it matches all the filters.

9. Click the **Save** button on the Access toolbar. Enter `FilteredPlants` as the query name and click **OK**.

10. Close the query datasheet.

note

Access sometimes alters what you enter as a filter. For example, if you type **Yarrow** (without quotes), you'll see it as "Yarrow" (with quotes) when you return to design view. This is nothing to be alarmed about. In fact, it's just Access's way of helping you.

Access supports a wide range of expressions in query filters. Table 7.1 shows some of the expressions you can use when designing a query. For more examples, search the Access help for the topic "Examples of Expressions."

TABLE 7.1   Query Filter Expressions

Expression	Meaning
`"Blue"`	Exactly the value `"Blue"`.
`"Blue" or "Red"`	Either `"Blue"` or `"Red"`.
`Like "B*"`	Anything starting with `"B"`. The * is a wildcard that matches any number of characters.
`Like "B??"`	`"Boo"`, `"Boy"`, `"Bay"`, or any other three-letter word starting with B. The ? is a wildcard matching precisely one character.
`< "N"`	Before *N* in the alphabet.
`333`	Exactly `333`.
`>= 333`	`333` or more.
`Between 5 and 100`	At least `5`, but no more than `100`.
`#3/5/2000#`	The date March 5, 2000 (applies to DateTime fields only).
`Not "Green"`	Anything other than `"Green"`.
`In ("Red", "Blue", "Green")`	Matches `red`, `blue`, or `green`.
`Is Null`	Field does not contain a value.
`Is Not Null`	Field contains any value (isn't blank).

Adding a Second Table

You can also develop queries that retrieve data from more than one table in design view. In this example, you'll build a query to retrieve all medicinal plants that come from catalogs in the U.S.:

1. Select the **Queries** shortcut in the Database window.

2. Click the **New** button on the Database Window toolbar.

3. In the New Query dialog box, select **Design View** and click **OK**.

4. In the Show Table dialog box, select the **Catalogs** table and click **Add**.

5. In the Show Table dialog box, select the **Plants** table and click **Add**.

6. Click **Close** to dismiss the Show Table dialog box.

7. Arrange the windows within Access so you can see both the query design window and the Database window.

8. Select the **Tables** shortcut in the Database window.

9. Drag the **Types** table from the Database window and drop it into the top pane of the query design window. This adds the Types table to the query. Figure 7.16 shows the query at this point. Note that Access automatically displays the relationships you have specified between the tables.

FIGURE 7.16

Multiple tables in query design view.

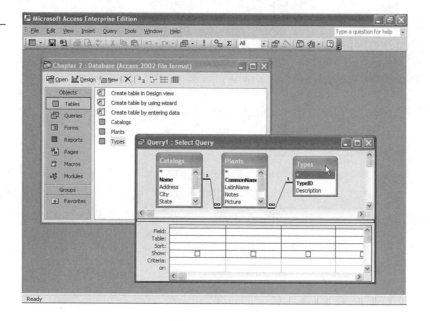

10. Add the **Name** and **Country** fields from the Catalogs table, the **CommonName** and **LatinName** fields from the Plants table, and the **Description** field from the Types table to the lower pane of the query.

11. Clear the **Show** check box for the Country field.

12. Specify **USA** as the filter for the Country field.

13. Specify **Medicinal** as the filter for the Description field. Be sure both filters are on the same row of the grid.

tip

To filter on a field without displaying the contents of the field, just uncheck the **Show** box, as you did in this example.

14. Specify **Ascending** as the sort for the CommonName field. Figure 7.17 shows the final query in design view.

FIGURE 7.17

Designing a complex query.

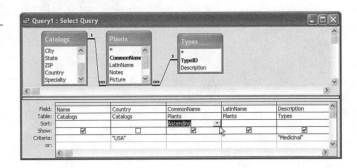

15. Switch to datasheet view to see the results of the query.

16. Save the query as `USAMedicinals`.

17. Close the query.

THE ABSOLUTE MINIMUM

In this chapter, you learned about Access queries. You'll find as you work with Access that queries provide you with a simple and flexible way to extract just the data you want from your database.

■ Queries provide a flexible way to display data from a database. You can combine data from multiple tables or display only the data of interest by using queries.

■ The Simple Query Wizard provides a quick way to build up queries that return records from one or more tables.

■ Query design view is a more flexible alternative to the Simple Query Wizard. With query design view, you can control the sorting order of the displayed records and set up complex filters to limit the amount of data returned by a query.

PART III

PUTTING A FRIENDLY FACE ON YOUR DATA

IN THIS CHAPTER

- Learn to create forms
- Use forms to view and edit data
- Find the data you need in form view

8

CREATING AND USING DATA ENTRY FORMS

Your database performs many tasks, and storing data is just one of them. After you have tables, you need a way to enter and modify data. The most efficient way to work with your data is through forms. Forms let you determine what data is displayed and what types of changes you can make to it.

A properly designed form will help you enter data more quickly and accurately. If you're creating an Access application to replace a process that currently uses paper forms, you can design your Access forms to look just like the paper forms. This will help ease the transition from paper to computer. You can also apply rules that limit the type of data the form accepts, which protects the data from some typos and other human errors.

At this point in your adventure, you have a few tables and queries, and now you're ready to advance to forms. In the next section, you'll create a couple of data entry forms for your gardening database using a few of the wizards that come with Access.

You can download the Chapter 8.mdb sample file, which is inclusive of all the examples in this chapter, from http://www.quepublishing.com/. If you want to follow along with our examples, download Chapter 7.mdb.

Creating Simple Forms

As with many other things in Access, there is more than one way to create a form. You can choose from the following three ways:

- You can use an AutoForm wizard, which automatically creates a form displaying all the data in a table or query.

- You can use the Form wizard, which automatically creates a form after you specify which fields you want the form to display (and a few formatting choices).

- You can create a form from scratch in design view.

The Wizard Way

Without a doubt, the quickest and easiest way to create a form is to let Access do the work for you—use a wizard whenever you can. The two types of form wizards are as follows:

- **AutoForm Wizard**—Creates a specific type of form and displays all the data in a table or query, without asking you any questions.

- **Form Wizard**—Lets you choose the type of form it produces and which data the form displays.

The AutoForm Wizard

Five AutoForm wizards are available, and each one automatically creates a specific type of form:

- **Columnar**—Stacks the fields, one on top of the other, beginning with the first field in the table or query until all the fields are lined up in a single column.

- **Tabular**—Aligns the fields beside each other in a row, positioning the first field in the table or query at the far left and adding subsequent fields in the same order they appear in the table or query.

- **Datasheet**—Displays all the fields in the table or query in the familiar table (or datasheet) row and column format. The form will look just like a table.
- **PivotTable**—The wizard opens the form in PivotTable view. (We won't review this wizard in this book.)
- **PivotChart**—The wizard opens the form in PivotChart view. (We won't review this wizard in this book.)

note

The PivotTable and PivotChart forms are for advanced analysis of large amounts of data. You won't need to use them in this book.

To quickly create a data entry form based on the Plants table, follow these steps:

1. Click the **Tables** shortcut in the Object bar, and then select the **Plants** table in the Database window.

2. Select **Form** from the Insert menu. Or, click the drop-down arrow next to the New Object button on the main Access toolbar and select **Form** from the list that appears.

3. In the resulting New Form dialog box, select the **AutoForm: Columnar** item, as shown in Figure 8.1, and click **OK**. Or, you can simply double-click the wizard. If you didn't choose the table beforehand, you can do so now by selecting a table or query from the drop-down control at the bottom of the dialog box.

FIGURE 8.1

Select the AutoForm: Columnar Wizard from the New Form dialog box.

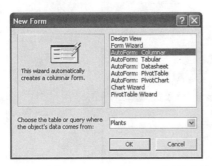

4. Save the resulting form, shown in Figure 8.2, by clicking the **Save** button on the Form view toolbar. Then, enter the name `Plants` in the Save As dialog box and click **OK**.

FIGURE 8.2

A columnar form stacks the controls vertically.

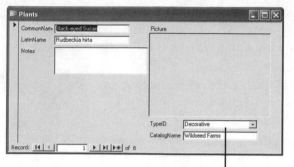

Inherited lookup field

Figures 8.3 and 8.4 show two more forms. Specifically, we used the AutoForm: Tabular Wizard to base a form on the Catalogs table and the AutoForm: Datasheet Wizard to base a form on the Types table. Creating these forms will help you practice with the AutoForm feature and show you the variety of forms you can get with a minimal amount of effort. Sometimes, though, you'll find that AutoForms just aren't good enough for what you want to do with the database. We'll show you how to create more complex and customized forms in the rest of the chapter.

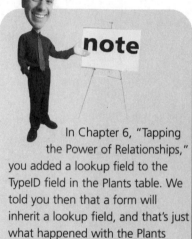

note

In Chapter 6, "Tapping the Power of Relationships," you added a lookup field to the TypeID field in the Plants table. We told you then that a form will inherit a lookup field, and that's just what happened with the Plants form. The TypeID control in the form shown in Figure 8.2 is a combo box control—you can tell by the drop-down arrow to the right of the control. You'll learn more about combo box controls in Chapter 13, "Customizing Forms."

FIGURE 8.3

The tabular form aligns the controls in the same row.

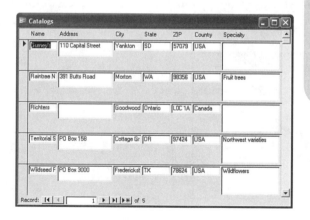

FIGURE 8.4

Datasheet forms look just like a table (or datasheet).

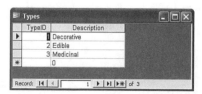

About Subforms

You might have noticed that the New Object button's list includes an AutoForm item, but you didn't select it in the previous example. This wizard automatically produces a columnar form similar to the AutoForm: Columnar Wizard used earlier. But there's an important difference between these two wizards: The wizard in the New Object list includes a table's relationships in the finished form. As you'll see, the relationship between tables translates into a relationship between forms. Specifically, the resulting form has a subform (an embedded form within the main form) that displays related data.

We'll show the difference between these two forms in the following steps. Let's use the AutoForm Wizard on the New Object list to base a form on the Catalogs table. To do so, follow these steps:

1. Click the **Tables** shortcut in the Object bar, and then Select **Catalogs** in the Database window.

2. Open the New Object button's drop-down list and select **AutoForm**. Figure 8.5 shows the new form. Note that the wizard uses the name of the main table (Catalogs) as the title of the form, even though the form shows data from both the Catalogs table and the Plants table. Save this form as `CatalogsAndPlants`.

FIGURE 8.5

The AutoForm Wizard accommodates the relationship between the Catalogs and Plants tables.

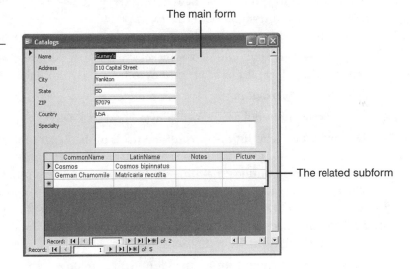

This form is special because it includes data from both the Catalogs and the Plants tables, even though you didn't tell the wizard to do so. That's because the wizard encountered the relationship between the two tables and included a subform to display the related plant information for the current catalog.

The main form displays the catalog records, and the subform displays plants where the primary/foreign key value in the two tables matches. In other words, the subform displays any plants where the CatalogName field matches the value in the main form's Name field. This might or might not be what you want. Just remember, you can always dump the form and use one of the other AutoForm wizards. Or, you can use the Form Wizard to exercise a bit more control over the results. Close the form before continuing. You'll learn more about building and customizing subforms in Chapter 13.

The Form Wizard

The Form Wizard creates the form for you but allows you to set limits to the data the form will display. You start the wizard the same way you do an AutoForm wizard, except in the New Form dialog box, you select Form Wizard.

Now, let's look at the options the Form Wizard enables you to select as you create a new form. Specifically, we'll base a form on both the Types and Plants tables. To do so, follow these steps:

1. Display the New Form dialog box by selecting **Form** from the New Object button's drop-down list or selecting **Form** from the Insert menu.

2. Select **Form Wizard** in the New Form dialog box.

3. Select **Types** from the drop-down control, and click **OK**.

4. The Available Fields list displays all the fields in the Types table. You'll move the fields you want to add to the form to the Selected Fields list by clicking one of the arrow buttons the same way that you did with the Simple Query Wizard in Chapter 7, "Retrieving Data with Queries." The single arrow button (>) moves one field at a time; the double arrow button (>>) moves all the fields to the Selected Fields list. For this example, click the double arrow button to move all the fields to the Selected Fields list, as shown in Figure 8.6.

5. Now, let's add some data from the Plants table. To do so, simply select **Table: Plants** from the Tables/Queries drop-down list, which updates the Available Fields list accordingly. Move the CommonName, LatinName, and CatalogName fields to the Selected Fields list, as shown in Figure 8.7. Click **Next** to continue.

Select a table or query

FIGURE 8.6
Include both
fields from the
Types table.

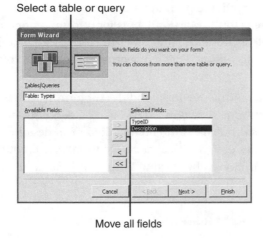

Move all fields

Select the Plants table

FIGURE 8.7
Include three
fields from the
Plants table.

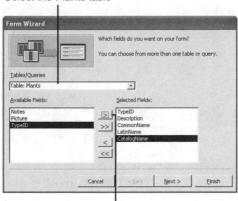

Move one field at a time

6. Because you selected fields from more than one table, the wizard offers three ways to display the related data. The wizard defaults to displaying the plant records data in a subform and shows you a schematic picture of this option.

7. To see the other options, select the **By Plants** item in the list to the left, and the wizard updates the sample form to the right accordingly. Notice that the wizard also selects the Single Form option at the bottom of the dialog box. Reselect the **By Types** item and click the **Linked Forms** option to view that sample, which creates two linked forms. Be sure to reselect the **Form with SubForm(s)** option before clicking **Next** to continue.

8. The next window enables you to choose the type of form you want: Tabular, Datasheet, PivotTable, or PivotChart. Select **Tabular**, and click **Next**.

9. At this point, you can choose from any number of autoformats. An *autofor-mat* lets you set the default colors and fonts for a form, among other things. The wizard defaults to Standard, and that's the format we'll keep. Click **Next** without changing this option. (You can learn more about autoformats in Chapter 13.)

10. In the last window, rename the form and the subform `TypesMain` and `PlantsSub`, respectively, as shown in Figure 8.8. You can also select to open the form in form view so you can start entering data or in design view, where you can modify the form's design. (It's common to tweak the product of a wizard.) Open the form in form view by clicking **Finish** without changing the wizard's selection.

FIGURE 8.8

Name the two forms (the main form and sub-form) and click Finish.

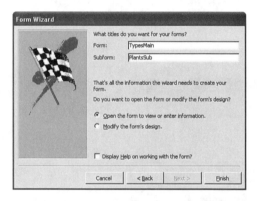

The new form, shown in Figure 8.9 lists the type possibilities in the main form. The subform displays the plant records for the type that's current in the main form.

You'll see that forms contain the same navigation buttons that you're already famil-iar with from datasheets. If you click the Next Record navigation button on the sub-form (refer to Figure 8.9), the selection arrow in the left margin of the subform advances one row, from Black-Eyed Susan to Cosmos. If you click the Next Record navigation button on the main form to display a new type, the subform updates the plant records accordingly. As you can see in Figure 8.10, type 2 (edible plants) cur-rently has no related plant records. Close the form.

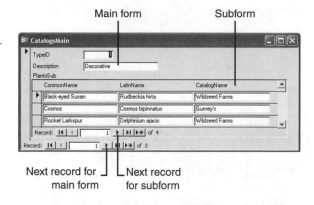

FIGURE 8.9
The wizard has
produced a form
that displays the
plant names in
a subform.

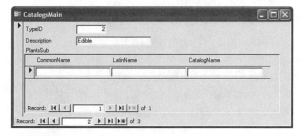

FIGURE 8.10
As yet, no edible
plants exist in
the database.

Creating a Form in Design View

You don't need a wizard to create a form. Although the wizards do a good job, sometimes simply starting from scratch can be more efficient. When this is the case, open
a blank form in design view and start adding controls. To open a blank form in
design view, do the following:

1. Select **Form** from the Insert menu. Or, select **Form** from the New Object button's drop-down list.

2. Design view is the default option in the resulting New Form dialog box, and
   this is the option you want.

3. If you didn't specify a table or query in step 1, select the appropriate table or
   query now in the drop-down control.

4. Click **OK** to open a blank form in design view, as shown in Figure 8.11.

In Chapter 13, you'll learn how to customize a form in design view by adding and
formatting controls and formatting the form itself. For now, just close the form without saving it.

FIGURE 8.11

A blank form in design view.

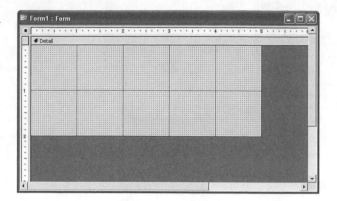

Quick Error Detection with Error-Checking

Access 2003's new error-checking smart tag warns you when you make common form and report errors. (You can learn more about smart tags in Chapter 5, "Building Your First Tables.") If you're familiar with Excel 2002, you may be familiar with the feature already, as Excel 2002 uses a similar smart tag to point out spreadsheet errors. In this section, you'll make a mistake on purpose, just so you can experience the error-checking smart tag:

1. Open the Plants form in design view by clicking the **Forms** shortcut in the Database window, selecting **Plants**, and then clicking **Design** in the Database Window toolbar.

2. In form view, double-click the **CommonName** control to display that control's properties in the Properties window.

3. Click the All Tab. The Control Source property is currently CommonName because this control is bound to the CommonName field in the Plants table. Change that setting to anything other than the name of a valid field in the Plants table. As you can see in Figure 8.12, we entered **Test** (there is no field named Test).

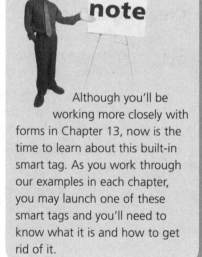

note

Although you'll be working more closely with forms in Chapter 13, now is the time to learn about this built-in smart tag. As you work through our examples in each chapter, you may launch one of these smart tags and you'll need to know what it is and how to get rid of it.

4. When you press Enter or try to move to another field, Access displays a smart tag icon next to the problem control in the form. Clicking the icon displays a list of possible errors and solutions, as shown in Figure 8.12. In this case, the error is an invalid Control Source property. Among other actions, you can select Edit the Control's Control Source Property to automatically select and highlight the Control Source property in the Properties window, or you can ignore the error. For now, just close the form without saving the change.

Click the smart tag icon

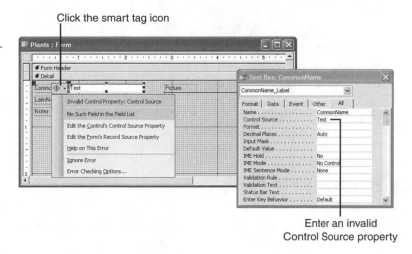

FIGURE 8.12
Enter a field name that doesn't exist to display the error smart tag.

Enter an invalid
Control Source property

Entering Data Through Forms

Now that you know how to create a form, let's learn how to use it to enter and modify data. First, open the Plants form by clicking the **Forms** shortcut on the Object bar and double-clicking **Plants** in the Database window. You'll see that some of the user interface for a form resembles the user interface you've already seen for tables and queries, but there are new things here as well. The form shown in Figure 8.13 can tell you a lot, such as

■ The title bar displays the form's name and purpose.

■ The record selector points out the active record. The sample form displays only one record at a time, but that isn't always the case. For example, in the subform in Figure 8.9 you can see more than one record at a time. On this form, the current record is for Black-eyed Susan.

■ The navigation bar displays the number of records and enables you to browse through those records. The current record is the first record of seven.

FIGURE 8.13

A basic form can give you a lot of information about your data.

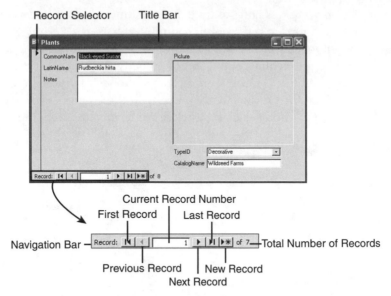

Navigating Fields and Records

In a table or query, you might refer to a particular column of data as a *field*. Forms use controls to display data. Right now the form displays the records you entered directly into the Plants table in earlier chapters.

When you open a form, Access selects the first control in the form. For instance, when you open the Plants form, Access selects the CommonName control—you can tell because the actual entry is highlighted. To move from one control to the next, simply press the Tab key. Sometimes the Enter key performs the same function, but not always, so the preferred method is the Tab key. For example, press the **Tab** key once to select the LatinName control. Then, press **Enter** to select the Notes control. While in the Notes memo field, pressing Enter simply moves the insertion point to the next line in the memo field. To move to the next control, the Picture control, you must press the Tab key. Table 8.1 lists helpful keystroke combinations for navigating a form, and Table 8.2 contains combinations for navigating in a form with a subform.

TABLE 8.1 Keyboard Shortcuts for Navigating Controls

Press	Result
F5+number	Selects a specific record
Tab	Moves to the next field
Shift+Tab	Moves to the previous field
End	Moves to the last field in the current record

Press	Result
Ctrl+End	Moves to the last field in the last record
Home	Moves to the first field in the current record
Ctrl+Home	Moves to the first field in the first record
Ctrl+Page Down	Moves to the current field in the next record
Ctrl+Page Up	Moves to the current field in the previous record

TABLE 8.2   Keyboard Shortcuts for Navigating Between a Main Form and a Subform

Press	Result
Tab	Enters the subform from the field that precedes the subform in the main form
Shift+Tab	Returns to the subform from the field following the subform in the main form
Ctrl+Tab	Exits the subform and moves to the next field in the main form or next record
Ctrl+Shift+Tab	Exits the subform and moves to the field that precedes the subform in the main form or previous record

Did you notice that the Notes control displayed a scrollbar when you selected it? That's because that control is based on a memo data type (at the table level). We chose that data type because it can store a lot more text than the normal text data type.

When you're ready to see the next record, simply click the **Next Record** button on the navigation bar. Or, keep pressing the **Tab** key until the last control is selected, which in this case is the CatalogName control. Then, press **Tab** one more time. When you do, Access displays the next record.

Entering data is simple: Just select a field and type the data. When you're done, press Tab or Enter, as the case may be. For example, with the Calendula record current, select the Notes control and enter the following text: `This plant loves cooler weather and full sun but will tolerate a hot spot if you keep well watered. You can expect lots of blooms well into fall.` When you're done, press **Tab** to select the Picture control. Right now, none of your records are displaying pictures, but you can fix that by following these steps:

1. With the Picture control selected, select **Object** from the Insert menu. (You can also right-click the **Picture** control and select **Insert Object** from the resulting submenu.)

2. Click the **Create from File** option to the left of the dialog box.

3. Click the **Browse** button to locate the picture file you want to display. We recommend you store pictures in the same folder with your database. When you find the correct graphics file, double-click it. Or, select it and click **OK**. Access will display the name of the graphic file in the File control, as shown in Figure 8.14. Click the Link option only if you plan to modify the graphic file. In this case, you won't be modifying the pictures, so don't select it.

FIGURE 8.14

Browse to the graphic file that you want to display with the current record.

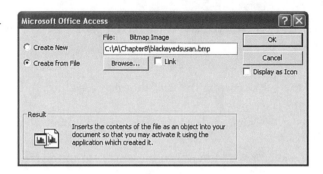

4. Click **OK**.

5. The control will probably display a small version of the file in the upper-left corner, as shown in Figure 8.15. If this happens, click the **Properties** button on the Form view toolbar.

FIGURE 8.15

Sometimes, the control displays a small version of the file.

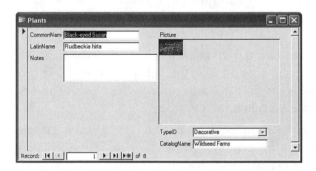

6. In the Properties list for the Bound Object Frame, open the **Size Mode** properties drop-down list and select **Stretch**, as shown in Figure 8.16. The default is Clip.

FIGURE 8.16

Select the Stretch Size Mode property.

7. Close the Properties window, and the control should display a full view of the file. You'll learn more about control properties in Chapter 13.

8. Repeats steps 1–4 to embed pictures of each plant.

9. When you're done, close the form and save it when prompted. You're not saving the data you just entered; Access automatically saves the new picture data. Remember during step 6 when you changed the Size Mode property? That's what you're saving now.

You might be curious about how a picture looks in datasheet view, so open the Plants table after you enter a few (or all) of the picture files. Figure 8.17 shows the Plants table after inserting a picture for each record. Each picture entry is a bitmap image. A table doesn't actually display a picture the same way a form or report does.

Of course, you won't always be adding new data via forms. Sometimes you'll delete data or replace an entry with something new. Fortunately, it's all very easy in a form. When you select a control, the form automatically highlights the entry. At this point, you can do any of the following:

■ Press Delete to delete the entry.

■ Start typing to replace the entry.

note

Did you notice that the CommonName label to the left of that control isn't completely visible? (Depending on your system's display properties, this might not occur in your form, so don't worry if it doesn't.) That's just one of the small annoyances you'll run into when using a wizard; it simply didn't allow enough room. In Chapter 13, you'll learn how to modify controls that don't behave the way you want them to.

Graphic files vary greatly, and there's no way to guarantee the quality of each file from record to record. You can improve a picture, but that's a bit beyond the scope of this chapter.

- Use the mouse to precisely position the insertion point so you can change one or just a few characters in the existing entry.

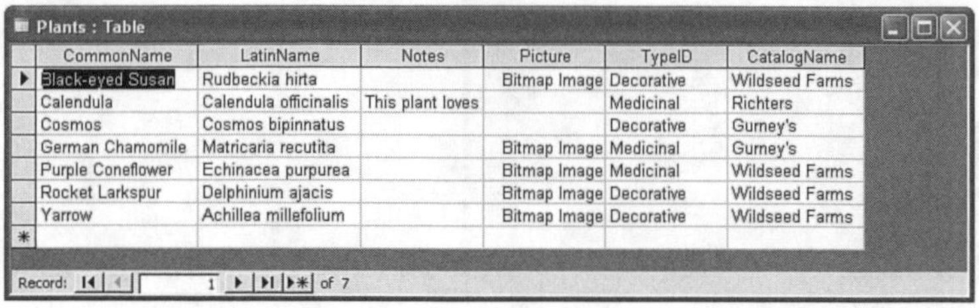

Plants : Table

	CommonName	LatinName	Notes	Picture	TypeID	CatalogName
▸	Black-eyed Susan	Rudbeckia hirta		Bitmap Image	Decorative	Wildseed Farms
	Calendula	Calendula officinalis	This plant loves		Medicinal	Richters
	Cosmos	Cosmos bipinnatus			Decorative	Gurney's
	German Chamomile	Matricaria recutita		Bitmap Image	Medicinal	Gurney's
	Purple Coneflower	Echinacea purpurea		Bitmap Image	Medicinal	Wildseed Farms
	Rocket Larkspur	Delphinium ajacis		Bitmap Image	Decorative	Wildseed Farms
	Yarrow	Achillea millefolium		Bitmap Image	Decorative	Wildseed Farms
*						

Record: 1 of 7

FIGURE 8.17
Graphic files appear as text in datasheet view.

When you're editing records, the record selector you saw earlier changes to the small pencil icon, just as it does on a datasheet (refer to Figure 8.15). You can demonstrate this in the Plants form by selecting the LatinName control and pressing the Delete key. If you try this yourself, press Esc to cancel the delete task so that you don't lose data.

Adding and Deleting Records

In the previous section, you learned how to enter and delete new data. Occasionally, you'll need to add or delete an entire record. You can add records in four ways:

- Click the New Record button on the form's navigation bar, as mentioned earlier.
- Click the New Record button on the form view toolbar.
- Select New Record from the Insert menu.
- Press Ctrl++.

All the previous methods display a blank record. Let's walk through the process of creating a new record. Do the following:

1. Use one of the methods mentioned above to display a new record. Notice that the record number control in the navigation bar displays the number `8`—you will be entering the eighth record. As soon as you begin to enter data, Access updates the record selector to display the editing symbol (the pencil icon).
2. With the CommonName control selected, enter **`French Lavender`** and press **Tab**.
3. Enter **`Lavandula stoechas`** and press **Tab** three times.
4. Open the TypeID control's drop-down list and select **Decorative**; then press **Tab**.
5. Enter **`Richters`**.
6. Save the record by selecting **Save Record** from the Records menu, pressing **Shift+Enter**, or simply moving to another record. Figure 8.18 shows the new record.

FIGURE 8.18
You haven't
entered a picture
of your new
plant yet.

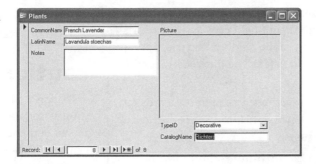

Deleting a record is even easier. After selecting
the appropriate record in your form, use one of
the following methods to delete that record:

- Click the Record Selector and then press
  the Delete key.
- Select Delete Record from the Edit menu.
- Click the Delete Record button on the
  form view toolbar.

After you attempt to delete the record, Access displays a confirmation message. You'd click Yes to
delete the record, or you'd click No to cancel the
delete task. Right now, click **No** because you don't
want to delete the record.

Finding Information with Forms

In Chapter 6, you learned how to sort and limit
the results of a query. You can also sort and limit
data in a form; we'll show you how to do so in
this section.

Sorting Records in a Form

Do you remember setting the sort order for a
query in Chapter 7? In the design grid, you selected
Ascending, Descending, or None in a field's sort cell. When you ran the query,
Access presented the records in the appropriate order. Sorting in a form is very similar, but there's no sort cell.

Let's look at a quick example using your Plants form. The form sorts the records by
the CommonName field because that field is the primary key for the Plants table.

tip

If you change your mind
while you're entering a
record, you can press Esc
twice to delete the record
before it's saved.

You won't always want to
view existing records while entering new ones. When that's the
case, select **Data Entry** from the
Records menu and Access will
remove existing data from the form
and update the record numbers in
the navigation bar. To return the
records, select **Remove Filter/Sort**
from the Records menu.

Not all forms allow you to enter
new records. If the New Record
button is disabled, you'll know the
form is just for browsing and editing existing data.

When you assign a primary key, Access automatically defines an index for that field and an index sorts the data according to the field's data type. For instance, if the field is text, the data sorts alphabetically.

Let's temporarily rearrange your plant records by sorting them by their LatinName entries. To do so, follow these steps:

1. Select the **LatinName** control for any record.

2. Click the **Sort Ascending** button on the Form view toolbar. Figure 8.19 shows the results. As you can see by the navigation controls, the first record is no longer Black-eyed Susan; instead it is Yarrow. If you browse the records, you'll find them in alphabetical order according to the LatinName entries.

> **caution**
>
> Don't assign a primary key just to sort data. From our discussion in Chapter 4, "Planning a Database," you might remember that a primary key's function is to uniquely identify a record—sorting is just a by-product.

FIGURE 8.19
Sorting the records by the LatinName entries.

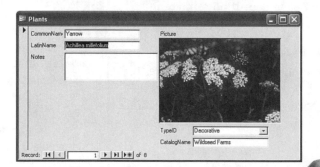

Sort tasks are temporary, unless you save the sorted form. In that case, Access remembers the new sort order the next time you open the form. To remove a temporary sort you've saved, select **Remove Filter/Sort** from the Records menu.

> **tip**
>
> A quick sort can filter records. It doesn't limit the records, but it does group the records by the sort field. You can then browse a particular group without first applying a more complex filter or query.

Using Filter by Selection

The Filter by Selection feature in forms is similar to the table feature you learned about in Chapter 5. You simply select a control and apply the filter—Access does the rest. The main difference is that the Filter by Selection feature limits the records it displays by eliminating all records that don't match the entry in the current control.

Now, let's suppose you want to browse only the decorative plants. To do so, follow these steps:

1. Select the **TypeID** control in the first record (or any record that displays Decorative in the TypeID control).

2. Select **Records, Filter, Filter by Selection**, or click the **Filter by Selection** button on the Form view toolbar. Figure 8.20 shows the results of the filter, and five records match the selected control (Decorative).

FIGURE 8.20

Use the Filter by Selection feature to limit the records in your form.

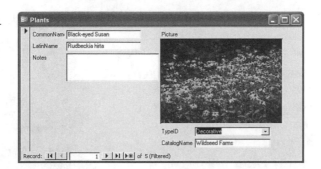

Notice that the navigation bar has updated the number of records. Specifically, there's a total of five records instead of eight. In addition, the toolbar now displays the text (Filtered). That way, you know you're looking at an incomplete set of records. To remove the record, click the **Remove Filter** button or select **Remove Filter/Sort** from the Records menu. Do that now to return your form to normal.

Using Filter by Form

The Filter by Form feature is similar to the Filter by Selection feature but more complex. Using this feature, you can specify the actual value that Access will attempt to match, instead of relying on existing data. You can also refer to more than one control.

Let's illustrate this filtering feature by finding the medicinal plants you purchased from Wildseed Farms. Do the following:

1. Select **Records, Filter, Filter by Form**, or click the **Filter by Form** button on the Form view toolbar.

2. Access displays the filtering form shown in Figure 8.21. Access remembers the last filter, which is why an entry exists in the TypeID control—that's a left over from the Filter by Selection exercise in the last section. You should clear any existing filters before you apply a filter by clicking the **Clear Grid** button on the Filter/Sort toolbar.

FIGURE 8.21

Using the Filter by Form feature to find all your medicinal plants purchased from Wildseed Farms.

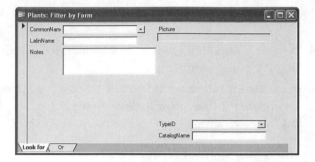

3. Select **Medicinal** from the TypeID control.

4. Select the **CatalogName** control, and Access displays a drop-down arrow to the right. Click it to display the possible entries by which you could filter. Then select **Wildseed Farms**.

5. Click the **Apply Filter** tool on the Filter/Sort toolbar to display the filtered set of records. The form shows only medicinal plants from Wildseed Farms.

The filtered set contains only one record—Purple Coneflower. To remove the filter, click the **Remove Filter** button on the Form view toolbar or select **Remove Filter/Sort** from the Records menu. Remove the filter now.

note

You might have noticed that the Remove Filter and Apply Filter buttons use the same icon. Don't let that confuse you because you can't make a mistake by clicking the button at the wrong time. The buttons perform the appropriate task.

Using the Find Dialog Box

So far, you've sorted and filtered. You can also search for a particular value in a record using the Find dialog box. This feature is similar to the Filter by Selection feature, but it doesn't filter the results and all the records are still available to you. Let's use this feature to find the record for purple coneflower. Follow these steps:

1. From any record other than the record for Purple Coneflower, select the **CommonName** control. Then select **Find** from the Edit menu or press **Ctrl+F**.

2. Enter `Purple Coneflower` as the data to find.

3. Click **Find Next**, and Access displays the record shown in Figure 8.22. You might need to move the Find and Replace dialog box to see the results of the search.

FIGURE 8.22

Access displays the first matching record when you click the Find Next button.

The record you see in Figure 8.22 might not be the only record that matches your entry. In this case it is, but if it weren't, you'd click Find Next again to see the next matching entry and continue doing so until you found the record you were searching for. Close the Find and Replace dialog box when you're done searching.

The Find and Replace feature lets you qualify a search by specifying the field you're searching, specifying just how much of the entry you want to consider, determining the direction of the search, matching the letter case, and considering any formatting.

note

Throughout this chapter, all the forms have been based on tables, but don't forget that you can also base a form on a query. Doing so provides a permanent means of filtering and sorting the form's data. Eventually, you might find that you seldom base a form on a table and that you rely a great deal on queries to provide the data for your forms.

THE ABSOLUTE MINIMUM

Storing data may be the purpose of a database, but it's your job to enter and maintain that data. Forms are the best way to enter new data, modify existing data, and even delete unwanted data. In this chapter, you learned to do the following:

- Create forms using wizards
- Navigate forms and enter new data
- Modify existing data
- Sort, filter, and search records

9

PRINTING INFORMATION WITH REPORTS

At this point, you've designed your database and built the basic tables to contain data. You know how to build queries to retrieve the information you'd want to work with. You've even seen how to build a user interface based on Access forms to quickly enter, display, and find information. What could be left?

Printing, that's what. The next step in your database journey is to learn how to print paper copies of information using Access reports.

Building Reports

Computers are convenient—but not for everything. Suppose you want to take your list of plants to the nursery to make sure that you know which varieties you already have when you're shopping? Or you might want to put your plant pictures into a physical photo album, as well as storing them on your computer. If you start treating your garden as a commercial activity, you'll also need to keep paper records to satisfy your accountant.

For all these reasons, you need to be able to get information from your database and send it to a printer instead of to the screen. Fortunately, Access includes the perfect object for this: It's called a *report*. In this chapter, you'll learn how to develop your own reports for those times when having the data onscreen just isn't enough.

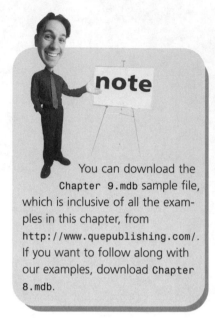

note

You can download the Chapter 9.mdb sample file, which is inclusive of all the examples in this chapter, from http://www.quepublishing.com/. If you want to follow along with our examples, download Chapter 8.mdb.

Why Not Just Print Forms?

While you were working with forms, you might have noticed the Print and Print Preview commands on the File menu. Maybe you could just use those commands to print your forms and save yourself the trouble of building additional objects? Well, you could—but you're not likely to be happy with the results. Here's how to take a look and judge for yourself:

1. Launch Access and load the Plants database.

2. Use the AutoForm: Tabular wizard to create a form named Catalogs, by selecting the Catalogs table in the Database window, choosing Form from the Insert command, and then double-clicking AutoForm: Tabular in the New Form dialog box.

3. Select **File, Print Preview**. This opens a print preview window showing the form.

4. Move the mouse cursor over the print preview window, so that it displays a magnifying glass cursor, and click the mouse button. This zooms in on the print preview window, as shown in Figure 9.1.

caution

Before you try to print or preview any objects in Access, make sure you've installed a printer in your Windows settings. Otherwise, things will look terrible!

FIGURE 9.1

Printing an
Access form.

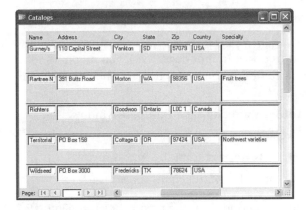

Not very inspiring, is it? Forms are great for onscreen
display, but printing a vast expanse of gray with
small bits of embedded information is not usually
what you want. For printed output that's actually
optimized for a printer, you need to use a report.

Creating Simple Reports

Access lets you easily create reports. As always,
there's more than one way to perform this particular task. In this section, you'll learn about three
ways that you can create reports in your Access
database:

- Using AutoReports
- Using a Report Wizard
- Using report design view

note

Access Print Preview is
practically identical to the
way things look when printed.
We'll be using print preview in this
chapter because there's no easy
way to take a screen shot of the
printed results!

These methods of building reports offer you a choice between the amount of work
you need to do and the amount of customization you can perform: Report design
view is the most flexible of the three, but it's also the most complex. For many of
your reporting needs, a simple AutoReport or a report generated by the Report
Wizard should be more than adequate.

Building an AutoReport

The easiest way to build a report in Access is to use the AutoReport wizard. You can think of AutoReport as a wizard that doesn't ask you any questions; it just makes the best guess that it can and then builds it. Here's how to create an AutoReport from the Catalogs table:

1. Select the **Tables** shortcut in the Database window.

2. Select the **Catalogs** table.

3. Select **Insert, AutoReport** from the Access menu.

4. Select **File, Save** and save the report as `CatalogsAuto`.

That's it! Access will design and open the report shown in Figure 9.2. The default AutoReport still wastes a lot of space, but it doesn't add unnecessary graphical clutter to the printed page.

FIGURE 9.2

An AutoReport based on the Catalogs table.

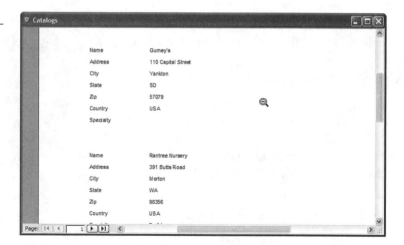

You'll note that the catalogs on this report are sorted in the same order in which they're sorted in the underlying table—that is, by the Name field, which is the primary key of the table. What if you want the report in a different order? One answer is that you can base a report on a query, which, as you know, can sort records in any order. For example, you might build an AutoReport that shows the catalogs sorted by specialty. To do so, follow these steps:

1. Select the **Catalogs** table in the Database window.

2. Click the drop-down arrow next to the **New Object** button on the Access toolbar, and select **Query** from the list.

3. In the New Query dialog box, select **Design View** and click **OK**.

4. In the Query1 design window, double-click the asterisk at the top of the list of fields in the Catalogs table. This is a shortcut for adding all the fields from the table to the query.

5. Drag the **Specialty** field from the field list to the query grid. Set the Sort for this field to **Ascending** and uncheck the **Show** box.

6. Select **File, Save** and save the new query as `CatalogsBySpecialty`, and close the query.

7. Select the **Queries** shortcut in the Database window.

8. Select the new **CatalogsBySpecialty** query.

9. Select **Insert, Report**.

10. In the New Report dialog box, select **AutoReport: Tabular**, as shown in Figure 9.3. Click **OK**.

FIGURE 9.3
Creating a tabu-
lar AutoReport
from a query.

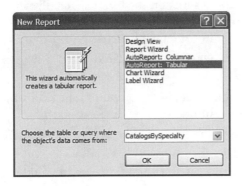

11. Select **File, Save** and save the new report as `CatalogsBySpecialty`. Figure 9.4 shows the new report.

As you can see, two styles of AutoReport are available in Access. The tabular AutoReport makes better use of space than the columnar AutoReport (which you saw in Figure 9.2). In its column headings and report title it also gives you the first hint of customization that you can bring to the printed page with Access reports.

tip

It's okay to have two different objects with the same name in an Access database, as long as they're different types of objects. For example, a query and a report can share a name, but you can't have two queries with the same name.

FIGURE 9.4
A tabular
AutoReport
based on a
query.

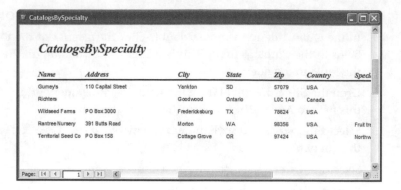

Using the Report Wizard

If you refer to Figure 9.3, you'll see that Access actually offers the following six ways to create a report:

- **Design view**—Although it's first on the list, it is actually the most complex option. We'll introduce you to design view later in this chapter and then cover it more extensively in Chapter 14, "Dressing Up Your Reports."

- **Report Wizard**—Offers you a flexible wizard-based way to create reports based on one or more tables. We'll cover this option next.

- **AutoReport: Columnar**—Creates a columnar report, in which all the fields are laid out in a single column.

- **AutoReport: Tabular**—Creates a tabular report, in which fields are laid out across the printed page.

- **Chart Wizard**—Creates a report containing a chart. You'll learn about this wizard in Chapter 14.

- **Label Wizard**—Creates a report you can use to print mailing labels. You'll learn about this wizard in Chapter 14.

In the next section of the chapter, we'll show you several ways to use the Report Wizard. You can base a report on a table, a query, or even more than one object at the same time.

Using the Report Wizard with a Table

To get started with the Report Wizard, you can build another report based on the Plants table. Here's how:

1. Select the **Reports** shortcut in the Database window.

2. Click the **New** button on the Database window toolbar to open the New Report dialog box.

3. Select the **Report Wizard** option in the list of report types. Then select the **Plants** table from the drop-down list of all the tables and queries in the database. Click **OK**.

4. On the first panel of the Report Wizard, shown in Figure 9.5, select the fields you want to see on your report. For this example, select the **CommonName**, **LatinName**, and **Picture** fields. Click **Next**.

FIGURE 9.5
Selecting fields in the Report Wizard.

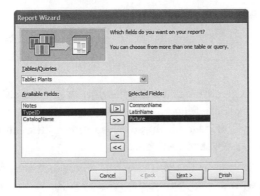

5. The second panel of the Report Wizard lets you specify grouping options for the report. You'll see how grouping works a bit later in the chapter. For now, just click **Next** to proceed.

6. The third panel of the Report Wizard enables you to sort your report by up to four fields. In this case, choose to sort by CommonName, as shown in Figure 9.6. Click **Next**.

FIGURE 9.6
Choosing a sort order for a new report.

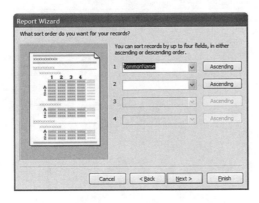

7. The fourth panel of the Report Wizard enables you to choose layout options for the report. In this case, we've chosen a tabular layout and specified landscape orientation for the paper in the printer. Figure 9.7 shows the options on this panel. Notice that the sample report to the left of the options changes to reflect your choices. Click **Next** after selecting layout options.

FIGURE 9.7
Layout options
for a report.

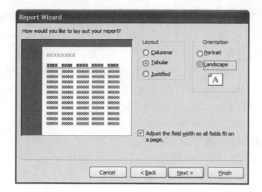

8. The fifth panel of the Report Wizard enables you to select a style for the report. Styles let you choose fonts and colors for the report. For this example, select the **Casual** style and watch the sample report to the left change to reflect that style. Click **Next** to continue.

9. The final panel of the report lets you assign a name to the report and then decide what to do with it next. Name the report **Plants** and click **Finish** to open the report in print preview mode. Figure 9.8 shows the finished report, maximized inside the Access window.

FIGURE 9.8
A new report
created by the
Report Wizard.

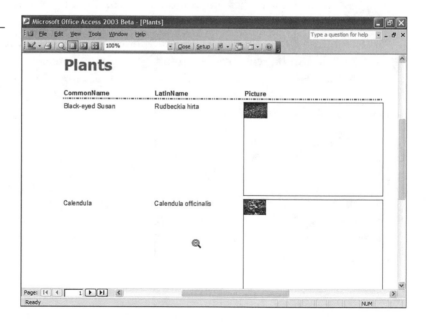

The Report Wizard seems to have made a strange decision about pictures on this report; they take up a lot of space, but the pictures themselves are tiny. We'll show you what happened and how to fix it a bit later in this chapter, in the section "A Peek at Report Design View."

Using the Report Wizard with a Query

You can also use the Report Wizard to create a report based on a query. You have the same options that you do when you base the report on a table. Here's how you might use the Report Wizard to base a report on the CatalogsBySpecialty query. You'll recall that this query retrieves all the catalogs in the database, sorted by their specialty. Do the following:

1. Select the **Reports** shortcut in of the Database window.

2. Double-click the **Create Report by Using Wizard** shortcut.

3. On the first panel of the Report Wizard, select the **CatalogsBySpecialty** query from the drop-down list of tables and queries. Select all the fields in the query and click **Next**. Remember, you can use the >> button as a way to select all the available fields in a single click.

4. On the second panel of the Report Wizard, don't select any grouping levels. Click **Next**.

5. On the third panel of the Report Wizard, choose to sort the report in descending order by state. Figure 9.9 shows these settings. You can click the Ascending button next to the sort field to change from an ascending sort to a descending sort. Click **Next**.

FIGURE 9.9

Choose a descending sort by state.

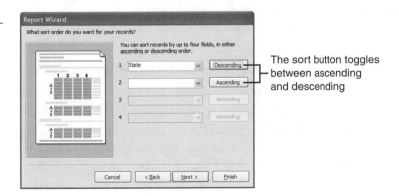

6. Create a tabular report in portrait orientation and click **Next**.

7. On the fifth panel of the Report Wizard, select the **Compact** style. Then click **Next**.

8. Name the report `CatalogsByStateDescending` and click **Finish**. Figure 9.10 shows the completed report.

FIGURE 9.10

A report based on a query.

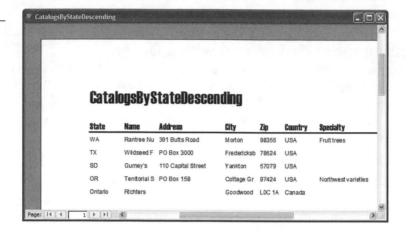

Selecting the State field on which to sort the report, as you did in step 5, has two consequences. First, the Report Wizard assumes that this field is important to you and therefore moves it all the way to the left on the finished report. Second, the sort you specified in the Report Wizard takes precedence over the original sort order that was specified by the query.

Using the Report Wizard with More Than One Table

For the most information in a single report, you can base your report on more than one table. For example, suppose you'd like to see a report of plants and the catalogs they came from? Here's how to do that:

1. Select the **Reports** shortcut in the Database window.
2. Double-click the **Create Report by Using Wizard** shortcut.
3. Select the **Catalogs** table in the list of tables and queries. Move the **Name**, **City**, and **State** fields from the Available Fields list to the Selected Fields list.
4. Now select the **Plants** table in the list of tables and queries. You'll see that this does not clear your existing selections. Add the **CommonName** and **LatinName** fields to the Selected Fields list and click **Next**.
5. Because the report includes fields from two tables, the Report Wizard displays an additional panel, shown in Figure 9.11. This panel provides a shortcut way to group the report. Select the **By Catalogs** entry (it should be the default choice) and click **Next**.
6. You don't want to add any grouping levels, so click Next again.

FIGURE 9.11

Grouping a report based on more than one table.

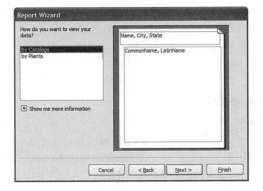

7. Choose to sort the records by CommonName and click **Next**.

8. Select the **Outline 1** layout and click **Next**.

9. Select the **Soft Gray** style and click **Next**.

10. Name the new report `CatalogsAndPlants` and open it in preview mode. Figure 9.12 shows the completed report.

FIGURE 9.12

A report of catalogs and plants.

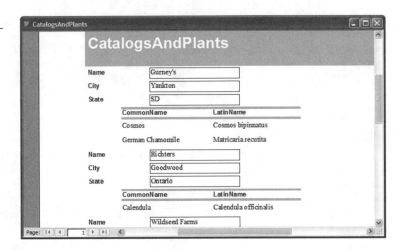

Although the layout could still be improved, for the moment concentrate on the information displayed by this report. It shows, in boxes, information about each catalog: the Name, City, and State fields from the catalog. After that, it lists the common name and Latin name of each plant from that catalog. Note that the catalog information is not needlessly repeated for every single plant.

That's the effect of grouping in a report. Because you chose to group this report by catalog, the information about each catalog is presented only once. You can think of Access as setting up a number of buckets internally, one for each catalog.

As it moves through the records for the report, it tosses each one in the appropriate bucket. Then each bucket is emptied onto the report in turn, showing the information that is shared by every item in the bucket followed by the information that is unique for each item.

A Peek at Report Design View

Similar to the other Access objects you've seen in this book, reports have more than one view. So far, you've been looking at reports in print preview view. The other view, design view, is analogous to the design view of tables, queries, and forms. It enables you to see the internal information that dictates the appearance of the report and the data it contains, and it enables you to make changes to this information.

Figure 9.13 shows a report open in design view. As you can see, quite a few windows and tools are available in this view.

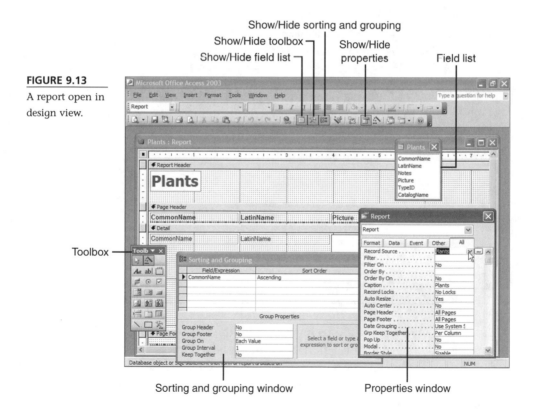

FIGURE 9.13
A report open in design view.

Report design view offers four windows for making design changes:

■ **Toolbox**—Lets you add new controls to a report. *Controls* are the containers that display data on a report.

- **Field List**—Lists all the data fields (from the underlying table or query) that are available to the report.
- **Sorting and Grouping window**—Lets you control the way the report sorts and groups the data.
- **Properties window**—Lets you change the appearance and behavior of controls on the report and the report itself.

As shown in Figure 9.13, toolbar buttons are available to show and hide each of these four windows. In addition, menu items appear on the **View** menu to show or hide each of these windows.

Although the Report Wizard creates useful reports, they're sometimes not quite perfect. A good example is the Plants report you created earlier in the chapter, which doesn't do a very good job of displaying pictures. Here's how you can use design view to fix the problem:

1. Select the **Reports** section in the Database window.
2. Select the **Plants** report.
3. Click the **Design** button on the Database Window toolbar.
4. After the report opens in design view, use the toolbar or menu items to hide the Toolbox, Sorting and Grouping window, and Field List (some of these might already be hidden). Make sure that the Properties window is visible; select **View, Properties** from the Access menus if it is not (or click the Properties button on the report design toolbar).
5. Click the drop-down arrow for the list at the top of the Properties window. This list shows all the controls on the report. Scroll through the list and select the **Picture** control. When you do this, the corresponding control on the report is selected, as indicated by the selection handles shown in Figure 9.14.
6. With the Picture control selected, the Properties window shows the settings that control the way this control looks and behaves. For example, the Control Source property indicates that data displayed in this control comes from the Picture field in the underlying (or bound) table or query. Click in the **Size Mode** control, where it currently says Clip. Now select **Zoom** from the drop-down list that appears when you click in the control.
7. Click the **Save** button on the toolbar.
8. Select **View, Print Preview**; the report displays with the pictures more nicely sized, as shown in Figure 9.15.

Select here

FIGURE 9.14

Selecting a control in report design view.

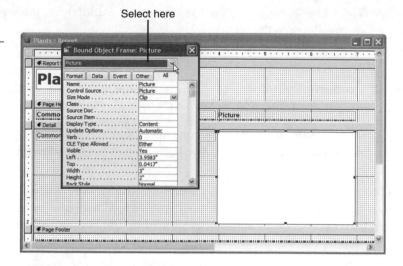

FIGURE 9.15

The Plants report after modifying its design.

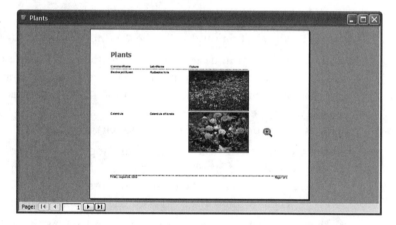

The reason the report looked bad in the first place is that the pictures in the database are of various sizes. Some are much larger than others. When the Report Wizard designed the original report, it made the control large enough to hold the largest picture. Then it set the Size Mode property of the control to Clip, which tells Access to display the pictures' actual sizes. So, although the largest of the pictures filled the control, the smaller pictures were left floating in a sea of white space.

By setting the Size Mode to Zoom, you told Access to expand or shrink the pictures to fit in the box, leaving as little empty space as possible without distorting the pictures. This way, the smaller pictures are increased in size to fill their allotted space on the page. The result is a much better looking report.

You might have noticed the third setting for the Size Mode property, Stretch. This setting tells Access to stretch the pictures to exactly fit their allotted space, distorting them if necessary.

You'll learn more about working with reports in design view in Chapter 14.

Using Reports

Now that you know how to build reports, you can take a closer look at their functionality. In this section of the chapter, we'll show you what you can do with a report in print preview mode and discuss the mechanics of actually printing a report.

Working with Print Preview View

You've already seen several of the pieces of the user interface that apply to a report open in print preview mode. The mouse cursor turns into a magnifying glass icon when placed over the report, and the bottom of the report window contains a navigation control, similar to those on tables, forms, and queries (refer to Figure 9.15).

Clicking the magnifying glass cursor on the report alternates between zooming in so you can see more details and zooming out so you can see the overall layout of the report. You can use the arrow buttons in the navigation control to move to different pages of the report. You can also type a page number into the navigation control and click Enter to move directly to that page.

In addition, a special toolbar is available for reports that are open in print preview view, as shown in Figure 9.16.

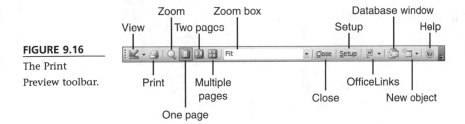

FIGURE 9.16
The Print
Preview toolbar.

The buttons on the print preview toolbar allow you to perform the following functions:

- **View**—Lets you switch between print preview view and design view.
- **Print**—Sends the report directly to your default printer.
- **Zoom**—Toggles between 100% zoom and "fit to window" zoom. This is the same as clicking the mouse on the print preview window.

■ **One Page**—Zooms to display a single page in the print preview window.

■ **Two Page**—Zooms to display two pages at the same time in the print preview window.

■ **Multiple Page**—Zooms to display multiple pages in the print preview window. You can select the number of rows and columns when you click this button. Figure 9.17, for example, shows a report displayed with two rows and two columns of pages at the same time.

■ **Zoom Box**—Lets you select from a number of predetermined zoom factors ranging from 10% to 1000%. You can also type a zoom percentage directly into the box and press Enter to apply that percentage.

■ **Close**—Closes the report.

■ **Setup**—Opens the Page Setup dialog box. You'll learn more about Page Setup in the section, "Printing a Report."

■ **OfficeLinks**—Lets you export the report to Word or Excel. You'll learn more about OfficeLinks in Chapter 16, "Sharing Data."

■ **Database Window**—Displays the main Database window.

■ **New Object**—Displays a drop-down list of new object wizards.

■ **Help**—Opens the Access help.

FIGURE 9.17

A report displaying four pages in print preview view.

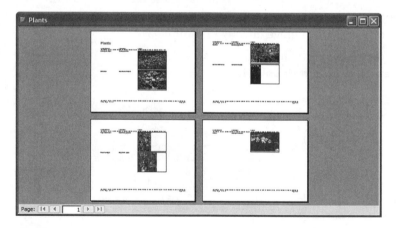

Printing a Report

Before you print a report, you might like to review the page setup settings. To do this, select the report in the Database window and select **File, Page Setup**. As an alternative, you can open the report in print preview view and click the **Setup** button on the toolbar. Either action opens the Page Setup dialog box, shown in Figure 9.18.

FIGURE 9.18
The Page Setup
dialog box.

The Page Setup dialog box is divided into three
tabs that let you perform the following actions:

tip

Checking the Print Data
Only check box lets you
print a copy of a report's
data more quickly. This is
useful when you want to verify the contents of the
report without worrying
about its appearance.

- **Margins**—Lets you specify the margins
  to maintain between the printed data
  and the edges of the paper. This tab also
  includes the Print Data Only check box,
  which suppresses all graphic content from
  the printout when checked.

- **Page**—Lets you choose between portrait
  and landscape orientation for the printed
  report, and lets you select a paper size
  and source. You can also select a different
  printer from this tab.

- **Columns**—Lets you control the grid settings when printing a multicolumn
  report. This tab is useful mainly with mailing labels, which you'll learn about
  in Chapter 14.

After you've created your report and set up the page the way you want it, you're
finally ready to print the report. You can do that in several ways:

- Select the report in the Database window and select File, Print.

- Select the report in the Database window and click the Print toolbar button.

- Right-click the report in the Database window and select Print from the shortcut menu.

- Open the report in print preview view and select File, Print.

- Open the report in print preview view and click the Print toolbar button.

- Open the report in print preview view, right-click the report, and select Print.

As always, Access tries to be flexible by offering you many ways to perform the same action. You might find this overwhelming at times, but when you get used to it, it's very convenient to have common actions at hand no matter where you're working.

THE ABSOLUTE MINIMUM

Reports provide a way to archive your Access data for posterity—or at least until the paper turns to dust! In this chapter, you learned the basics of working with reports:

- You can create a report using the AutoReport facility, the Report Wizard, or design view.

- The Report Wizard offers you a flexible way to create a report based on a single table, a query, or multiple tables.

- Print preview view lets you experiment with layout options and see reports onscreen without wasting paper.

- When your report is ready to print, Access offers multiple options for sending it to the printer.

IN THIS CHAPTER

- Interact with your Access database via an Internet connection and the page object
- Compare objects to other Access objects
- Create and modify page objects

10

TAKE YOUR DATA TO THE WEB WITH PAGES

Most of us are using the Web in some way, even if it's just to play or to research a favorite hobby. Others are connecting to the Internet and using it to solve business problems. Chances are, if you're reading this entry-level Access book, you'll not be asked to produce a Web-enabled application right away, but that's no reason to not be prepared!

A *data access page (DAP)* is an Access object, but unlike the other objects you've learned about so far, the page is actually a Dynamic Hypertext Markup Language (DHTML) file. This file is stored outside of your database (MDB) file, although you can still view it in the database window. A page looks and responds like an Access form or report, but you can view the page using a Web browser and update a connected database via an Internet connection. In this chapter, we'll show you how to create a data access page—one of Access's current solutions for working with data via the Internet.

A Quick Overview of the Page Object

Before you actually learn how to create a page, let's look at a few and compare them to forms and reports. Northwind (the sample database that comes with Access) has a few pages we can use to demonstrate their design.

Launch Northwind (close the opening splash screen and close the switchboard forms if necessary). Remember, you can launch Northwind by selecting Help, Sample Databases, Northwind Sample Database from the Access menu. Click the **Pages** shortcut on the Database window's Object bar, and Access displays a list of page objects. Hover the mouse pointer over any part of the page objects list. You'll notice that Access displays a ScreenTip that contains the name of the page, as shown in Figure 10.1. Access doesn't do this for other objects.

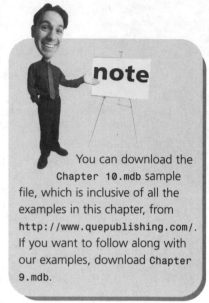

note

You can download the Chapter 10.mdb sample file, which is inclusive of all the examples in this chapter, from http://www.quepublishing.com/. If you want to follow along with our examples, download Chapter 9.mdb.

FIGURE 10.1

Access displays the page object's name in a ScreenTip.

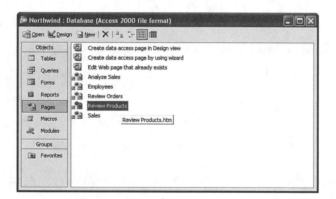

Did you also notice that the object name contains an .htm extension? That's because a page object is really an HTML file. Unlike other Access objects, Access doesn't actually store page objects in the MDB file. The items listed in the Database window are shortcuts (hyperlinks) to the HTM files stored outside the MDB file.

Now, double-click the **Review Products** page to open it. Then, click the **Maximize** button so you can view more of it. This page lists all the products in alphabetical order, but they're grouped by their first letters. When you first open the page, it doesn't show any products. Click the arrow next to the letter *A*.

Figure 10.2 shows the result of clicking this control, called an *expand/collapse control*. After expanding a section, the arrow points down. To hide, or *collapse*, a section, simply click the arrow again.

Group data

Heading

Expand/Collapse control

FIGURE 10.2
Click the arrow next to the letter A to display products that begin with that letter.

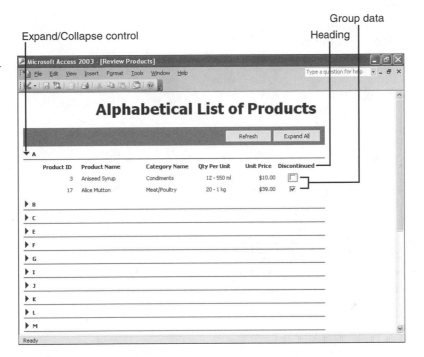

After you expand a group, you can see that a page can be similar to a grouped report. In this case, each group consists of the products that begin with a common letter. A group heading of labels describes the data, and just below it, the group displays the actual data.

As is, this page is read-only. That means, even if you viewed it in a Web browser, that's all you'd be doing—viewing data. It's a read-only object, and as such, you can't modify the actual product records in the Northwind database.

Comparing Forms, Reports, and Pages

The page object is similar in look and purpose to both the form and the report objects. Table 10.1 compares the three objects.

note

A *lookup field* is a table-level user-defined data type that stores a value other than the value it displays. Learn more about lookup fields and how to create them in Chapter 6, "Tapping the Power of Relationships."

TABLE 10.1   Features of Forms, Reports, and Pages

Object's Purpose	Form	Report	Page
Updates data in an Access database application.	Yes.	No.	Yes.
Interacts with live data via the Internet or an intranet.	No.	No.	Yes.
Prints data for distribution.	You could, but you probably won't.	Yes.	You might.
Can base the object on one or more tables or queries.	Yes.	Yes.	Yes.
Inherits lookup fields.	Yes.	Yes.	No.
Supports graphics files.	Yes.	Yes.	No, but you can embed your own graphics directly in the page.

Creating Simple Pages

Now that you're familiar with the page object, let's look at the various ways you can create one. As you might expect, there's more than one way to create a page. You can

- Use the AutoPage Wizard.
- Use the Page Wizard.
- Save an existing form or report as a page.
- Save an existing Web page as a page.
- Create the page yourself in page design view.

Running the AutoPage Wizard

By now, you can probably guess that the easiest way to create a page is to use a wizard. At this point, you've used wizards to create several objects, queries, forms, and reports, so the following section will probably seem familiar to you.

You can choose from two wizards—the AutoPage wizard and the Page Wizard. The AutoPage Wizard includes all the data in a fixed format (columnar). In this example, you'll use the AutoPage Wizard to create your first page based on the Plants table. Open your sample Plants database and then, follow these steps:

1. Click the **Tables** shortcut in the Database window.
2. Select **Plants**.

3. Select **Page** from the New Object button's drop-down list, or select **Page** from the Insert menu.

4. Select **AutoPage: Columnar** in the New Data Access Page dialog box.

5. You can change (or choose) the data source from the drop-down control at the bottom of the dialog box. In this case, the control already displays Plants because we selected that table before we launched the wizard. Click **OK** to create the page shown in Figure 10.3. The page will display all the fields and all the records in the Plants table. As you can see, the page also contains familiar icons for many navigation tasks, including moving between records, sorting, and filtering. The arrangement of these controls is a bit different from that on forms, but the basic function of each is the same.

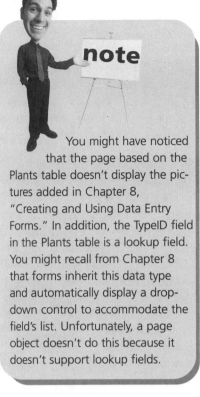

You might have noticed that the page based on the Plants table doesn't display the pictures added in Chapter 8, "Creating and Using Data Entry Forms." In addition, the TypeID field in the Plants table is a lookup field. You might recall from Chapter 8 that forms inherit this data type and automatically display a drop-down control to accommodate the field's list. Unfortunately, a page object doesn't do this because it doesn't support lookup fields.

By now, you're probably familiar with the columnar format the wizard uses and the navigation tools you'll use to browse the records. These tools serve the same purpose they do in a table, form, or report.

FIGURE 10.3
Use the AutoPage Wizard to create this page.

Plants
CommonName: Black-eyed Susan
LatinName: Rudbeckia hirta
Notes:
TypeID: 1
CatalogName: Wildseed Farms
Plants 1 of 8

Using the Page Wizard

The Page Wizard takes a few more clicks, but you can better control the results. In this example, you'll use this wizard to create a page based on two of your tables, Plants and Types. More specifically, you'll group all the plants of a specific type. Follow these steps:

1. Launch the Page Wizard by selecting **Page** either from the New Object button's drop-down list or from the Insert menu. Then, select **Page Wizard** from the resulting New Data Access Page dialog box and click **OK**.

2. In the first panel of the wizard, you must select all the fields you want in the page. First, select **Table: Types** from the Tables/Queries drop-down control; then click the double arrow button to move all the fields in Types to the Selected Fields list.

3. Select **Table: Plants** from the Tables/Queries drop-down control and move all those fields to the Selected Fields list. Figure 10.4 shows all the fields in the Selected Fields list. Click **Next** to continue.

FIGURE 10.4

Move all the fields from both the Plants and the Types tables to the Selected Fields list.

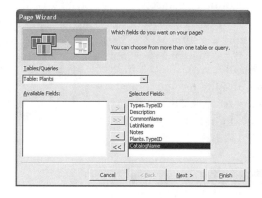

4. In the next panel, you can group the records by the type value. Select the **Types.TypeID** item in the list to the left; then click the single right arrow button to create a group based on that field (see Figure 10.5). The control to the right updates according to your grouping selection.

   Notice that the list contains two TypeID fields. That's because both tables have a TypeID field—it's a primary key in the Types table and a foreign key in the Plants table. (You can learn more about primary and foreign keys in Chapter 4, "Planning a Database," and Chapter 6, "Tapping the Power of Relationships.") Click **Next** when you're ready to continue.

5. We won't use the following panel in our example, but you could sort records in this window. Click **Next**.

FIGURE 10.5
Group the page by the type values.

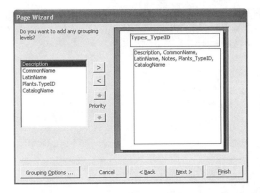

6. In the final panel, enter a new name for the page (or accept the wizard's choice). We named ours TypesAndPlants, as shown in Figure 10.6. Select the **Open the Page** option, and then click **Finish** to create the page.

FIGURE 10.6
Name the page.

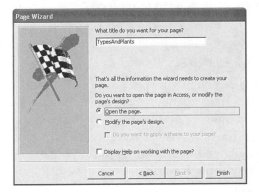

Initially, the page shows only the type fields and has only two type records (remember, the database doesn't have any records for type 2 yet). With the page displaying the record for type 1, click the **Expand** control (the + symbol) to see all the plants that match that type, as shown in Figure 10.7.

Interestingly, the page displays a second navigation bar so you can browse all the plants that match the current type. This behavior is similar to forms and subforms—both display their own navigation bar as well. You can browse records in both sections with the plant group fully expanded. However, if you collapse that section, you won't see the matching plants as you browse the type records.

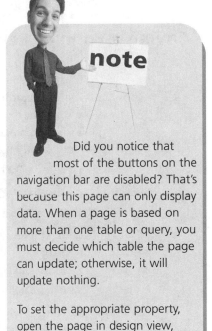

note

Did you notice that most of the buttons on the navigation bar are disabled? That's because this page can only display data. When a page is based on more than one table or query, you must decide which table the page can update; otherwise, it will update nothing.

To set the appropriate property, open the page in design view, select the appropriate data section, open the Properties window, click the **Data** tab, and set the **UniqueTable** property to the table you want to update.

FIGURE 10.7
Display type 1
plants.

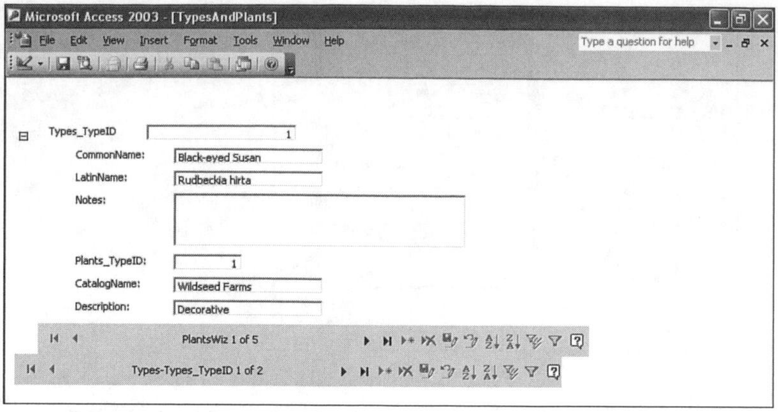

You might want to tweak the results a bit. The current page displays the TypeID
value twice. After you're familiar with pages, correcting such a minor problem will
be a snap. (Learn how to modify a page in the section "A Peek at Page Design
View," later in this chapter.)

Saving a Form or Report As a Page

You might already have the beginnings of your page in an existing form or report.
That happens frequently if you're expanding an existing database application to an
intranet. Fortunately, Access can save that form or report as a page object. You won't
always get the exact results you need, but sometimes a form or report provides a
good starting place. Let's see what happens when you save the Plants form you created in Chapter 8 as a page. Do the following:

1. Click the **Forms** shortcut on the Database window's Object bar.

2. Highlight **Plants** in the list of forms.

3. Select **Save As** from the File menu.

4. In the resulting dialog box, give the page a name and select **Data Access
   Page** from the drop-down control. We named our new page
   PlantsSavedFromForm.

5. Click **OK**.

6. In the New Data Access Page dialog box, you can select a new location in
   which to store the page. To save it in the same folder as your database,
   accept the default choices. Click **OK**.

Figure 10.8 shows the new page. It's similar to the page shown in Figure 10.3, but
the record selector to the left is a good clue that the page started as a form.

FIGURE 10.8

A page created by saving the Plants form as a page.

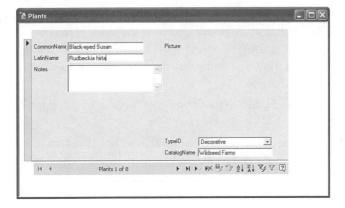

A Peek at Page Design View

So far, you've viewed all your new pages in page view. However, you can also view (and modify) the page object in design view. The process is similar to modifying tables, queries, forms, and reports in design view (we reviewed design view for other objects in Chapter 5, "Building Your First Tables"; Chapter 7, "Retrieving Data with Queries"; Chapter 8, "Creating and Using DataEntry Forms"; and Chapter 9, "Printing Information with Reports"). In design view, you can change the way the page looks and even the data with which it interacts. Figure 10.9 shows the TypesAndPlants page created earlier in design view.

FIGURE 10.9

A page in design view.

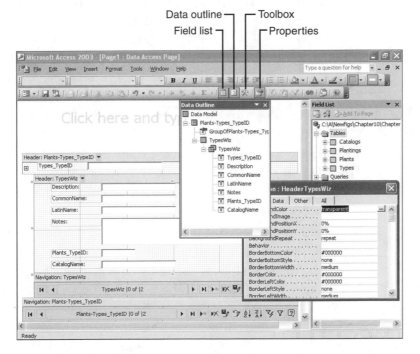

You'll be using several windows to modify a page. Sometimes it can get crowded, which is why Access lets you display and hide these windows as you need them by clicking the appropriate button on the Page Design toolbar or selecting the window from the View menu. Feel free to display these windows and familiarize yourself with them. They are as follows:

- **Field List**—Lists all the fields you can include in the page (refer to Figure 10.9).

- **Data Outline window**—Displays the page's structure in a tree view hierarchy. This window displays the data source and all the fields, including any calculated controls the page might have. A *calculated control* displays the results of an expression.

- **Toolbox**—Always found in design view for all objects. The tools it offers change from object to object, and page controls are unique to the page object.

- **Properties window**—Lets you change the properties for the page and its controls. The properties are always unique and specific to the current object.

Now, let's make a few changes to the TypesAndPlants page in Design view. Perform the following steps:

1. Open the page in design view, if you haven't already. (Click the **Design** button on the Page view toolbar.)

2. Select the **Plants_TypeID** Text Box control (just below the Notes control). You'll know it's selected because it will have selection handles around it, as shown in Figure 10.10. The Properties window will also show the control's name in its title bar.

3. To remove this control from the page, press **Delete**. This will also delete the associated label control.

4. Select the **CatalogName** control and drag it up to fill in the empty space left by the Plants_TypeID control.

5. The next two steps will allow you to modify the plants data. Double-click the TypesWiz header to display that section's properties.

6. Click the Data tab and then select Plants from the UniqueTable property field's dropdown list.

7. Save the change by clicking the **Save** button on the design view toolbar. Confirm changes if prompted to.

8. Next, drag the **Description** control to the right of the Types_TypeID control in the page's header section. At this point, your page should resemble the one shown in Figure 10.11.

FIGURE 10.10

Access displays selection handles around a control's border when it's selected.

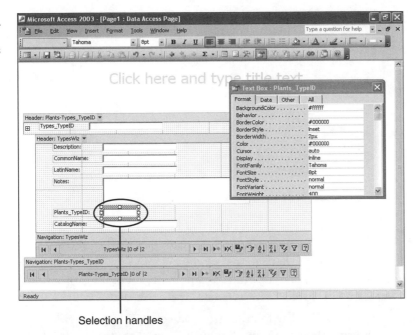

Selection handles

FIGURE 10.11

After making your changes, your page will look like this one in design view.

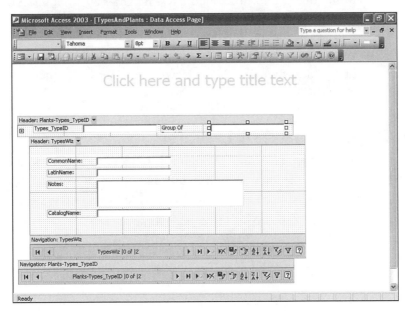

7. Click **View** on the Design toolbar to return the page to page view. Then, click the **Expand** control (+) to display the plants for the current type, as shown in Figure 10.12. The duplicate TypeID control is gone, and the Description and TypeID controls are now side by side.

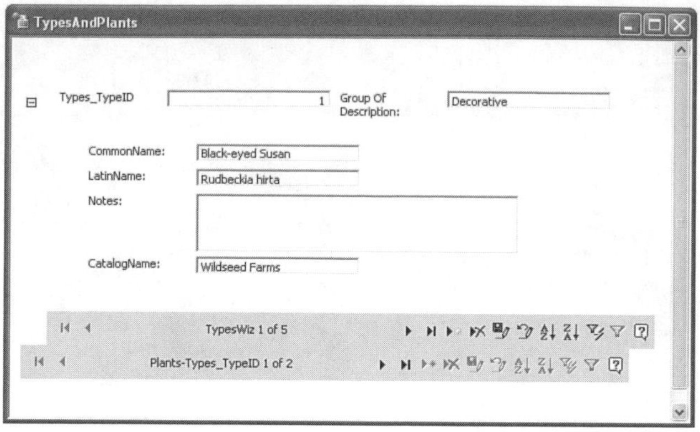

FIGURE 10.12
Display the
modified form in
page view.

Using Pages

Pages are similar to both forms and reports, and the type of page determines how you use it. If the page is meant for data entry, treat it just like a form (see Chapter 8). However, a few differences do exist, such as

- Use the Tab key to move from one control to another just as you do in a form. (Unlike a form, though, pressing Enter does not select the next control.) The Tab key also selects the tools on the navigation bar. You must use the tools on the navigation bar to move to other records.

- You must click the Save button on the navigation bar to save new records and editing changes. The page won't save those changes automatically like a form does.

Browsing Pages in Internet Explorer

Pages are meant to be viewed in a browser so you can update data via an Internet connection. This example shows you how to launch the page from inside Access.

Launch the Plants page from inside Access by following these steps:

1. Open the **TypesAndPlants** page in page view.

2. Right-click the page's title bar.

3. Select **Web Page Preview** from the resulting shortcut menu, shown in Figure 10.13.

4. You may receive warning messages about trusting the page. If so, click OK to view the page.

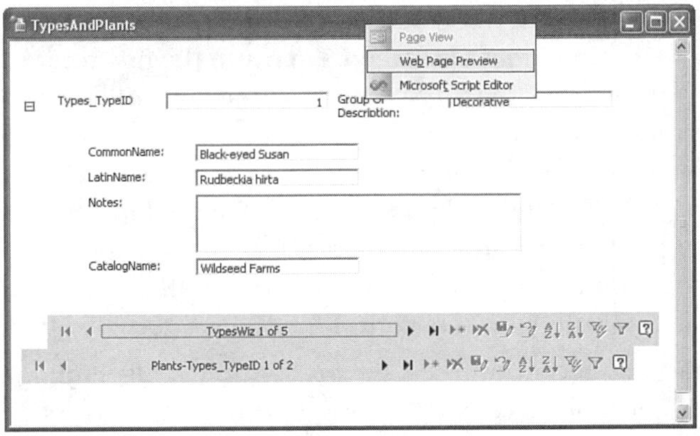

FIGURE 10.13
Select Web Page
Preview.

Figure 10.14 shows the page in Internet Explorer with the plants group expanded. The Address control displays the complete path to the .htm file (the page object). You could've launched the browser and entered that path to view the page.

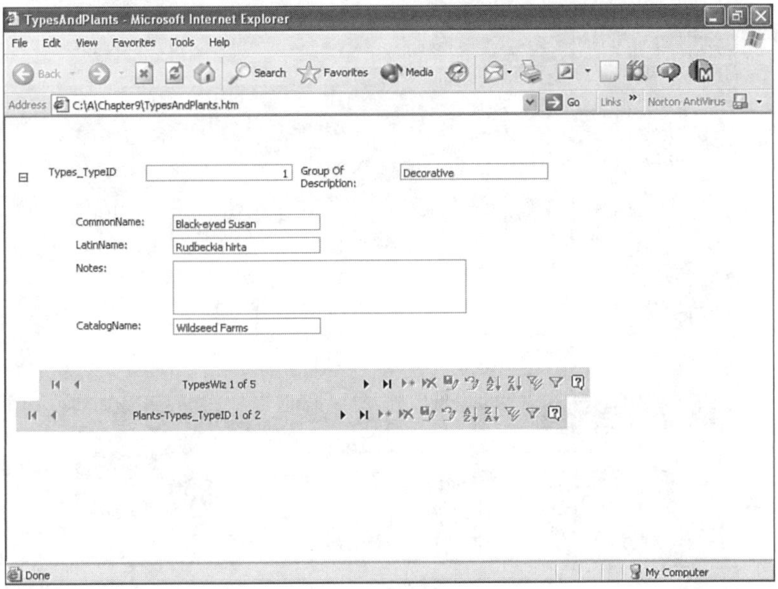

FIGURE 10.14
View the page in
your browser.

Now let's see what happens when you try to modify some data with the page open in the browser. First, highlight **Wildseed Farms** in the first record and try to delete the word Farms. Then, click the **Save** button on the navigation bar, which causes the following error message to pop up: You cannot add or change a record because a related record is required in table 'Catalogs'. That's because the CatalogName value is a foreign key value, and you enabled referential integrity in Chapter 6. Therefore, you can't enter a catalog unless it first exists in the Catalogs table. Currently, there is no catalog named Wildseed. Click **OK** to clear the error message, and then click the **Undo** button to cancel the change you tried to make.

Let's try another change. Select the **CommonName** value, highlight **Susan**, and delete it. Then, click the **Save** button. Now, return to your Access database, display the Database window by pressing **F11**, and open the Plants table. As you can see in Figure 10.15, the Black-eyed Susan entry appears as just Black-eyed. Because the page and the database are connected, the change you made was dynamic—you actually changed the underlying data in the connected database. While you've got the table open, change the CommonName back to its original value.

FIGURE 10.15

The change you made in your browser updated the actual database table.

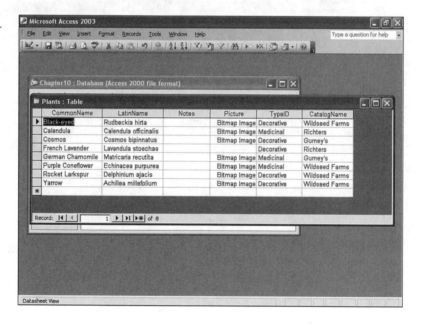

How You'll Use Pages

The technology that produces these objects is impressive. Imagine creating a Web page with just a few clicks! On the other hand, that same technology is somewhat limited:

- You can view the page object only in Internet Explorer 5 and later.

- You must publish a page on a Microsoft server. Specifically, you must have Internet Information Server (IIS) 4 or later if you want to share the page and data with others across the Internet. You can use a page on your own system, if you want, without IIS.

- The client PC (the PC with the Web browser) must have an Office license to interact with a page object. Without that license, you can still view the page but you can't interact with it. If you're just publishing static data via a page, this limitation won't really matter.

- Pages run on Microsoft Script, a complex scripting language. Consequently, page objects are hard to automate and modify. If the wizard does a good job of creating what you need, this limitation probably won't have much impact on you.

The technology provides a great tool for creating and implementing dynamic data using your Web browser. More than likely, you'll use the page object to share data on an intranet. Or, you can use the page object to create a quick mock-up or prototype of a Web page during the design and development process.

THE ABSOLUTE MINIMUM

The Access page object might be your first step toward Web development. The technology involved is impressive and complex. There's a lot going on behind the scenes, and we can't begin to cover it all in this short chapter. This chapter introduced you to the page object, and you learned the following:

- How to create a page using a wizard or design view
- The differences between a page and the similar form and report objects
- How to launch a page in a browser and make changes to the connected database

PART IV

MAKING ACCESS WORK YOUR WAY

11

CUSTOMIZING YOUR TABLES

By now, you should be pretty comfortable with the Access user interface. You've learned how to create the objects that will make up most of your databases, and you've had practice customizing those objects. Now it's time to look a bit more at the underpinnings of those objects. Although Access lets you get up and running quickly, it also lets you customize your database in almost any way you can imagine. In this chapter, you'll learn more about tables and how you can use table design view to further improve your database.

Using Data Types Wisely

In Access, every field in a table is assigned a data type. You got a glimpse of data types in Chapter 5, "Building Your First Tables," when you used table design view to build the Plants table. Now it's time to understand more about this aspect of table design.

The *data type* of a field controls the type and amount of data you can store in that field. This is an important part of keeping your data safe. For example, suppose you build a table that keeps track of your friends and their anniversary dates. That table might have a field for name and a field for anniversary dates. A good design for this table would use a field with the data type of date/time (usually just called a *date/time field* for short) to store anniversary dates. The data type would limit the field to just storing dates; if you tried to put anything else there (such as accidentally typing a name instead of a date), Access would warn you that the data cannot be saved to that field.

note

You can download the Chapter 11.mdb sample file, which is inclusive of all the examples in this chapter, from http:// www.quepublishing.com/. If you want to follow along with our examples, download Chapter 10.mdb.

Figure 11.1 shows the Plants table open in table design view. As you can see, Access supports nine data types (in addition to the Lookup Wizard, which you learned about in Chapter 6, "Tapping the Power of Relationships").

FIGURE 11.1

The variety of Access data types.

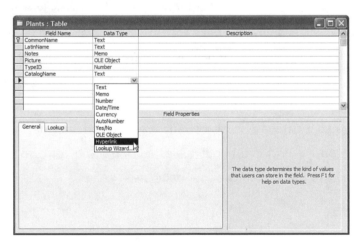

Here's a quick explanation of the available data types and what you can use them to store:

- **Text**—The text data type is suitable for storing any sort of textual information (letters, numbers, punctuation, or symbols). But there's a limit to the text data type: A single text field can store no more than 255 characters of data.

- **Memo**—You can think of the memo data type as an unlimited text data type. Like the text data type, the memo data type can store any kind of textual information. But a memo field can hold more than 65,000 characters of information entered from the user interface. Why not just use memo fields for everything? Because they're a bit slower than text fields.

- **Number**—The number data type can store only numeric data. This might be a simple integer value, such as 37, or a value with a decimal point, such as 42.1857392.

- **Date/Time**—The date/time data type can store dates, times, or both.

- **Currency**—The currency data type is meant to store currency values. It's similar to a number data type, except that it's limited to four digits after the decimal point. Also, the currency data type is designed to avoid rounding errors, so that calculations involving money will be precise.

> **note**
>
> Access stores text and memo data in a format called *Unicode*. This format handles accented characters, foreign alphabets such as Greek or Hebrew, and even mathematical symbols with ease. So, there's no need to worry about what kind of data your text fields can hold!

- **AutoNumber**—AutoNumber is a special variant of the number data type. An autonumber field is filled in by Access, not by the user. This is useful when you want to generate a unique key for a record but don't have a good key in the data.

- **Yes/No**—The yes/no data type can store yes or no. It's designed to keep track of simple on/off information.

- **OLE object**—The OLE object data type stores information in a format that is accessible to other programs, rather than to human beings. For example, the Picture field in the Plants table uses the OLE object data type. You can store any type of document in an OLE object field: Word documents, Excel spreadsheets, images, music files, and so on.

- **Hyperlink**—The hyperlink data type is a special text field designed to store hyperlinks to Web sites and other Internet resources.

Setting Field Properties

Although only nine data types are available in Access, each data type can be customized in many ways. This customization is done through *properties*. This is the first time we've formally discussed properties in this book, so we'll explore the concept a bit further.

Saying that a data field is a text field, number field, or hyperlink field is a bit like saying that a piece of food is a fruit, vegetable, or meat. When you know that there's a fruit on the menu, you know something about the meal—but there are still many possibilities. The fruit might be a grape, watermelon, tangerine, or nectarine. If I tell you the fruit is red, you can narrow the possibilities a bit. If you know it's red, sweet, juicy, and about the size of a marble, you might properly guess that the fruit is a cherry.

The color, flavor, texture, and size of the fruit are its properties—the things that describe that particular fruit and distinguish it from all other fruits. In addition, each property has a particular value: The color is red, the flavor is sweet, and so on. Moving back to Access, fields have properties, too. A text field, for example, has properties such as field size, input mask, caption, and default value. If you know the values of those properties, you know a lot more about the particular field.

Of course, properties have uses beyond simply distinguishing one field from another. The field size property, for example, dictates how much data you can store in a field. So, you can use the properties to help limit your database to storing reasonable data, as well as for other purposes.

In the next section of this chapter, we'll introduce you to some of the most important properties of the various data types.

Text Field Properties

To explore field properties, you'll build a new table named Plantings, which will track information about exactly which seeds you planted in the garden and when. You'll build this table entirely in design view. To get started with a single field in the table, follow these steps:

1. Launch Access and load the Plants database.
2. Select the **Tables** shortcut in the Database window.
3. Double-click the **Create Table in Design View** shortcut.
4. Enter **Bed** as the field name in the first row of the design grid, and select **Text** as the data type. Figure 11.2 shows the new table at this point.

Take a moment to examine the design view of this table. You already know about field names and data types. To the right of the data type is a space for the field description; type **Bed where the planting is located** in this area for the Bed field. The description is one of the properties of the field. Beneath the grid of field names, data types, and descriptions is another area for properties, divided into two tabs. For this chapter, you'll work with the General tab; the properties on the Lookup tab are used by the Lookup Wizard, and you usually won't modify them directly. (You can get a brief look at the Lookup properties in Chapter 6.)

Field names   Data type   Description

FIGURE 11.2

The table in
design view.

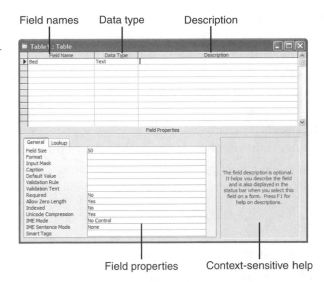

Field properties   Context-sensitive help

Each data type has its own set of properties on the General tab. The properties you're seeing now are all the properties that describe a text field. Some of these are advanced properties you won't need to worry about—for example, you probably won't need to change the Unicode Compression or IME Mode property. As you select different properties in the list, you'll notice that the area to the right of the properties list changes to show you a short bit of help on the current property. Of course, you can also click F1 at any time if you need more help.

Here's a list of the text field properties you might need to work with as you're learning:

- **Field size**—This property dictates the maximum number of characters you can store in the field. You can have fewer characters in the field, but Access won't let you enter more than this number. As mentioned previously, the maximum field size for a text field is 255.

- **Format**—The format property controls the way in which the data in a field is displayed. You'll learn more about this when we discuss date/time fields in the section "Date/Time Field Properties."

- **Input mask**—The input mask property supplies a pattern that data entered into the field must match. We'll show you an input mask when we discuss date/time fields.

- **Caption**—The caption property is used in place of the field name when the field name is displayed. For example, the columns in a datasheet will be labeled by captions instead of field names if you supply a caption. This enables you to use friendlier names where people will see them, while still using names without spaces for the fields themselves.

- **Default value**—The default value property supplies a value to be used for the field in a new record. If you don't overwrite the default value with other data, it is saved with the record.

- **Validation rule**—The validation rule property lets you specify a formula that limits the data entered into a field. You'll see an example when we discuss the number data type in the section "Number Field Properties."

- **Validation text**—The validation text property supplies a message that Access displays if the user tries to break a validation rule.

- **Required**—The required property is just what it sounds like: If you set it to Yes, you can't save a record in the table without filling in this field.

To continue working with the Plantings table, set some properties of the Bed field by doing the following:

1. Enter **30** as the Field Size property.

2. Set the Caption property to **Garden Bed**.

3. Set the Required property to **Yes**.

4. Set the Bed field as the primary key for the new table by selecting it in the list of fields and clicking the **Primary Key** toolbar button.

5. Select **File, Save** and save the new table with the name **Plantings**. Figure 11.3 shows the saved table, still in design view.

FIGURE 11.3

The table in design view with properties set.

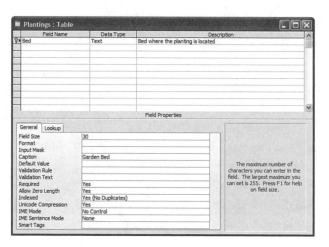

Now switch the Plantings table from design view to datasheet view using the View button on the toolbar. Drag the mouse to make the column a bit wider, and enter some data, as shown in Figure 11.4. You can see that some of the properties you set for the field make a difference in the user interface.

FIGURE 11.4

Entering data in a field with a caption and description.

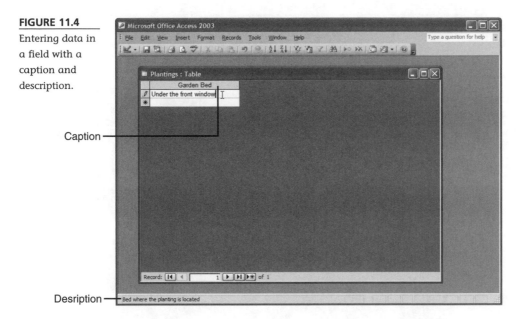

Caption

Description

You'll also find other effects of the properties that you can't immediately see. If you try to enter more than 30 characters in the Bed field, for example, Access refuses to accept the extra characters. The field size property sets an absolute limit here.

The effects of property settings go beyond the table itself because properties in Access are inherited whenever such inheritance makes sense. To see how this works, try following these steps:

> **tip**
>
> To change the value of a property such as Required from No to Yes, or vice versa, just double-click the property. If you don't want to use the mouse, enter just the first letter or two of the setting, and Access will fill in the rest for you.

1. Close the Plantings table.
2. Select the **Plantings** table in the Database window.
3. Click the **New Object: AutoForm** button on the toolbar.

Figure 11.5 shows the AutoForm's results. Access has reused the Caption and Description properties of the field on the form. The Status bar displays the Description property's text. Often, a quick glance at the Status bar during data entry can answer questions about the type of data you're entering. Inheritance applies to queries, reports, and pages as well as forms. If you'd like, save the form as Plantings, and then close it.

FIGURE 11.5

A form including a field with a caption and description.

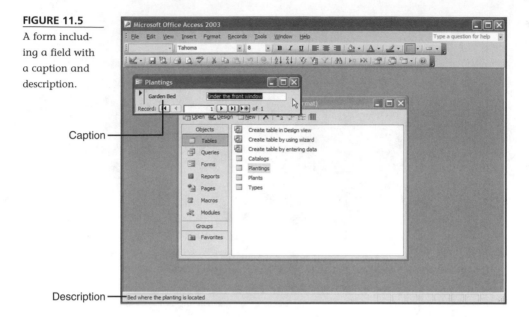

Caption

Description

Memo Field Properties

To continue working with field properties, you'll add a memo field to the Plantings table by following these steps:

1. Open the Plantings table in design view.

2. Enter a new field named **Notes**. Set its data type to **Memo**. You'll see that the properties section of the design view changes to show a slightly different set of properties for a memo field than for a text field.

3. Set the Description of the new field to **Notes about the planting**.

4. Set the Caption of the new field to **Planting Notes**.

If you compare the property list for a memo field with the property list for a text field, you'll see that they are almost identical. That makes sense because a memo field is just a big text field.

Number Field Properties

With a numeric field, you'll see some new properties and some new twists on some old ones. Here's how to add a numeric field to the Plantings table:

1. Add a new field named **NumberPlanted**. Set its data type to **Number**.

2. Set the Description of the new field to **Number of plants planted**.

3. Click in the Field Size property to reveal the drop-down arrow to the right of the property. Then click the drop-down arrow to see the choices for numeric field sizes, as shown in Figure 11.6. Select the **Byte** field size for this field.

FIGURE 11.6

Selecting a field size for a numeric field.

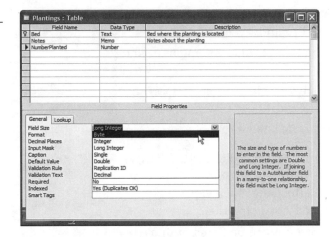

4. Set the Decimal Places property to **0**.

5. Set the Caption property to **Number Planted**.

6. Set the Default Value property to **1**.

7. Set the Validation Rule property to **<=50**.

8. Set the Validation Text property to **You can't plant more than 50 at one time.**

9. Set the Required property to **Yes**.

Similar to the field size property of a text field, the field size property of a number field imposes a limit on the amount of data you can enter in the field. But unlike the field size for a text field, the field size for a number field is the name of a type of number. Table 11.1 shows you how to translate these names into the actual ranges the field can store.

TABLE 11.1   Field Sizes for Numeric Fields

Name	Minimum Value	Maximum Value	Exact?	Maximum Decimal Places
Byte	0	255	Yes	0
Integer	−32,768	32,767	Yes	0
Long Integer	−2,147,483,648	2,147,483,647	Yes	0
Single	-3.4×10^{38}	3.4×10^{38}	No	7
Double	-1.8×10^{308}	1.8×10^{308}	No	15
Replication ID	n/a	n/a	n/a	n/a
Decimal	-1×10^{38}	1×10^{38}	Yes	28

When choosing a field size for a numeric data type, you need to keep in mind several things:

- What's the largest value you might need to store?
- Is the value a whole number, or does it have a fractional part?
- Are you worried about rounding errors?

Whole numbers are best stored in byte, integer, or long integer fields. Choose the smallest type that will actually hold the data you're expecting because the smaller types are faster.

Numbers with fractions can be stored in single, double, or decimal fields. Again, you can choose based on how large the data is, but the other factor to keep in mind is rounding. Single and double fields might return a number slightly different from the one you typed if the original number had many decimal places. The decimal data type stores the decimal places exactly—but it's slower to process than single or double.

We've also included a validation rule for the NumberPlanted field. In English, you might express this rule as "the number entered must be less than or equal to 50." If this is a true statement, Access will let you enter the number. If it's not true, Access will display the validation text instead. Here's how you can see this in action:

note

Replication IDs are coded values that are most useful in databases that are maintained on multiple computers simultaneously. You'll probably never use a replication ID in your own database.

tip

For most data, you'll be safe using long integer fields for numbers without fractions and double fields for numbers with fractions.

1. Save the Plantings table. When you do this, you'll see the somewhat scary warning shown in Figure 11.7. That's because Access wants to know whether to apply the new validation rule to the existing rows in the table. The table doesn't have any rows, so you can just click **No** here.

2. Switch to datasheet view. Notice that the NumberPlanted field already has the value 1 in the new record row, as specified by its default value property. If you entered a record earlier, you might notice that Access doesn't enter the default value of 1 for the existing record. That's because you set the Default Value property after entering that record, and the Default Value only applies to new records.

FIGURE 11.7

Data validation warning.

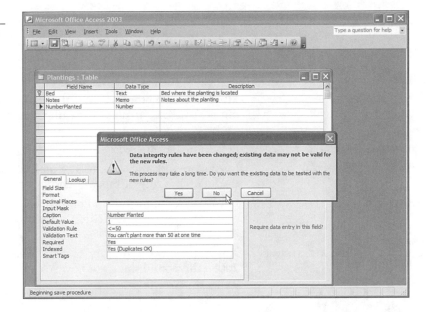

3. Enter some data in the new record, including a value of **52** for the number planted. When you attempt to leave the field, you'll get the error message shown in Figure 11.8. Until you correct the validation error, you can't leave the field or save the record.

FIGURE 11.8

Attempting to violate a valida-tion rule.

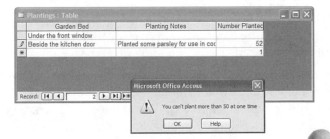

4. Click **OK** and change the value in the Number Planted field to **48**. Now you'll be able to tab out of the field and save the record.

Access supports a complex syntax that allows you to build a wide variety of validation rules. Fortunately, you don't need to learn the entire syntax to get started! Table 11.2 shows you examples of some common validation rules.

tip

Whenever you set the Validation Rule property, you should also set the Validation Text property. That's the best way to give feedback to database users when they make a mistake.

TABLE 11.2 Examples of Validation Rules

Rule	Meaning
<=50	Less than or equal to 50.
<>5	Not equal to 5—any value *except* 5 is allowed.
Is Not Null	Must enter something, rather than leaving the field blank. This is equivalent to setting the required property to Yes.
<10 or Is Null	Less than 10; otherwise, blank.
Like "B*"	Must start with the letter *B*. The asterisk is a wild card that matches any number of characters.
Like "?????X"	Must be six characters and end with the letter *X*. The question mark is a wild card that matches precisely one character.
Between #1/1/2004# And #12/31/2008#	Any date between January 1, 2004, and December 31, 2008. The pound signs are how Access indicates dates in an expression.

Date/Time Field Properties

The date/time data type gives you a chance to practice using the input mask and format properties. Here's how:

1. Switch back to design view of the table.

2. Create a new field named `DatePlanted` and set its data type to **Date/Time**. You'll notice that the date/time data type doesn't have a field size property. All dates and times are stored the same way by Access.

3. Set the Description of the new field to `Date that the plants were planted`. When you enter the new description, Access will display the Property Update Options icon (a type of smart tag) next to the description. If you click the icon, you'll get two choices, "Update Status Bar Text everywhere DatePlanted is used" And "Help on propagating field properties." Because there's a form based on this table, Access monitors the table for property changes that might affect the form. DatePlanted is a new field, so there's no need to continue with the updates. These icons will continue to pop up as you work with the table, as long as you have a form based on the table.

4. Click in the **Format** property to reveal the drop-down arrow to the right of the property. Click the drop-down arrow to see the choices for a list of formats, as shown in Figure 11.9. Select the **Short Date** format for this field.

Smart Tag icon

FIGURE 11.9

Selecting a for-
mat for a
date/time field.

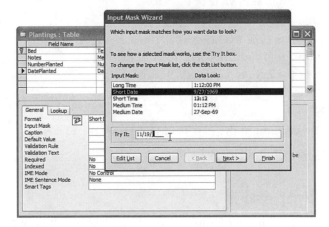

5. Click in the **Input Mask** property. A little button with three dots, called a
builder button, will appear to the right of this property; click it. Access will
prompt you to save the table; click **Yes**. Then the Input Mask Wizard will
open.

6. Select the **Short Date** input mask. You can try it by typing in the indicated
area, as shown in Figure 11.10. You'll discover that the input mask prevents
you from typing characters that don't fit into the short date format.

FIGURE 11.10

Testing an input
mask.

7. Click **Finish** to save the input mask to the table. You'll see that Access converts your choice in the wizard into a code in the property.

8. Set the Caption property to `Date Planted`.

The format and input mask properties complement each other. The input mask controls what you can type into a field, and the format property controls how the results

are displayed. Although you'll often use the same standard for both properties (as in this example), that's not required. You could use a short date input mask and a long date format, for example.

To see how the properties work, switch the table back to datasheet view and enter some dates in the DatePlanted field. You'll see that the input mask characters are displayed when the cursor is in that field, as shown in Figure 11.11.

FIGURE 11.11

An input mask in a datasheet.

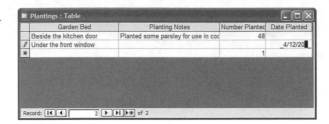

Currency Field Properties

You won't find any surprises when you create a currency field. By now, you should find the properties of this field type familiar. But add one to the table anyhow, just for practice, by doing the following:

1. Switch back to design view of the table.

2. Create a new field named **PurchasePrice** and set its data type to **Currency**. You'll see that this automatically sets the format property of the field to Currency, which displays the proper currency symbol for your locality.

3. Set the Description of the new field to **Cost of the plants.**

4. Set the Caption property to **Purchase Price.**

tip

The format Access uses for currency is taken straight from Windows. You can modify this in the Regional Settings application in Control Panel if you want.

AutoNumber Field Properties

You might recall from Chapter 5 that autonumber fields are used when you want Access to create primary key values for your table. So far in this table, you really don't have a good candidate for a natural primary key. So, follow these steps to add an autonumber primary key:

1. Add another field to the list in table design view, and name it **PlantingKey.**

2. Set the data type of the new field to **AutoNumber.**

3. Set the description to `Unique key for this record (generated by Access)`.

4. Right-click the field name and select **Primary Key** to make the new field the primary key of the table replacing the current primary key.

5. Save the table.

6. Switch to datasheet view. You'll find that Access has assigned a unique value to the PlantingKey field in each existing record, as shown in Figure 11.12. If you add a new row, it too will be assigned a unique primary key.

tip

Access doesn't let you enter (or change) a value in an autonumber field yourself. If you try typing in an autonumber field, Access just beeps at you.

FIGURE 11.12

An autonumber field is assigned by Access.

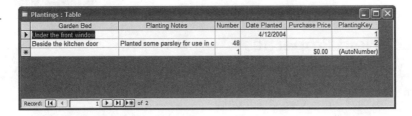

In most cases, you won't need to change the properties of an autonumber field. You might want to add a caption or description to aid in identifying the field in datasheets and on forms and reports. The field size property lets you choose between Long Integer and Replication ID, whereas the new value's property lets you choose between Increment and Random. You should generally leave these set to their defaults—Long Integer and Increment.

Yes/No Field Properties

You've already seen all the properties of Yes/No fields on other fields. This data type displays a small check box, which you'll select during data entry to indicate a yes value. Leaving the check box unselected (or unchecked) indicates a no value. Here's an example:

1. Switch back to table design view. Add another field to the list in table design view and name it `Future`.

2. Set the data type of the new field to **Yes/No**.

3. Set the description to `Plant this variety again in the future?`

4. Set the caption to `Future Planting`.

5. Set the default value to `Yes`.

6. Save the table.

7. Switch to datasheet view. Access automatically displays the yes/no field as a check box, which is checked for yes and unchecked for no. Again, notice that Access doesn't check Yes, as the default value for existing records. Only the new record row's field is checked Yes.

If you investigate the choices for the format property of a yes/no field, you'll see that such fields are also suited to represent on/off or true/false choices.

OLE Object Field Properties

We just have a few more field types to look at! From the properties point of view, OLE object fields are very simple. Here's an example that shows you how to set the properties for an OLE object field:

1. Switch back to table design view. Add another field to the list in table design view and name it `Photo`.

2. Set the data type of the new field to **OLE Object**.

3. Set the description to `Picture of the planting`.

4. Set the caption to `Photo`.

5. Save the table.

The only properties for an OLE object field are the caption and required properties because these fields don't really store data Access needs to describe. Instead, they store data from outside Access. You can think of an OLE object field as a box into which you can put files saved by other programs. Access only knows which label to paste on the box and whether to insist that you put something inside it.

Hyperlink Field Properties

Finally, Access includes support for a special field type, the hyperlink. A *hyperlink* is similar to a text field, except that it's designed to work as a live link to online material. Here's how you can add a hyperlink field to the table you've been working with:

1. Add another field to the list in table design view, and name it `OnlineReference`.

2. Set the data type of the new field to **Hyperlink**.

3. Set the description to `Online reference material for this plant`.

4. Set the caption to `More Info`. You'll see that the hyperlink data type has most of the properties of the text data type. Figure 11.13 shows the table design with the full variety of data types included.

5. Save the table.

6. Switch to datasheet view; then enter a URL (an Internet address, such as `http://www.quepublishing.com/`) in the new hyperlink field.

7. Click the data in the hyperlink field to open the linked Web site in a separate browser window, as shown in Figure 11.14.

tip

To edit the data in a hyperlink field, click in the previous field in the table and then press the **Tab** key to move to the hyperlink field.

FIGURE 11.13

A table with a variety of data types.

Field Name	Data Type	Description
Bed	Text	Bed where the planting is located
Notes	Memo	Notes about the planting
NumberPlanted	Number	Number of plants planted
DatePlanted	Date/Time	Date that the plants were planted
PurchasePrice	Currency	Cost of the plants
PlantingKey	AutoNumber	Unique key for this record (generated by Access)
Future	Yes/No	Plant this variety again in the future
Photo	OLE Object	Picture of the planting
OnlineReference	Hyperlink	Online reference material for this plant

Field Properties

General | Lookup

Format	
Caption	More info
Default Value	
Validation Rule	
Validation Text	
Required	No
Allow Zero Length	Yes
Indexed	No
Unicode Compression	Yes
IME Mode	No Control
IME Sentence Mode	None
Smart Tags	

The label for the field when used on a form. If you don't enter a caption, the field name is used as the label. Press F1 for help on captions.

Plantings : Table

FIGURE 11.14

Clicking a
hyperlink field
opens a browser
window.

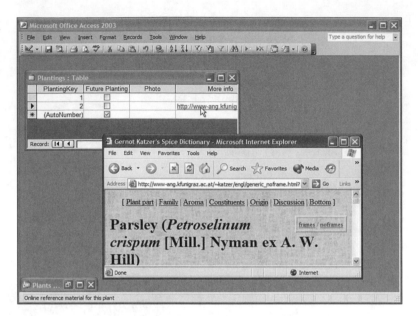

Working with Indexes

There's one important property we skipped over in the chapter so far: the Indexed property. That's because we wanted to discuss indexes as a separate subject. Deciding which fields to index in a table is an important part of designing a database.

An index in a database works much the same way as an index in a book. Suppose you want to find a particular topic in a book. You can leaf through every page in the book, looking for mentions of that particular topic. Or, more sensibly, you can turn to the index and use it to find the exact page where the topic is covered.

In an Access database, the indexes are not for your benefit, but for the benefit of Access. Although it might not seem like it at first, Access frequently has to look things up in the data you've entered. Suppose you create a query to display all the medicinal plants. Access can find that information by starting at the top of the Plants table and reading down, looking for plants that are medicinal. But if you add an index to the Type field in the table, Access can use that index to find the appropriate rows without searching for them.

Here's how you can add some indexes to the Plants table to make your database more efficient:

1. Open the Plants table in table design view.

2. Click in the **LatinName** field.

3. Set the indexed property for the field to **Yes (Duplicates OK)**. This tells Access to create an index on the field but to allow you to enter the same value in this field in more than one record of the table.

4. Click in the **CatalogName** field.

5. Set the indexed property for the field to **Yes (Duplicates OK)**.

6. To view all the indexes in the table, select **View, Indexes** or click the **Indexes** button on the toolbar. This opens a separate Indexes window, as shown in Figure 11.15. You can see that indexes have their own set of properties; when you're building your first databases, you should leave these properties set to their default values.

7. Close the indexes window and save the table.

FIGURE 11.15

Viewing the indexes for a table.

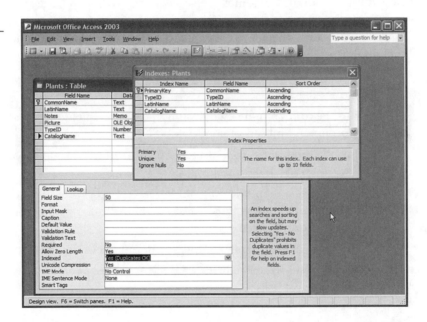

If you examine Figure 11.15 closely, you'll see that this table has some indexes you didn't add—Access sometimes creates indexes on its own when it knows they will make things work better. For example, the primary key field is automatically indexed, and numeric linking fields are automatically indexed as well.

You normally shouldn't add indexes to every field of your table because indexes make adding or updating data in the table slower. This is due to Access having to spend time updating the indexes. But remember, you usually enter data only once and then work with it many times. Here are some rules of thumb for deciding which fields need indexes:

- Add an index to any field that is used to join two tables in a relationship (Access adds most of these indexes for you).

- Add an index to any field that contains data you frequently search.

- Add an index to any field by which you frequently sort.

- Add an index set to Yes (No Duplicates) to any field where you want each record in a table to contain its own unique value. Access automatically adds such an index to the primary key field of your table.

The Absolute Minimum

Access makes working with most objects easy through its wizards and other tools, but sometimes you just have to get under the hood and make things better. In this chapter, you learned about some of the things you can do in table design mode, including the following:

- How to control the data that goes into a field by carefully choosing the data type for the field

- How the caption and description properties of a field let you supply helpful information for users of your database

- How the input mask and format properties of a field let you control what data is entered and displayed

- How the validation rule and validation text properties of a field help you limit the data to acceptable values and how to show a friendly error message in case of any problems

- How indexes let Access find and sort data in your database more quickly

12

GETTING DOWN TO BUSINESS WITH QUERIES

So far, you've learned how to create and use almost every Access object. That means you can probably do quite a lot now. However, there's more to learn.

There's a lot more to queries than just retrieving data. As your data and your needs grow, your queries will probably become more complex.

Occasionally, you might need more help than the Simple Query Wizard provides. When this happens you have several options:

- The Find Duplicates Query Wizard creates a Select query that locates duplicate records in the same table.

- The Find Unmatched Query Wizard creates a Select query that locates records in one table that don't have related records in another table.

- The Crosstab Query Wizard creates a type of Select query that summarizes data by categories.

- Parameter queries prompt you to enter criteria when you run the query. As a result, you can reuse the same query for a number of results.

- Action queries act on data by inserting new data, modifying existing data, and deleting records.

In this chapter, you'll work with a few query solutions that can handle some of your more complex data questions.

Running the Query Wizards

A *query* is really just a question. You ask the question, and Access returns an answer in the form of data. For instance, you might ask Access which medicinal plants came from a particular catalog. That's a very specific question, and Access will return only those plants that are tagged as medicinal plants and were also ordered from the catalog you specify. This type of query is known as a *Select query*—Access retrieves and displays the records that answer your questions.

The Simple Query Wizard you learned about in Chapter 7, "Retrieving Data with Queries," is only one of several query wizards. There are three more query wizards:

- The Find Duplicates Query Wizard
- The Find Unmatched Query Wizard
- The Crosstab Query Wizard

These three queries make easy work of some rather complicated tasks.

The Find Duplicates Query Wizard

Before we can show you how to use the Find Duplicates Query Wizard, we must define just what a duplicate is. Some fields can repeat entries, and some can't. For instance, you learned in Chapter 4, "Planning a Database," and Chapter 6, "Tapping the Power of Relationships," that every entry in a primary key field must be unique, and you learned why. Furthermore, some fields require a *unique index*, and these types of fields accept only unique entries. You can learn more about indexes in Chapter 11, "Customizing Your Tables."

On the other hand, some fields repeat many entries. For instance, the CatalogName field in the Plants table repeats catalog names, and the Country field in the Catalogs table repeats the USA entry. You'll find several repeated values in your tables.

Duplicate entries can mean duplicate records. That isn't always the case, but it's something you'll need to check for because duplicate records can cause errors. For instance, suppose you have a table of orders and one of those orders is entered twice. As a result of that mistake, your customer might receive a duplicate invoice or be billed twice the appropriate amount—and that isn't good business.

A *duplicate record* is one in which every field is the same except for the primary key field if you're using an autonumber data type. (You can learn more about the autonumber data type in Chapter 11.) Or, the repeated values could be in just a few critical fields. For example, suppose your gardening database contains hundreds of plants, which makes keeping up with just which plants you've entered and which plants you haven't difficult. Several hundred plants later, you reenter Purple Coneflower. You might use a different picture, and you might even enter a different purchasing catalog, but the common and Latin names are the same. Such an entry could constitute a duplicate record, even though all the data isn't exactly the same.

Right now, our examples don't have any duplicate records, so we'll have to create one, just so we can find it using the Find Duplicates Query Wizard. To that end, open the Catalogs table and enter a new record for Gurney's, repeating all the same data, except for the name entry. This time, enter the catalog name as Gurneys (without the apostrophe). Remember, this field is the primary key, so every entry must be unique.

Now, follow these steps to launch the wizard and see whether it can find the duplicate record:

1. Select **Query** from the Insert menu; then double-click **Find Duplicates Query Wizard** in the New Query dialog box shown in Figure 12.1. Or, select the query item and click **OK**.

FIGURE 12.1

Select the Find
Duplicates
Query Wizard.

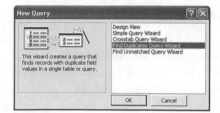

2. Figure 12.2 shows the query's first pane, which defaults to the Catalogs table (because it's the first table in the database). That's the table you need, so click **Next** to continue.

FIGURE 12.2

Selecting the
Catalogs table.

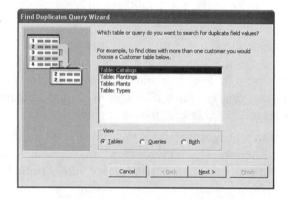

3. To search for duplicates on the Name field, double-click **Name** in the Available Fields list to add it to the Selected Fields list, as shown in Figure 12.3. Click **Next** to continue.

FIGURE 12.3

Searching for
duplicate Name
entries.

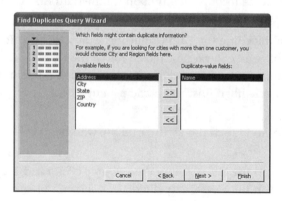

4. In the next pane, you can add a second field to help you identify any records that are found. However, because you're working with the catalog names, that step isn't necessary, so just click **Next**.

5. In the final window the wizard assigns a default name to the query. Accept this name, and click **Finish** to display the results shown in Figure 12.4.

FIGURE 12.4

The query says no duplicate entries exist in the Name field.

Are you surprised by the results? Oddly enough, the query doesn't return any records. You know you entered a duplicate record—in fact, you did so on purpose. Even so, the wizard isn't wrong. If you remember, you purposely entered the name a little differently the second time (without the apostrophe). The wizard can't tell that Gurney's and Gurneys really are the same because as far as data is concerned, they aren't. You didn't actually compare every field—you only searched for duplicates in the Name field, and the wizard didn't find any.

Close the wizard's first results and try again. This time, let's rely on a different field and see what happens. Repeat steps 1–5, but this time, look for duplicates in the Address field instead of the Name field. In addition, in step 4, specify the Name field; then name the query `CatalogDuplicates` in the wizard's last window.

The results of this query are shown in Figure 12.5. This time the query returned two records because the address 110 Capital Street appears twice in the table. Including the Name field allowed you to determine which catalog you entered twice. Although you can't tell by viewing the results, the wizard uses a totals view to determine duplicates (see "Summarizing Results Using a Totals View" later in this chapter).

FIGURE 12.5

This time the query found two duplicates in the Address field.

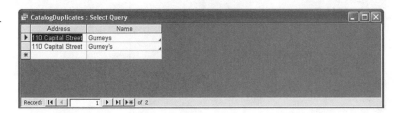

You're not limited to searching just one field as you did in both examples. You can search for duplicate entries in many fields. For instance, you might want to see whether any employees share the same first and last name. In that case, you'd search on both the first and last name fields. You can even include every field in the table, except for the primary key field. Because that field always contains a unique entry, the wizard would never find any duplicates, even if every other value in the record was exactly the same as at least one other record.

You might want to try a few more examples by finding duplicate Country entries or City entries. When you're done, be sure to delete the duplicate record for Gurneys in the Catalogs table.

The Find Unmatched Query Wizard

The Find Unmatched Query Wizard finds records not related to another table in the same database. For instance, you might want to see which customers haven't placed an order or which employees haven't taken any sick days. You could build these queries yourself, but often, the Find Unmatched Query Wizard is quicker.

Now, let's use this wizard to find catalogs with no matching record. In other words, let's find catalogs from which you've not ordered. To do so, follow these steps:

1. Launch the wizard by selecting **Query** from the Insert menu and double-clicking **Find Unmatched Query Wizard** (refer to Figure 12.1).

2. In the wizard's first pane, select the table that contains the primary key records. In this case, that's the Catalogs table, but because that table is selected by default, you can just click **Next**.

3. In the next window, select the table that contains the related records, or the foreign key values. In this case, that's the Plants table. After selecting Plants, click **Next**.

4. The wizard wants to know which field contains the related values and will attempt to select the right fields. Figure 12.6 shows that the wizard's guess was correct. The wizard correctly matched the related fields—Name and CatalogName—so click **Next** when you're ready to continue.

FIGURE 12.6

The wizard guesses which fields are related between the two tables.

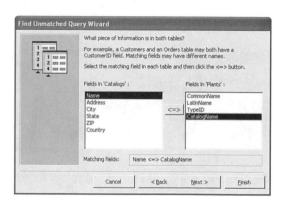

5. In the next window, identify the fields you want displayed in the query's results. We just need to see the Name field, as shown in Figure 12.7. Click **Next**.

6. The last window assigns a name to the query. Accept this name by clicking **Finish** to display the query's results shown in Figure 12.8.

FIGURE 12.7

You need to view only the Name field in the query's results.

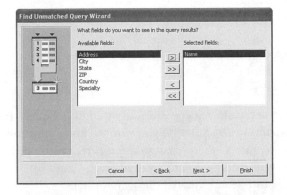

FIGURE 12.8

The wizard found two catalogs from which you haven't ordered yet.

The wizard found two catalog entries that have no related plant records—Raintree Nursery and Territorial Seed Company. If you open the Plants table, you can quickly see that this is true. On the other hand, if you had several plant records to review, you wouldn't want to depend on visual confirmation—the wizard makes the job much easier.

The Crosstab Query Wizard

A crosstab query is a curious query and can be a bit difficult to create yourself. That's why the Crosstab Query Wizard is such a useful wizard.

In a nutshell, a *crosstab query* summarizes data by categories. The main claim to fame for this type of query is the amount of data it can display in a small area, yet easily readable format. For instance, you might want to total the number of orders placed each day. Or, you might want to review the number of sick days used by each employee totaled by the month. In both cases, a crosstab query would do the trick.

note

If you need to base a crosstab query on more than one table, you must create a query and work from that. Considering the results, this isn't such a big deal. You just need to be aware of the requirement.

Every crosstab query must contain three elements:

- A column heading
- A summary field
- A row heading

We'll point out these elements as you use the wizard to create a crosstab query.

Building the Query

The first step to using the crosstab query is usually building a query that contains all the data you want to summarize. Suppose you want to know how many plant types you ordered from each catalog—the perfect solution is a crosstab query. You want to summarize (total) the type using the catalog name as a category. To create the query on which you'll base your crosstab query, follow these steps:

1. Select the **Plants** table in the Database window.

2. Select **Query** from the Insert menu, and double-click **Design View** in the New Query dialog box.

3. Add the **Types** table to the Query Design grid by clicking the **Show Table** button on the Query Design toolbar. Then, double-click **Types**, and click the **Close** button.

4. Drag the following fields to the grid: CatalogName from the Plants table and TypeID, and Description from the Types table as shown in Figure 12.9.

5. Save the query as **CrosstabQuery** and close it. If you need more help creating this query, refer to Chapter 7.

FIGURE 12.9
Add the CatalogName, TypeID, and Description fields to the query.

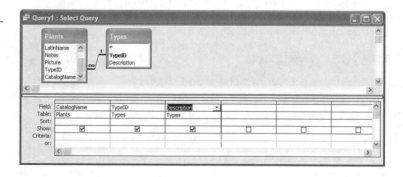

Now you're ready to launch the Crosstab Query Wizard and build the crosstab query. Follow these steps:

1. Select **Query** from the Insert menu; then double-click **Crosstab Query Wizard** in the New Query dialog box.

2. In the wizard's first pane, select the query's data source. This time, you're using a query, so click the **Queries** option in the View section to update the contents of the list control, accordingly. Then, select **CrosstabQuery**, as shown in Figure 12.10.

FIGURE 12.10

Selecting the query that contains the data for the crosstab query.

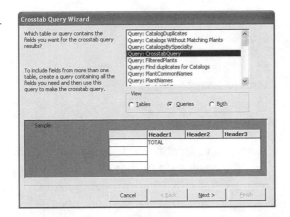

Notice how the Sample query at the bottom of the pane displays an example of how the data will be arranged in the actual query results. Pay attention to this panel as you continue and when you're using the wizard on your own. It'll help you make decisions as you go. Click **Next** to continue.

3. In the next pane, identify the row heading field. Because you're summarizing plants by their types, select the **Description** field, as shown in Figure 12.11. That way, the query will display the type text and not the primary key value. Click **Next**.

FIGURE 12.11

Identify the Description field as the crosstab's row heading field.

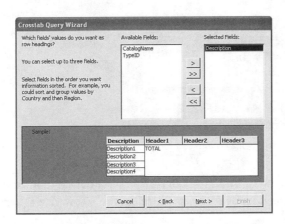

4. In the following pane, select the column headings. Figure 12.12 shows the CatalogName field selected. Click **Next** to continue.

FIGURE 12.12

Select the CatalogName field as the crosstab's column heading field.

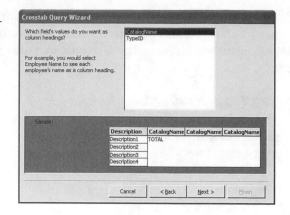

5. Now the wizard wants you to identify the field you're summarizing, so select **TypeID**. The wizard also needs to know how to summarize the data in the TypeID field. You can see from the Functions list that you can summarize the data in a variety of ways, from counting or averaging the records to using more advanced statistical functions such as standard deviation. You just want to count the number of records, so select **Count** from the Functions list. Figure 12.13 shows the updated Sample panel, which displays the Count(TypeID) expression in the detail section of the query. Click **Next**.

FIGURE 12.13

Summarize the TypeID field by counting the number of entries for each catalog.

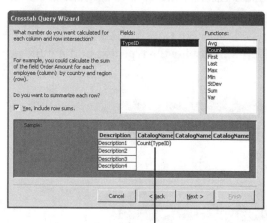

The summarizing function

6. The last dialog box names the query; you won't change it for this example. If you want to view the query's results, select the **View the Query** option.

Otherwise, select the **Modify the Design** option to open the query in design view, where you can tweak it just a bit if necessary. When you need help, you can select the Display Help on Working with the Crosstab Query check box. Doing so automatically opens the Help window to information on crosstab queries. Don't select that option now, though. In fact, you don't need to change any option; just click **Finish** to display the crosstab query shown in Figure 12.14.

FIGURE 12.14

The wizard displays these records.

Description	Total Of TypeID	Gurney's	Richters	Wildseed Farms
Decorative	5	1	1	3
Medicinal	3	1	1	1

Record: 1 of 2

The first record tells you that you have five decorative plants and that one came from Gurney's, one came from Richters, and three came from Wildseed Farms. The second record summarizes medicinal plants in the same way. There's a total of three, with one plant coming from each of the listed catalogs. Even though you don't have a lot of data to summarize, it's easy to see how this format could be useful when analyzing many records.

Working in Query Design View

Wizards are a great way to get a lot of work done quickly, but there isn't a wizard for every question you might want to ask. In Chapter 7, you learned how to create Select queries in the query design view window. Specifically, you learned how to base a query on more than one table and how to limit the results by displaying only the fields you need. In this section, you'll work exclusively in design view to work with some other query possibilities, including

- Using action queries to modify and delete data
- Using parameters to create more efficient and interactive queries
- Displaying summary values in a totals view

note

Access also supports an append query (which adds records to an existing table) and a make-table query (which makes a brand-new table). Both are considered action queries, but we won't review them in this book.

About Action Queries

An action query is so named because it actually changes the data in some way. We'll show you two types of action queries in this chapter:

- An update query modifies existing data based on some condition. For instance, you might reduce the price of all products under $20 by 15% for a limited sale event.

- A delete query removes records based on some condition. For instance, you might delete discontinued items instead of just flagging them as discontinued.

Modifying Data Using an Update Query

Data entry tasks often include modifying existing data. You search for the appropriate record and then update one or more fields for that record. Sometimes updates aren't confined to just one record. When this is the case, an update query is a more efficient solution because you can modify a large number of records with one simple query.

Suppose you want to change all the USA entries in the Country field in the Catalogs table to United States. With so few records, you could easily update them one at a time, but let's use an update query to illustrate how easily and quickly you could change a large number of records. Do the following:

1. Make a copy of the Catalogs table.

2. Select Catalogs in the Database window and then choose **Query** from the Insert menu. Double-click **Design View** in the New Query dialog box.

3. In Design view, add Country to the grid.

4. Select **Update** from the Query menu, which adds the Update To row to the grid.

5. You want to limit the update to only those fields that contain the string USA. To do so, enter USA in the Country column's Criteria cell. (Access will enclose the string in quotation marks for you.)

> **caution**
>
> Before executing any action query, take two steps to protect your data. First, make a copy of the table that will be changed. If the query doesn't return the appropriate results, you still have a copy of the unchanged data. Second, run the action query as a select query. This lets you see which records will be changed without actually making the change.

6. Because you want to change these USA entries to United States, enter `United States` in the Country column's Update To cell. At this point, your query should resemble the one shown in Figure 12.15. (We won't run the select query to avoid confusion during this first attempt, but we will add this step in the next example.)

FIGURE 12.15

The update query specifies which records to change and how to change them.

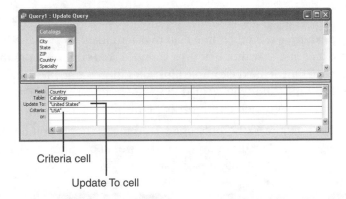

Criteria cell

Update To cell

7. Execute the query by clicking the **Run** button on the Query Design toolbar.

8. Unlike a select query, the update query displays a confirmation message: You are about to update 4 row(s). Once you click Yes, you can't use the Undo command to reverse the changes. Are you sure you want to update these records? Click **Yes** to continue. (You could click No to abandon the query if necessary.)

9. Open the Catalogs table so you can see for yourself that the query really did change all those records with just a few clicks. Figure 12.16 shows the modified Catalogs table.

10. Close the query and delete the copy you created in step 1 if you want. You can save the query as UpdateCountry if you like, but you don't need to as we won't use it again.

note

To make a copy of a table, select that table in the Database window and then choose **Copy** from the Edit menu. Next, select **Paste** from the Edit menu, then enter a name for the copy in the Paste Table As dialog box, and click **OK**.

FIGURE 12.16

The query changed all the USA entries to United States.

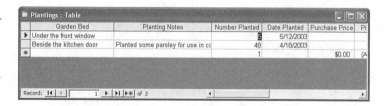

The previous example used the same field to determine the condition by which a field was changed and just how that field was changed. You can use more than one field in an update query. The next example illustrates this by updating the Future entries in the Plantings table (that you created in the last chapter) to Yes (or checked) for any record where the corresponding number of plants planted is five or less.

As you can see in Figure 12.17, only one record meets that condition. You could easily update this manually, but an update query would be more efficient in a table with numerous records that might be affected.

FIGURE 12.17

The Plantings table has only one record that meets the update condition of five plants or less.

To update the Plantings table, perform the following steps:

1. In the Database window, right-click the **Plantings** table and select **Copy**. Then right-click in the Database window and select **Paste**. Enter a name for the copy in the Paste Table As dialog box and click **OK** to make a copy of the Plantings table for safekeeping.

2. Select Plantings in the Database window, choose **Query** from the Insert menu, and double-click **Design View** in the New Query dialog box.

3. Add the `NumberPlanted` and `Future` fields, and add the criteria expression `<=5` to the NumberPlanted column's Criteria cell, as shown in Figure 12.18.

4. Run a select query to see whether the criteria chooses the right records. It should choose just one record—the one for "Under the front window" because it's the only record with the value 5 or less in the NumberPlanted field. You therefore know the criteria expression is correct. The query also returns the value 1 because that's the default value for any new records, but the query doesn't actually make any changes to that record because it doesn't exist yet.

FIGURE 12.18

These two fields determine which fields are modified and how they are changed.

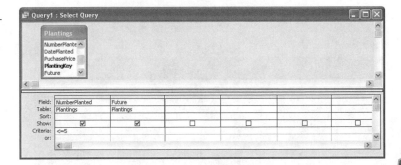

5. Return to design view and select **Update Query** from the Query menu.

6. Then, add the expression -1 to the Future column's Update to cell, as shown in Figure 12.19.

7. Run the query, and click **Yes** to confirm the query.

8. Open the Plantings table, shown in Figure 12.20, to see the results. As you can see, the Future Planting checkbox for the first record is now checked. A checked box equals True or -1. That's why you entered the value -1 in step 6.

caution

To open a select query, you can double-click it in the Database window. The same is true with an action query such as an update or delete query. However, Access doesn't just open the action query, it runs it. Be careful not to double-click these queries and run them by accident.

FIGURE 12.19

Add the update expression before running the update query.

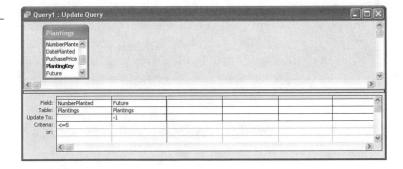

9. Delete the copy you made in step 1 if you want.

10. Close the update query. Save it as UpdatePlantings if you want to keep it, but you don't need to as we won't use it again.

FIGURE 12.20
The Future
Planting field in
the first record is
now checked.

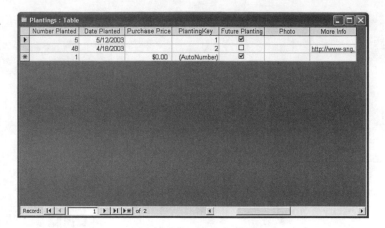

Deleting Data Using a Delete Query

Deleting records in bulk is just as easy as modifying records—simply run a delete
query. The premise is almost identical to the update query except that you delete
records instead of modifying existing data.

To illustrate this action query, let's delete all the medicinal plants from the Plants
table. To do so, follow these steps:

1. Make a copy of the Plants table and name it `PlantsCopy`. This time, work with
   the copy because you really don't want to keep these changes.

2. Select **PlantsCopy** in the Database window and then select **Query** from the
   Insert menu. Double-click **Design View** in the New Query dialog box.

3. Add `TypeID` to the grid; then enter the number `3` in the Criteria cell, as shown
   in Figure 12.21. Run a select query to view the results, which should return
   only three records. Also, each field should contain the string `Medicinal`.
   Remember, the TypeID field in the Plants table is a lookup field so it displays
   that string but stores the value 3. (Review Chapter 6 for information on
   lookup fields.)

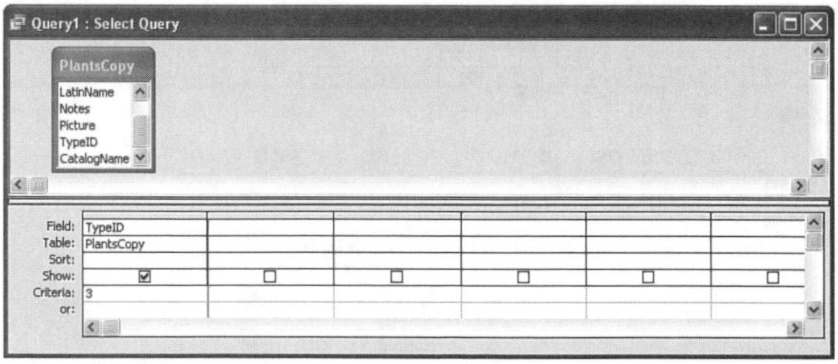

FIGURE 12.21

Add the value 3
to limit the
delete task to
just the medici-
nal records.

4. Return to Design view and select **Delete** from the Query menu.
5. Run the query, and Access will warn you that you're about to delete three records. Click **Yes** to continue the delete task. Open the **PlantsCopy** table to see that you have only decorative plants left, as shown in Figure 12.22.

FIGURE 12.22
The delete query has removed all the medicinal plants from the PlantsCopy table.

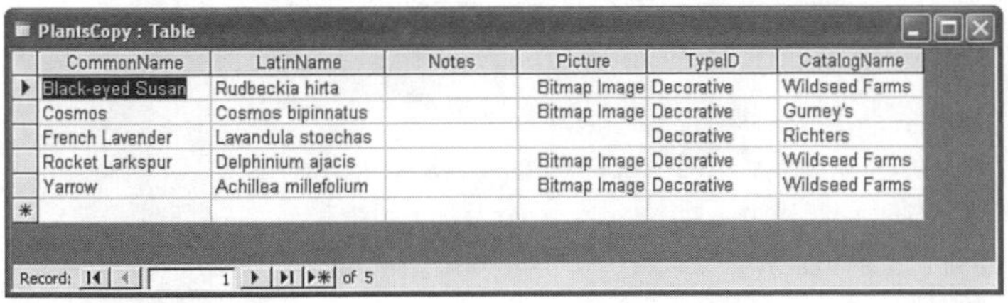

CommonName	LatinName	Notes	Picture	TypeID	CatalogName
Black-eyed Susan	Rudbeckia hirta		Bitmap Image	Decorative	Wildseed Farms
Cosmos	Cosmos bipinnatus		Bitmap Image	Decorative	Gurney's
French Lavender	Lavandula stoechas			Decorative	Richters
Rocket Larkspur	Delphinium ajacis		Bitmap Image	Decorative	Wildseed Farms
Yarrow	Achillea millefolium		Bitmap Image	Decorative	Wildseed Farms

6. You can delete the PlantsCopy table when you're done. Also, close the delete query. You can save it as DeleteTypes if you like, but you don't need to as we won't use it again.

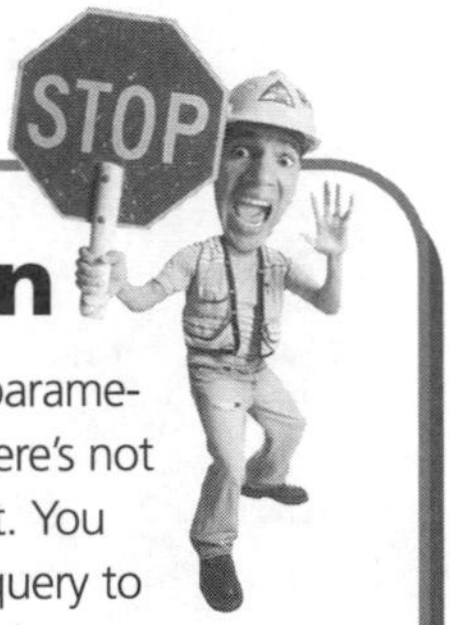

caution

You can ignore a parameter prompt, but there's not much point to that. You might expect the query to return all the records because you're not limiting the records in any way, but that's not how Access interprets the empty prompt. If you leave the prompt empty, Access most likely won't return any records. Access thinks you want to see those records that are null (empty), and because none of the Country fields are blank, the query fails to match any records and returns nothing.

Interact with Your Query by Adding a Parameter

Until now, queries have just done what they're supposed to do. After you add a parameter (a type of expression), the query stops and asks for more information before actually executing the query. That way, you can change the results using the same query.

A *parameter query* isn't really a type of query in the same sense as a select or action query. A parameter simply lets you interact with the query when you execute it.

Now, suppose you want to view plants, but you often need to limit which plants the query returns by the country from which you purchased the plants. You can create a simple parameter query that prompts you for a country and then returns only those records that match your response. To do so, follow these steps:

1. Select the **Plants** table in the Database window, and then select **Query** from the Insert menu. Next, double-click **Design View** in the New Query dialog box.
2. In design view, add the Catalogs table to the grid by clicking the **Show Table** button on the Query Design toolbar, double-clicking **Catalogs**, and then clicking **Close**.

3. Add all the fields in the Plants table to the grid. Then, add the Country field from the Catalogs table.

4. Add the parameter expression `[Please enter a country]` to the Country field's Criteria cell, as shown in Figure 12.23. Be sure to include the square brackets when you type the expression.

5. Run the query, and Access displays a dialog box asking you to enter a country. Enter `United States`, as we've done in Figure 12.24. Then, click **OK**. The results are shown in Figure 12.25. As you can see, the query returned only those plant records you purchased from USA catalogs. (If you didn't change the USA entries to United States in the earlier update example, be sure to enter USA instead of United States.) Save the query as ParameterCountry if you want to keep it.

Access can handle more than one parameter expression in the same query. For instance, you could add a second prompt that returns only medicinal plants purchased from United States catalogs by adding the parameter expression [Enter a TypeID value] to the TypeID field's Criteria cell.

FIGURE 12.23
Enter a parameter expression in the Country's Criteria cell.

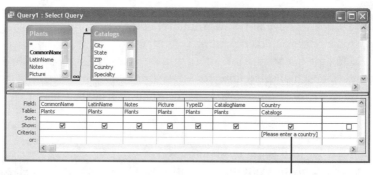

Parameter expression

FIGURE 12.24
Access displays a parameter prompt asking you for more information.

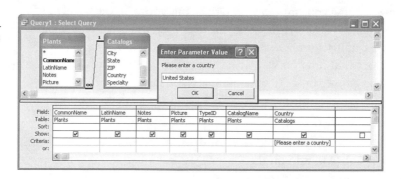

FIGURE 12.25

The query returns only United States records.

CommonName	LatinName	Notes	Picture	TypeID	CatalogName	Country
Cosmos	Cosmos bipinnatus		Bitmap Image	Decorative	Gurney's	United States
German Chamomile	Matricaria recutita		Bitmap Image	Medicinal	Gurney's	United States
Black-eyed	Rudbeckia hirta		Bitmap Image	Decorative	Wildseed Farms	United States
Purple Coneflower	Echinacea purpurea		Bitmap Image	Medicinal	Wildseed Farms	United States
Rocket Larkspur	Delphinium ajacis		Bitmap Image	Decorative	Wildseed Farms	United States
Yarrow	Achillea millefolium		Bitmap Image	Decorative	Wildseed Farms	United States

Record: |◀| ◀ | 1 | ▶ |▶|| |▶*| of 6

Summarizing Results Using a Totals View

A totals query provides a special view of your data—one in which you summarize the data. Remember how the earlier crosstab query summarized your data by categories? Think of a totals view as a simplified version of a crosstab query because it summarizes the data but doesn't categorize it.

A totals query actually groups the data so you can analyze the group in some way, usually by performing some type of calculation on each group. For instance, you could use a totals query to tell you how many plants of each type you have. Here's how to do so:

1. Select the **Plants** table in the Database window, select **Query** from the Insert menu, and then double-click **Design View** in the New Query dialog box.

2. Add the `TypeID` field to the grid twice (yes, twice). Don't try to add more fields to the grid than you actually need because doing so will change the nature of the group(s).

3. Select **Totals** from the View menu to add a Totals row to the grid. Both Totals cells will display the Group By aggregate function by default. Change the second to **Count** by selecting that function from the cell's drop-down list, shown in Figure 12.26.

4. Run the query to display the summarized results shown in Figure 12.27. Currently, you have five decorative plants and three medicinal plants.

FIGURE 12.26

Select the Count aggregate function from the Totals drop-down list.

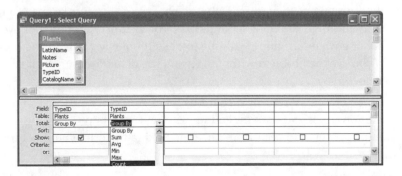

The query counts the number of records in each category.

An *aggregate* function acts on a set of records. (Earlier, you chose the Count aggregate.) Twelve options are available in that totals list, and nine of those twelve are aggregate functions:

- **Sum**—Totals the value in each group
- **Avg**—Returns the average value in a group
- **Min**—Returns the lowest value in a group
- **Max**—Returns the highest value in a group
- **Count**—Returns the number of items in each group (excluding nulls and blanks)
- **StDev**—Returns the standard deviation for each group
- **Var**—Returns the variance for each group
- **First**—Returns the first value in each group
- **Last**—Returns the last value in each group

> **caution**
>
> Sometimes a query that groups records returns the error `Cannot group on fields selected with "*"`. That can happen if you use the asterisk (*) to specify all the fields in your query, which you can't do in a totals query. If that isn't the problem, check the query's Output All Fields property. If it's set to Yes, change it to No. A totals view can display only those fields considered by the aggregate functions selected in the totals cells.

The other three totals options are as follows:

- **Group By**—Defines the group by reducing the records to unique values
- **Expression**—Evaluates a calculation based on an aggregate function
- **Where**—Specifies a condition that limits the values in each group

In step 2 of the previous exercise, we warned you about adding fields to a totals view that aren't part of the group. Doing so changes the nature of the group and consequently returns a different set of records. For instance, suppose you want to view the name of each plant along with the total count of each type in the previous exercise. Can you see the problem without viewing the actual query? We'll explain it and then show you.

The previous query returns a count by types. You can't attach a single plant to each type or group. If you try, you end up with several groups—one for each plant. For example, if you add the CommonName field to the grid, you'll get the results shown in Figure 12.28. See how the result of the Count function is now 1 for each record? That's because each group is based on both the CommonName and TypeID fields and not just the TypeID field, as before. Be careful when designing your totals views to include only the fields that pertain to the group.

FIGURE 12.28

The query counts each plant as a group.

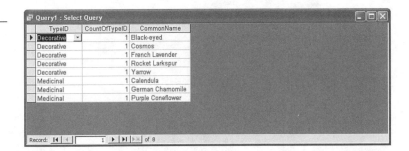

THE ABSOLUTE MiNiMUM

Queries are one of the most powerful tools you'll use, and fortunately, Access provides a number of query wizards and query types to take care of most situations. In this chapter, you learned how to solve some complicated problems using queries, including

- How to find duplicates and unmatched records and how to summarize data by categories using wizards
- How to modify and delete groups of records using action queries
- How to interact with your query by adding parameters
- How to summarize groups of data using aggregate functions

IN THIS CHAPTER

- Working with form properties
- Creating your own controls
- Using sections and subforms effectively

13

CUSTOMIZING FORMS

By now you've got a good handle on how to manage the data in your Access applications. You can create and customize tables to store your data, and you know how to build the queries to present that data as information. Now it's time to turn your attention back to the user interface of your Access database. So far, you've let Access do most of the work of building forms for you. In this chapter, we'll show you how to tap the power of form design view to make your Access forms more usable and flexible and to make them look the way you want. This is also a good time for you to learn about the object dependencies task pane, which helps you keep track of how everything in your database fits together.

Setting Form Properties

Like just about everything else in Access, forms have properties. The properties of a form control some of its behavior, as well as its look and feel. For example, you can use form properties to prevent data from being accidentally deleted or to change the background color of a form from gray to lime green. In this section, you'll learn about two ways to set the properties of your forms. For a quick facelift, you can use the AutoFormat function. On the other hand, for complete control over all aspects of your forms, you can use the Properties window.

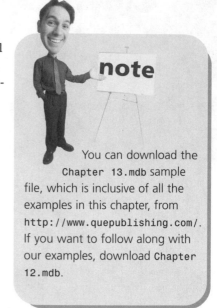

note

You can download the `Chapter 13.mdb` sample file, which is inclusive of all the examples in this chapter, from `http://www.quepublishing.com/`. If you want to follow along with our examples, download `Chapter 12.mdb`.

Using AutoFormat

AutoFormat in Access provides an easy way to change the overall appearance of a form. Although this tool is easy to use, it requires you to work with your form in design view. That's nothing to be scared of—we're going to work almost exclusively with design view in this chapter—but you need to be careful. In design view, you can change any aspect of a form, including things (such as its connection to the underlying data) that you might not want to alter.

Here's how you can use AutoFormat to dress up the Catalogs form:

1. Select the **Forms** shortcut in the Database window.

2. Select the **Catalogs** form.

3. Click the **Design** button on the Database Window toolbar to open the form in design view.

4. Select **Format, AutoFormat**, or click the **AutoFormat** button on the toolbar. Either way, the AutoFormat dialog box will open, as shown in Figure 13.1.

tip

If you make a mistake in design view (such as deleting a control you meant to keep), just close the form and click No when Access asks if you want to save changes.

Notice that the Standard option is the default format; this feature defaults to the format last used, so don't worry if your system choose a different option.

FIGURE 13.1
The AutoFormat
dialog box.

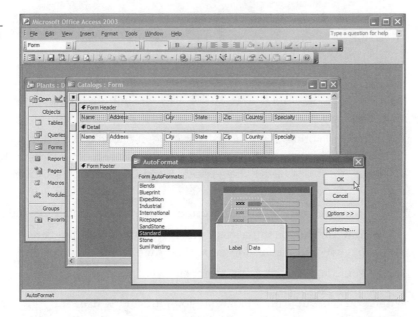

5. The list at the left side of the AutoFormat dialog box includes all the available AutoFormats. As you click each one, the center section of the dialog box changes to show you a preview of the format. Select the **Blends** AutoFormat.

6. Click **OK** to apply the AutoFormat.

7. Select **View, Form View** to see the form with the selected AutoFormat applied, as shown in Figure 13.2.

FIGURE 13.2

In just a few
quick steps, you
completely
reformatted this
form.

8. Click the **Save** button on the toolbar to save the changes to the form. Close the form when you're done inspecting the results.

Applying an AutoFormat to a form doesn't affect any of the form's functions. Instead, it makes changes to the form's appearance. In particular, it can change the font used for labels and text, the color used for controls, the image used for the form's background, and the borders used around controls.

You can do two other things in the AutoFormat dialog box. First, if you click Options, you can selectively choose whether to apply the AutoFormat to fonts, colors, and borders or to leave them alone. Second, you can click Customize to modify the available AutoFormats as follows:

- You can create a new AutoFormat based on the contents of the current form.
- You can change the selected AutoFormat to match the current form (instead of changing the form to match the AutoFormat).
- You can delete an AutoFormat entirely.

When you come up with a look that you particularly like for a form, you can use the AutoFormat options to turn this look into a new AutoFormat. Then, you can apply that AutoFormat to the other forms in your database, allowing you to easily create a consistent user interface. You'll learn more about customizing AutoFormats in Chapter 14, "Dressing Up Your Reports."

Using the Properties Window

You'll recall from previous chapters that properties are the values that describe a particular object. Similar to other objects in Access, forms have a set of properties that control their appearances and behaviors. To change the properties of a form, you can use the Properties window. Some properties you can even change in form view. Here's an example:

1. Open the **Plants** form in form view. You'll see the first record in the Plants table displayed on the form.

2. Do one of the following: select **View, Properties** or click the **Properties** toolbar button (as usual, Access provides more than one way to do things). This

note

AutoFormats are stored in Access itself, not in individual databases. So, if you create a new AutoFormat in one database, you can use it in all your databases.

opens the Properties window, as shown in Figure 13.3, which displays the properties of the control that has the focus (in this case, the CommonName text box). (Pressing F4 will open the Properties window in design view.)

FIGURE 13.3
Viewing the Properties window.

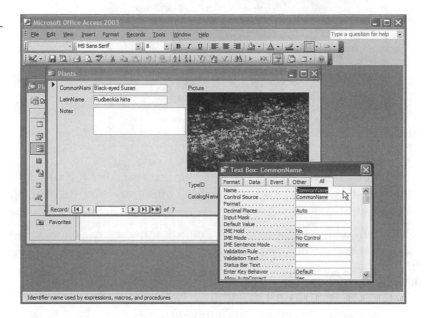

3. Click twice—slowly (don't double-click)—in the gray area between the controls on the form. The Properties window changes to show the properties of the form itself.

4. Click the **Format** tab in the Properties window.

5. Scroll down the list of properties to locate the Picture property, which is currently set to (None). Click in this property to reveal a build button.

6. Click the build button to open the Insert Picture dialog box. Browse to the Windows directory on your computer, and select the FeatherTexture.bmp file. Click **OK**.

7. Select the **Picture Tiling** property and change its value from No to **Yes**. Figure 13.4 shows the resulting form.

8. Close the Properties window and save the form.

Unlike AutoFormat, you can use the Properties window no matter which view you're using to display a form—either design view or form view. As you saw in this example, changes made through the Properties window take effect immediately (in form view). The changes aren't permanent, though, unless you save the form after making the changes.

FIGURE 13.4

A form with
new properties.

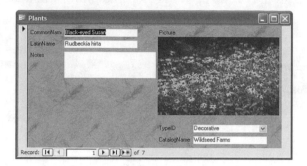

What else can you change with the Properties window? Anything! Well, just about. In fact, if you look at the properties that appear for the form, you'll find an almost frightening array of properties. Fortunately, you won't need to use most of these.

Five tabs appear at the top of the Properties window. As you click these tabs, the window displays different sets of properties. These tabs are as follows:

- **Format**—Properties that control the appearance of the selected item
- **Data**—Properties that control the data displayed by the selected item
- **Event**—Properties that control the code executed by the selected item
- **Other**—Properties that don't fit into one of the three previous classes
- **All**—All the properties of the item in one big list

We won't discuss event properties in this chapter; you'll learn a bit about them in Chapter 15, "Automating Your Database." In this chapter, you'll work only with properties from the Format, Data, and Other categories.

Table 13.1 lists some of the properties of the form that you might find useful.

TABLE 13.1 Properties of an Access Form

Property	Meaning
Record Source	The table or query from which the form gets its data
Caption	The text displayed at the top of the form
Allow Edits	Controls whether the form can be used to edit data
Allow Deletions	Controls whether the form can be used to delete data
Allow Additions	Controls whether the form can be used to add data
Scroll bars	Controls whether scrollbars appear on the form

Property	Meaning
Record Selectors	Controls whether record selectors (the bars to the left of the data) appear on the form
Navigation Buttons	Controls whether the navigation bar appears at the bottom of the form
Dividing Lines	Controls whether lines appear between the records when the form is displayed in continuous forms view, as well as whether lines appear between sections of the form, such as the detail section and footer section
Auto Resize	Controls whether the form automatically resizes to show all its controls when it is opened
Auto Center	Controls whether the form is automatically centered on the screen
Picture	The picture (if any) to use for the form's background
Picture Size Mode	Specifies whether any background picture should be stretched to fill the form
Picture Tiling	Controls whether any background picture should be repeated to fill the form
Moveable	Controls whether the form can be moved onscreen after it has been opened

Here's how you might use some of these properties to further customize the Catalogs form:

1. Open the **Catalogs** form in design view.
2. If the Properties window is not already open, press **F4** to open it.
3. Select the **Format** tab.
4. Double-click in the **Dividing Lines** property to change its value from Yes to No.
5. Change the Navigation Buttons property to **No**.
6. Select the **Data** tab.
7. Change the Allow Deletions property to **No**.
8. Close the property sheet.
9. Select **Form View** from the View drop-down list on the toolbar. The form will display as shown in Figure 13.5. Note that the dividing lines and navigation bar are gone.
10. Click in the navigation bar to the left of one of the records, and then press the **Delete** key. Access will beep, and the status bar will display the message `Records can't be deleted with this form`.
11. Save and close the form.

FIGURE 13.5

The Catalogs form after further design work.

Name	Address	City	State	Zip	Country	Specialty
Gurneys	0 Capital Stre	Yankton	SD	57079	USA	
Rantree	391 Butts Road	Morton	WA	98356	USA	Fruit trees
Richters		Goodwoc	Ontario	L0C 1	Canada	
Territoria	PO Box 158	Cottage (	OR	97424	USA	Northwest varieties
Wildsee	PO Box 3000	Frederick	TX	78624	USA	

Using the Field List

Another tool that's available only in design view is the Field List. The Field List enables you to easily add new data to be displayed on a form. To see the Field List in action, you'll build a new form based on the Plantings table, which doesn't yet have a user interface in the database. To add one, follow these steps.

caution

Setting Allow Deletions to No only prevents deleting entire records. You can still delete the contents of any individual control.

1. Select the **Forms** shortcut in the Database window.

2. Click the **New** button on the Database Window toolbar.

3. In the New Form dialog box, select **Design View**. Then select the **Plantings** table in the data source combo box, as shown in Figure 13.6.

4. Click **OK** to create the form and open it in design view.

5. Access might automatically display the Field List. If it doesn't, either click the **Field List** button on the toolbar or select **View, Field List**. The Field List (shown in Figure 13.7) lists all the fields in the table or query on which the form is based—in this case, the Plantings table.

6. To add controls to the form, you can drag and drop items from the Field List. For example, select the **DatePlanted** field in the Field List; then drag and drop it onto the form. When you release the mouse button, Access creates a label and text box for this field.

7. Drag and drop the **Notes** and **Future** fields from the Field List to the form.

FIGURE 13.6

Creating a new form from scratch.

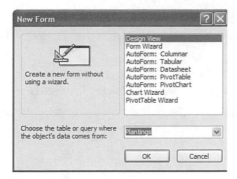

FIGURE 13.7

The Field List.

8. Click the **Save** button on the toolbar. Name the form `Plantings` and click **OK**.

9. Select **View, Form View** to see your new form.

Chapter 11, "Customizing Your Tables," discussed the fact that properties in Access can be inherited from one object to another. The new Plantings form provides a good example of this. Because you set properties on fields when you built the Plantings table, the form automatically makes some settings for you:

■ The Caption property for each field is used as the text for the label on the form.

■ The Description property for each field is displayed on the status bar when that field is active.

■ The data type for each field is used to determine the type of control to display. That's why the Future field (which accepts only Yes or No values) is displayed as a check box rather than as a text box.

■ The Format and Input Mask properties control the appearance and function of the control that holds the Date field.

Access 2003 also keeps track of inherited properties as you work with the database. For example, follow these steps to change a property in the Plantings table:

1. Close the Plantings form.

2. Select the **Tables** shortcut in the database window.

3. Open the Plantings table in design view.

4. Change the Description property of the DatePlanted field to `Date that these plants were planted`.

5. When Access displays the Property Update Options icon, click it and select the **Update Status Bar Text everywhere DatePlanted is used** option.

6. In the resulting Update Properties dialog box, select only the forms that you want to display the new Description, and click **Yes**.

7. Save and close the table.

8. Select the **Forms** shortcut in the database window.

9. Select the **Plantings** form.

10. Click the **Open** button.

11. Check the status bar of Access. You'll see that the status bar text for the DatePlanted control has been updated.

Using the Toolbox

The last major form design aid you need to know about is the Toolbox. The Toolbox is used to add new controls (labels, text boxes, check boxes, and so on) to forms. These controls can be attached to data (such as the text boxes and check box you just created on the Plantings form), or they can be independent of any data (such as the labels that contain the captions for those controls).

To see the Toolbox, place a form in design view and either click the **Toolbox** button on the toolbar or select **View, Toolbox**. Figure 13.8 shows the Toolbox and the buttons it contains (your Toolbox might be shaped differently; you can drag the borders to control its size and shape).

Most of the buttons on the Toolbox are used to select the type of control with which you want to work. We'll show you how to use the following six common buttons later in this section of the chapter:

In Access, a control that is attached to data is called a *bound* control. A control that is independent of data is called an *unbound* control.

- **Label**—Used to display unbound text
- **Text box**—Used to display an area in which the user can type
- **Check box**—Used to allow making a yes or no choice

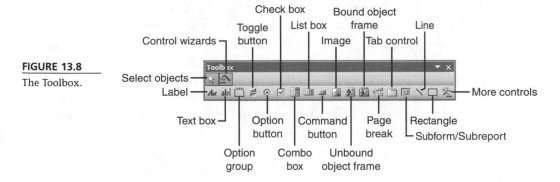

FIGURE 13.8
The Toolbox.

- **List box**—Used to display a list of information
- **Combo box**—Used to display a drop-down list of information
- **Command button**—Used to display a button

Three of the buttons in the Toolbox have special meanings:

- **Select Objects arrow**—Used to choose an already existing control with which to work.
- **Control Wizards button**—Turns the Control Wizards on or off. You should have them turned on for now.
- **More Controls button**—Allows you to add more controls to the Access Toolbox. We won't be using this button in this book.

Labels

Perhaps the simplest of all controls is the Label control, which is designed for displaying information, not editing information. When you see field names or captions displayed on a form, those are all Label controls. Although Label controls are not as complex as other controls, they do offer an easy way to practice some essential form design operations: placing, moving, sizing, and changing the properties of controls. Start by following these steps to add some Label controls to the Plantings form:

tip

When you're learning your way around design mode, the Control Wizards can save you a lot of time. Later, when you're more of an expert, you might want to turn them off and set the control properties by hand.

1. Open the **Plantings** form in design view. If the form is still on your screen in form view, you can select **View, Design View** to change it back.

2. Click the **Label** control in the Toolbox, and move your cursor to the form. It will display a crosshair and a capital letter *A*, indicating that it is ready to create a label. Click and hold the mouse button where you want the upper-left corner of the new label to be on the form. Then, drag the cursor down and to the right. A box will appear as you drag, indicating the dimensions of the new control.

3. Release the mouse button; the label will be displayed as a blank, white box with a blinking cursor. Type the text `Number Planted` and click **Enter** to finish creating the label. Access will place an alert Smart Tag next to the new label. If you hover your cursor over the alert, you'll see the text "This is a new label and is not associated with a control." That's nothing to worry about; you'll create the associated control later.

4. Create a second label beneath the first one, following the same steps. Enter the text `Purchase Price` for the second label.

You might not have managed to place the controls precisely where you want them when you created them. That's okay because Access offers flexible ways to control the sizes and positions of controls. Try these steps to see how you can alter the placement of the new controls:

1. Click in the **Number Planted** control, and Access displays eight dark boxes around the control. These boxes are called *sizing handles*; there's one at each corner of the control and one in the middle of each side of the control.

2. To resize the control, click one of the sizing handles, hold down the mouse cursor, and drag the handle in the direction in which you want to move that part of the control.

3. To make the control exactly the right size to display its contents, double-click any one of the sizing handles.

4. To move the control, move the cursor until it is over one of the sides of the control, between sizing handles. The cursor turns into an open-palmed hand at this point. Click and hold the mouse button, and you can drag the control wherever you want to place it.

5. Press **F4** to display the Properties window if it's not already visible.

6. Click the **Format** tab of the Properties window.

7. Four properties dictate the size and position of the control. The Left property measures the distance between the left side of the control and the left side of the form, whereas the Top property measures the distance between the top of

the control and the top of the form. The Width property measures the width of the control, and the Height property measures the height of the control. Type a new value in one of these properties, and you'll see the control immediately change in response.

8. With the Number Planted control still selected, hold down the **Shift** key and click the **Purchase Price** control. This results in both controls being selected, as shown in Figure 13.9. Note that the Properties Window now displays values for the properties that the two controls have in common. For example, they're both the same height, so the Height value is displayed; but they have different widths, so the Width value is missing.

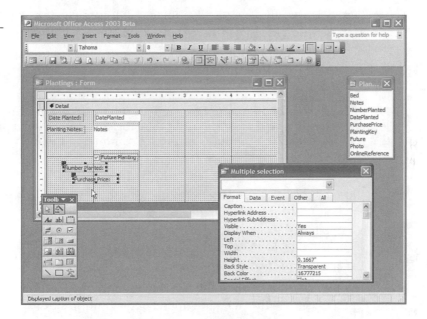

9. Type a value in the Properties window for the Left property. You'll see that the new value is applied to both selected controls.

10. Select **Format, Size, To Widest** to make both controls the same width. The other choices on the Format, Size submenu offer other ways to make multiple controls the same width or the same height.

11. Hold down **Shift** and click the **Purchase Price** control again. This deselects that control, leaving only the Number Planted control selected.

12. Drag the **Number Planted** control to the left or right so that the two controls are not lined up vertically.

13. Place the mouse cursor at a point below and to the right of both controls. Now hold down the mouse button and drag the mouse up and to the left; Access draws a box that follows the mouse pointer as you do this. When the box includes both controls, release the mouse button. Both controls are now selected.

14. Select **Format, Align, Left** to set the Left property of both controls to the same value. The Format, Align submenu contains other choices for aligning controls.

Besides the sizing and placement properties, many other properties are available, even for a control as simple as the Label. Inspecting the Properties window with a Label selected shows you the entire list. Table 13.2 lists some of the properties that you'll most likely find useful as you're starting out.

TABLE 13.2   Properties of the Label Control

Property	Meaning
Name	Each control on a form has a unique name. Until you start writing code, you won't need to worry about this. The caption of the Properties window shows both the control type and the control name when you have a control selected.
Caption	Specifies the text displayed in the control.
Left	Specifies the distance between the left edge of the control and the left edge of the form.
Top	Specifies the distance between the top edge of the control and the top edge of the form.
Width	Specifies the width of the control.
Height	Specifies the height of the control.
Back Style	Specifies whether the background of the control is transparent.
Back Color	Specifies the background color of the control.
Special Effect	Specifies the 3D appearance (if any) of the control.
Border Style	Specifies the style of line used to draw the box around the control in form view.
Border Color	Specifies the color of the line around the control in form view.
Border Width	Specifies the width of the line around the control in form view.
Fore Color	Specifies the color of the text in the control.
Font Name	Specifies the font used to display text in the control.
Font Size	Specifies the size of the text in the control.
Font Weight	Specifies the boldness of the text in the control.

Property	Meaning
Font Italic	Controls whether the text in the control appears in italic.
Font Underline	Controls whether the text in the control appears underlined.
ControlTip Text	Specifies the control tip to appear when the user hovers the cursor over the control.

You can set any of the properties listed in Table 13.2 by making entries directly in the Properties window. However, user interface shortcuts exist for some of these properties as well. Follow these steps to explore some of the properties of the Label control:

tip

Most of the properties of the Label control also apply to other types of controls.

1. Select the **Purchase Price** control.

2. Click the drop-down arrow next to the **Fill/Back Color** button on the toolbar. Select a background color for the control by clicking one of the color patches that appears.

3. Click in the **Fore Color** property in the Properties window. A build button appears to the right of the property—click it.

4. Select a color from the **Color** dialog box and click **OK** to assign that color to the text of the control.

5. Click the drop-down arrow next to the **Special Effect** button on the toolbar; then select the **Shadowed** special effect.

6. Click in the **Font Name** property in the Properties window. A drop-down arrow appears; click a font name to assign that font to the control.

7. Double-click in the **Font Italic** property in the Properties window to switch the property value from No to **Yes**.

8. Double-click one of the sizing handles for the control to ensure that it can still display all its text.

You might have noticed that the Fore Color and Back Color properties display numbers in the Properties window. That's because Access assigns a numeric code, ranging from 0 to 16 million, to each of the colors it can display. If you pick a number at random for a color property, you'll get a random color—although generally it's more useful to use the toolbar buttons or the Color dialog box to select the color you want!

Text Boxes

Text boxes provide a control that can display data from a table and that a user can use to edit or enter data. Most of the controls you've been working with on forms so far in this book are text boxes. You'll find that all your skills from manipulating labels apply equally well to text boxes. In fact, all controls are sized, placed, and so on using the same techniques.

Follow these steps to add some text boxes to the Plantings form:

1. Select the **Text Box** tool in the Toolbox. The Properties window displays the default properties for a text box control. Set the Auto Label property to **No**.

2. Now move your cursor to the form. It displays a crosshair and control with letters in it, indicating that it is ready to create a text box. Click and hold the mouse button where you want the upper-left corner of the new label to be on the form; start just to the right of the Number Planted label. Then, drag the cursor down and to the right. A box appears as you drag, indicating the dimensions of the new control.

3. Release the mouse button, and the text box is displayed with the contents Unbound.

4. Click in the **Control Source** property to display both a drop-down arrow and a build button. Click the drop-down arrow and select **NumberPlanted** from the list.

5. Hold down **Shift** and click the **Number Planted** label so that both the text box and the label are selected. Use the Format menu to size and align the two controls.

6. Click the **Text Box** control in the Toolbox again.

7. Set the Auto Label property to **Yes**.

8. Draw another text box on the form. This time, however, when you release the mouse button, Access creates both a Text Box control and a Label control. Both controls will be selected.

9. Move the cursor until it is over the edge of one of the controls and displays the open hand.

10. Click and drag the cursor; both controls move together.

11. Move the cursor over the upper-left sizing handle of one of the controls. At this point, the cursor displays a hand with one finger sticking up. Click and drag the cursor to move just that control, without moving the other control.

12. Set the Control Source property of the new text box to **Bed**.

The Text Box control has many of the same properties as the Label control. However, it also has other properties because it can contain data. Figure 13.10 shows the Data tab of the Properties window with a Text Box control selected.

FIGURE 13.10
Data properties
for a Text Box
control.

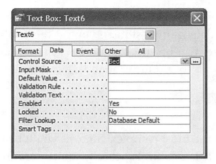

Many of the data properties of a Text Box control are familiar to you from table design (and indeed, these properties inherit their values from the values assigned to the corresponding table field). This includes the Input Mask, Default Value, Validation Rule, and Validation Text properties. Three of the other properties on this tab will be important to you as you design forms:

- **Control Source**—Specifies the data field to which this control will be bound. The Control Source will be a field from the Record Source specified for the form.

- **Enabled**—Controls whether the control is displayed as a live control. If you set the Enabled property to No, the control is grayed out and the user is not able to type in it.

- **Locked**—Controls whether the user can enter data in the control. If you set the Locked property to yes, the user cannot edit the data contained in this control, but the control itself isn't grayed out.

Check Boxes

Check boxes are an appropriate control to use when you want the user to make a yes/no choice. Indeed, the Form Wizard and the Field List use Check Box controls to represent any data field with the Yes/No data type. That's why the Future control on the Plantings form is a check box.

If you select the Future control on the Plantings form, you'll see that we've already discussed many of the properties of the control. The following are two more properties we want to point out:

■ **Status Bar Text**—Holds the text to be displayed on the Access status bar when this control is selected. Access automatically initializes this property from the description property of the corresponding table field, but you can override that here if you want.

■ **Triple State**—Controls whether the control is just a yes-or-no choice or whether it has a third, indeterminate state. If you set the Triple State property to Yes, a Check Box control can be checked, unchecked, or grayed out. The grayed-out state corresponds to a null value in the underlying table.

List Boxes and Combo Boxes

List boxes and combo boxes are the most complex controls you'll be working with as you design your first databases. These controls actually relate data from one table to data from another table. You can think of the List Box and Combo Box as little machines that allow the user to pick a value from one table and then pump that value into a field from another table.

Fortunately, although these controls are complex, they aren't hard to build because Access includes a Control Wizard to help you build them. Here's how you can create a simple List Box control:

1. Open the **Plants** form in design view.

2. Make sure that the **Control Wizards** button in the Toolbox is selected. If it isn't, click it before you continue so Access will automatically launch the appropriate control wizard. This button is a toggle button and remains selected until you click it to deselect it.

3. Select the **List Box** control in the Toolbox.

4. Use the cursor to draw a control in the empty area of the form, just as you earlier drew Label and Text Box controls. When you release the mouse button, instead of creating the new control, Access launches the List Box Wizard, as shown in Figure 13.11.

5. On the first panel of the List Box Wizard, select **I Want the List Box to Look Up the Values in a Table or Query**. Then, click **Next**.

6. On the second panel of the List Box Wizard, select the **Types** table as the source of data for the List Box. Click **Next**.

7. On the third panel of the List Box Wizard, click the >> button to move both the TypeID field and the Description field from the Available Fields list to the Selected Fields list. Click **Next**.

FIGURE 13.11
The first panel
of the List Box
Wizard.

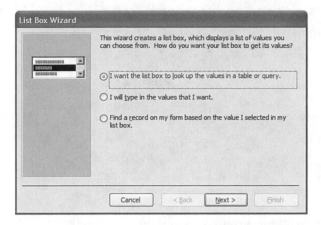

8. The next panel of the List Box Wizard allows you to specify a sort order for the data. Select **Description** in the first combo box on this panel and then click **Next**.

9. The next panel of the List Box Wizard, shown in Figure 13.12, displays the way the List Box control will look. You'll see that Access has chosen to hide the TypeID column. Click **Next**.

FIGURE 13.12
Setting column
options in the
List Box Wizard.

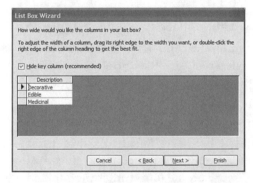

10. On the sixth panel of the List Box Wizard, select **Store That Value in This Field**. Select the **TypeID** field from the drop-down list and click **Next**.

11. Assign the name `Type` to the List Box. Then click **Finish** to create the list box.

12. Select **View, Form View** to see the effects of your changes. Figure 13.13 shows the form at this point.

FIGURE 13.13

The form with a
new List Box
control.

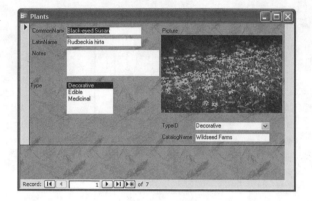

As you scroll through the records displayed by this form, you'll notice that the new
List Box control and the existing Combo Box control always show the same selected
value. The reason is that they're both bound to the same underlying field in the
Plants table. There's nothing to prevent you from displaying the same data in two
different controls, although users of your database might find this a bit confusing.

The major difference between a list box and a combo box is that the list box shows
the entire list at all times, whereas the combo box shows only the selected value
until you click the drop-down arrow. A list box is also limited to the values that are
already in the list. A combo box, on the other hand, can let the user enter a value
that's not in the list, although this capability is usually turned off.

To see the properties that control the behavior of a combo box or list box, switch the
Plants form back to design view and click the **TypeID** combo box (the one that
existed before you added the list box). Here's what you'll find:

- **The Control Source property is set to TypeID**—This is the field in the
  Plants table in which the user's selections are stored.

- **The Row Source Type property is set to Table/Query**—In most cases,
  this is the setting you'll want here. You can also choose Value List, which lets
  you embed the list directly on the form rather than taking it from another
  table.

- **The Row Source property is set to SELECT Types.TypeID,
  Types.Description FROM Types**—You might recognize this as a select
  query. Fortunately, you don't have to build the row source by typing such
  code in; when you click in the Row Source property, the Properties window
  displays a build button that opens the query design grid. The row source
  specifies the source of the list of values in this control. In this case, it's using
  all the TypeID and Description values from the Types table to build the list.

- **The Column Count property is set to 2**—This tells the form that there are two columns in the row source.
- **The Column Widths property is set to 0"; 1"**—This tells the form that the first column should be hidden (by setting its width to 0) and the second column should be 1" wide.
- **The Bound Column property is set to 1**—This tells the form that when the user selects a row in the list, the value from the first column of that row should be stored in the field specified by the control source property.
- **The List Rows property is set to 8**—This is the maximum number of rows Access will display in the drop-down list at once. If more than eight rows are in the list, Access displays a scrollbar.
- **The Limit to List property is set to Yes**—This prevents the user from entering a value not in the list.

Access also offers a useful tool to change the type of a control, which comes in handy when you change your mind about the best user interface for a form. For example, the Plants form currently contains a text box to enter the catalog, but you know that all the catalogs are listed in the Catalogs table. By converting this control to a combo box, you can let the user select from a list rather than forcing her to type in a value:

1. Select the **Type** list box you created earlier in this section, and press the **Delete** key to remove it from the form. This will also remove the associated label control.
2. Select the **CatalogName** text box.
3. Select **Format, Change To, Combo Box**.
4. Click in the **Row Source** property for the new combo box, which displays a build button. Click the build button.
5. Select the **Catalogs** table in the Show Table dialog box and click **Add**.
6. Click **Close** to dismiss the Show Table dialog box.
7. Drag the **Name** column from the field listing in the Query Builder down to the query grid. Set the Sort property for this field to **Ascending**.
8. Click the **Close** button to close the Query Builder.
9. Access displays an error message, as shown in Figure 13.14. Even though this is not the friendliest dialog box possible, its appearance is completely normal. Click **Yes** to finish building the Row Source property.

FIGURE 13.14

The prompt you
see when setting
the Row Source
property.

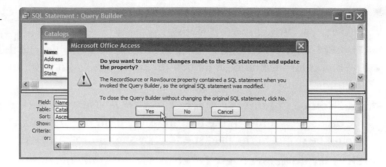

10. Set the Column Widths property by typing 1.5".

11. Set the Limit to List property by selecting **Yes**.

12. Save the form.

13. Switch to form view. Now you can select the catalog name from a list, instead
    of having to type it in for each record.

Command Buttons

The last important control that we'll look at in this chapter is the Command Button
control. Command buttons, as you might guess from their name, are used to tell
Access to do something. To get deeply into the subject of commands requires more
programming than you'll learn in this book, although there's a short introduction in
Chapter 15. But for now, you'll use one of the Control wizards to construct a command button to give you a feel for what they can do. Follow these steps:

1. Open the **Plants** form in design view.

2. Click the **Command Button** button in the Toolbox.

3. Click in an empty area on the form to launch the Command Button Wizard,
   shown in Figure 13.15.

FIGURE 13.15

The Command
Button Wizard.

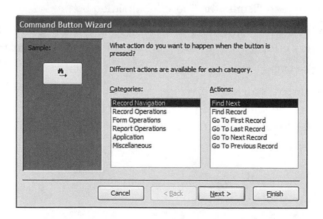

4. Select **Report Operations** in the Categories list. Then select **Preview Report** in the Actions list and click **Next**.

5. On the second panel of the wizard, select the Plants report. Click **Next**.

6. On the third panel of the wizard, accept the default picture and click **Next**.

7. On the final panel of the wizard, accept the default name and click **Finish**.

8. Save the form and switch back to form view.

9. Click the newly created button. The Plants report opens in print preview view.

Working with Sections and Subforms

Now we'll take a brief look at two more form design topics: sections and subforms. Access forms can have multiple sections and can display subforms.

Form Sections

Form sections provide a way to logically group some of the controls on forms. The list of available sections is fixed by Access. In practice, the following are the three sections you're likely to use:

- **Form header**—This section appears at the top of the form, above all the records.

- **Form detail**—This section is where the actual records appear. The detail section might be displayed many times, if you have the form set to continuous view.

- **Form footer**—This section appears at the bottom of the form, below all the records.

To see form sections in action, you can work with the Catalogs form by doing the following:

1. Open the **Catalogs** form in design view.

2. In design view, you'll see several gray bars running the width of the form. You might have ignored these, but now you can see that they mark the sections of the form. Place your cursor at the bottom of the Form Footer bar and drag it downward to create an actual footer section.

3. Click the **Command Button** control in the Toolbox.

4. Click in an empty area in the footer section of the form to launch the Command Button Wizard.

5. Select **Record Navigation** in the Categories list. Then select **Go To Last Record** in the Actions list and click **Next**.

6. On the second panel of the wizard, accept the default picture and click **Next**.

7. On the final panel of the wizard, accept the default name and click **Finish**.

8. Save the form and switch back to form view.

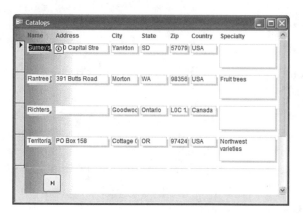

> **tip**
>
> To change the background color of a form that doesn't have a picture for a background, select the detail section of the form and edit its Back Color property.

Figure 13.16 shows the modified form. You can see that the controls in the form header (the labels for Name, Address, and so on) appear only once at the top of the form. The controls in the detail section appear multiple times, and the command button control in the form footer appears only once at the bottom of the form.

Subforms

You first saw a subform in Chapter 8, "Creating and Using Data Entry Forms." Now we'll take a brief look at using subforms in design view. As you'll recall, a subform lets you show a group of related records on a parent form. For example, on the CatalogsMain form, the main part of the form (the parent form) displays information on types, whereas the subform displays a list of plants of the currently displayed type.

FIGURE 13.16

Form sections in action.

To see the details of how forms and subforms work together, follow these steps:

1. Open the **TypesMain** form in design view.

2. Click the subform area in design view. You can tell the subform because it has its own set of rulers and its own header and detail section.

3. Inspect the Properties window for the subform. The Link Child Fields and Link Master Fields properties specify how the form and subform are related. At any time, the subform displays records whose Link Child Fields have the same value as the current Link Master Fields values on the main form.

4. Although you can edit the subform directly in the main form, this can get confusing. Click outside of the subform to deselect it. Then right-click the subform and select **Subform in New Window** to edit the subform in a new window, as shown in Figure 13.17.

FIGURE 13.17
Working with a subform in design view.

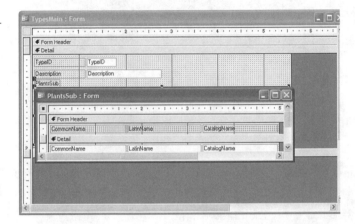

5. Select the form header in the subform by clicking the gray bar above the header.

6. Change the Back Color property of the subform header by clicking in the property and using the build button to select a new color.

7. Click the **Save** button to save the changes to the subform.

8. Close the subform.

9. Switch the main form back to design view; the subform now has the colored header you selected.

Object Dependencies

By now you're starting to accumulate quite a few objects in your database. Access keeps track of the relationships between these objects, and it can show them to you as well. To see this in action, follow these steps:

1. Click the **Tables** shortcut in the database window.

2. Right-click the **Catalogs** table and select **Object Dependencies**.

3. Access may ask whether to update the dependency information in the database. Click **OK**.

4. Access will display the dependency information in a task pane at the side of the screen, as shown in Figure 13.18.

FIGURE 13.18

Displaying the dependencies of the Catalogs table.

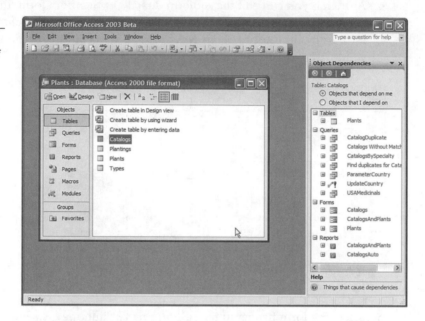

The dependent objects are presented in a treeview. You can click the plus signs to expand the treeview, up to four levels deep. For example, in this case clicking the + sign next to the Plants table will show you the objects that depend directly on that table.

This default view allows you to perform easy impact analysis. You can immediately see which objects in your database will be affected by a change to the selected object. This lets you see the repercussions of major changes (such as deleting an object or changing the columns returned by a query) before you make them.

You can also reverse the process and see the ancestors of the selected object by clicking the **Objects That I Depend On** option button in the Object Dependencies task pane.

THE ABSOLUTE MINIMUM

We covered a lot of ground in this chapter, and yet we did not see everything that you can do in form design mode. This is one of the areas of Access where there is much more depth than we can cover in an introductory book. As you're working with forms in design mode, keep these points in mind:

- AutoFormats enable you to quickly change the appearance of a form.

- The Field List can be used to add new bound controls to a form.

- Both forms and the controls on forms have properties that control their appearances and behaviors. You can alter these properties by manipulating the controls directly or by changing values in the Properties window.

- The Toolbox enables you to add new controls of various types to your Access forms.

- Sections and subforms provide more advanced ways of managing the design of forms.

- You can use the Object Dependencies task pane to see how the objects in your database are related.

IN THIS CHAPTER

- Quickly format a report using AutoFormat
- Customize your reports by modifying report properties
- Print labels using the special Label Wizard
- Add a chart to a report

14

DRESSING UP YOUR REPORTS

After storing and manipulating all your data, you might want to print hard copies so you can share the information in a meaningful way with other people. Or, you just might prefer to view your data on paper instead of onscreen. Fortunately, Access provides one of the most flexible and easy-to-use report managers around.

In Chapter 9, "Printing Information with Reports," you learned how to use a few report wizards, but they won't always be adequate. In this chapter, you'll learn how to format reports so they look and display your data the way you want. We'll also review two wizards; one will help you print labels and another displays charts in your reports.

Formatting Reports

In Chapter 13, "Customizing Forms," you learned about form properties; reports also have properties, and you can change them to create just the right look for your reports. You can add subtle shading to controls or entire sections. Or, you might want to apply a border or other special effects to a control. In this section, you'll use AutoFormat and the Properties window to set report properties.

Using AutoFormat

The AutoFormat feature quickly applies an overall display scheme to a report, the same way it does to a form (which you learned about in Chapter 13). Although Access comes with several predefined formats, you can create your own.

Now, let's get to work and apply an AutoFormat to quickly format a new report by performing the following steps:

1. Select **Catalogs** in the Tables section of the Database window, and then select **Report** from the Insert menu.

2. Double-click **AutoReport: Tabular** in the New Report dialog box.

3. After Access displays the report, review it carefully so you'll be able to identify the changes after you reformat it. Next, click the **View** (Design View should be the default) button on the Print Preview toolbar to open the report in design view.

4. In design view, select **AutoFormat** from the Format menu; then select any of the predefined formats other than the currently selected one. As you select each format, the sample report to the right changes to reflect the new format. That enables you to see what the new format looks like before you

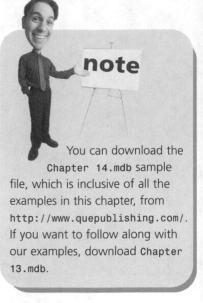

note

You can download the Chapter 14.mdb sample file, which is inclusive of all the examples in this chapter, from http://www.quepublishing.com/. If you want to follow along with our examples, download Chapter 13.mdb.

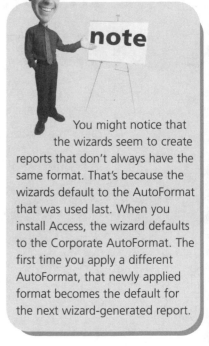

note

You might notice that the wizards seem to create reports that don't always have the same format. That's because the wizards default to the AutoFormat that was used last. When you install Access, the wizard defaults to the Corporate AutoFormat. The first time you apply a different AutoFormat, that newly applied format becomes the default for the next wizard-generated report.

actually apply it. Our wizard chose the Corporate AutoFormat. Figure 14.1 shows the Soft Gray option selected. After you've selected an AutoFormat, click **OK**.

FIGURE 14.1

Choose a predefined AutoFormat for your report.

5. Click **View** on the Report Design toolbar to view the changes shown in Figure 14.2. If you chose a format other than Soft Gray, your report won't look like the one in the figure. Close and save the report as Catalogs.

FIGURE 14.2

Selecting an AutoFormat is a quick way to apply a complete scheme to a report.

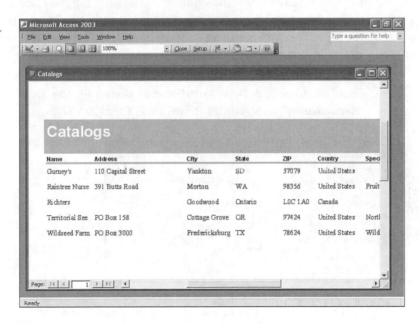

Customizing AutoFormat

We mentioned earlier that you can create your own AutoFormat options. Doing so can save you a lot of time if you routinely apply the same formatting to your reports. There are two ways to create your own: You can base a new AutoFormat on an existing format, or you can modify an existing AutoFormat.

More than likely, you'll just create your own, rather than change the built-in choices, so let's look at the first method. Specifically, let's base a new AutoFormat on Corporate and change some fonts. To do so, follow these steps:

1. Return to the report you created in the previous exercise. If you didn't save it, open any report. Just be sure not to save any of the changes you make during this exercise.

2. In Design view, select all the controls in the Page Header section. Clicking the ruler to the left of the section automatically selects the controls in that section. Click the **Italic** button on the Report Design toolbar. Then, select any color other than black (or the current color) from the Font/Fore Color list.

3. Select all the controls in the Detail section, and then select **Shadowed** from the Special Effect list.

4. Now, select **AutoFormat** from the Format menu.

5. In the AutoFormat dialog box, click the **Customize** button to open the Customize AutoFormat dialog box. The default option is Update Soft Gray with values from the Report *'ReportName'*, where *ReportName* is the name of the report that's currently open in design view. This option modifies the current AutoFormat with the formats in the current report. This isn't the option you want, though.

6. Select the **Create a New AutoFormat Based on the Report *'ReportName'***, as shown in Figure 14.3. Then click **OK**.

FIGURE 14.3

Base a new AutoFormat on an existing format.

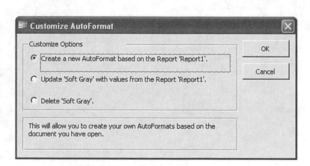

7. Enter a name, such as Custom1, for the new AutoFormat in the resulting dialog box; then click **OK**.

8. Access automatically selects the new format in the AutoFormat dialog box. Click **OK** to apply the new format to the current report. Then, take a look at the report in Print Preview. Anytime you want a report to look like the one shown in Figure 14.4, just assign the Custom1 AutoFormat.

FIGURE 14.4

Apply this report's format to another by selecting the Custom1 AutoFormat you just created.

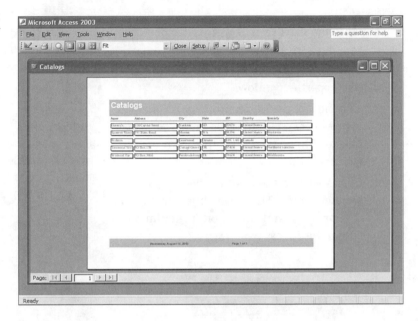

Using the Properties Window

You're probably familiar with the Properties window because you used it to set properties for forms in Chapter 13. Reports also have properties you can use to determine the way reports look or the data they display.

To change report properties, open the report in design view. Then, double-click the **Report Selector**—the gray square at the intersection of the two rulers—to open the Properties window. The title bar displays the word Report, which means the offered properties belong to the report object.

To change a property, select an option from the field's drop-down list or simply type over the current property. If the field offers a list of options, you can also double-click the property name to

caution

In design view, you can set properties for a form or a report, which also includes many other objects such as controls. Fortunately, the Properties window's title bar always displays the current object's type. You can take advantage of this behavior by checking the Properties window's title bar to make sure the correct object is selected before you start changing properties.

cycle through the options. Simply stop clicking when the field displays the property you want.

Now, let's look at a quick example by changing the Catalog report's Caption property. To do so, follow these steps:

1. Open the **Catalogs** report you've been working with in design view.

2. Double-click the **Report Selector** to open the Properties window.

3. Currently, the Caption property is Catalogs. Type `Seed Catalogs` into the Properties window to change the value, as shown in Figure 14.5.

4. Click **View** on the Print Preview toolbar to see the change. The Access title bar displays the caption text if the report is maximized within the Access window.

The Properties window displays properties for the current object. To open the window, double-click an object or select **Properties** from the View menu. Clicking the Report Selector always displays the report's properties.

FIGURE 14.5
Change the Caption property.

Caption property

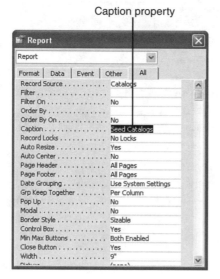

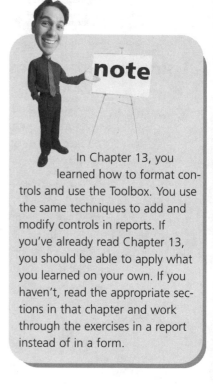

In Chapter 13, you learned how to format controls and use the Toolbox. You use the same techniques to add and modify controls in reports. If you've already read Chapter 13, you should be able to apply what you learned on your own. If you haven't, read the appropriate sections in that chapter and work through the exercises in a report instead of in a form.

Specialized Wizards

Access provides a number of wizards for creating quick reports. A few of them were discussed in Chapter 9. Sometimes a report isn't as simple as a hard copy of your data—you can also print labels and display charts in a report. Don't worry, though, both reports are simple to create as long as you let an Access wizard do the work.

Creating Label Reports

A label report is a little different from most reports. You can print name tags, mailing labels, file labels, or even inventory labels for storage. The uses are limited only by your imagination—if the data's in a table, you can print a label for it.

Let's use the Label Wizard to print a mailing label for each catalog in your plants database. Do the following:

1. Select **Report** from the Insert menu.

2. In the New Report dialog box, select the **Label Wizard**, select **Catalogs** from the drop-down control, and then click **OK**.

3. The wizard already knows all the dimensions for a number of labels. Most of the time, you can find your label listed among these options. For this example, select **English** and **Sheet Feed** from the Unit of Measure and Label Type sections, respectively. Then, select **Avery** from the Filter by Manufacturer drop-down control. Doing so limits the number of label choices.

4. Select Product Number **5095**, as shown in Figure 14.6. Access has built-in information for many common label types from various manufacturers. If you don't find a suitable label, you can click the **Customize** button to enter your label's dimensions. Click **Next** to continue.

FIGURE 14.6

Choose a label by its product name, number, or dimensions.

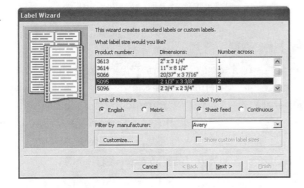

5. In the next window, you can specify fonts and other font attributes. Accept the default options by clicking **Next** without making any changes.

6. Now you're ready to list the fields that contain the data you want to print on labels. You can also include literal characters. You'll add the catalog name and address fields as follows: Double-click **Name** in the Available Fields list to move it to the prototype label; then press **Enter** to move the insertion point to the next line. Double-click **Address** and press **Enter**. Double-click **City**, and then type a comma and space character. Next, double-click **State**, add a space, and then double-click **ZIP** to create the prototype shown in Figure 14.7. Click **Next**.

FIGURE 14.7
Add labels to the Prototype label.

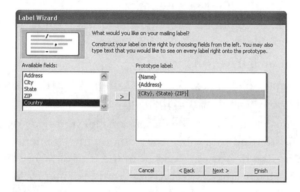

7. You can sort the labels by any field in the table. Select **Name** and click **Next**.

8. The wizard assigns a default name to the label report in the final window. You can change it, but don't. Click **Finish** to generate the report shown in Figure 14.8.

All that's left to do is to insert the label sheets and click Print!

Displaying Charts in a Report

The Chart Wizard embeds a chart in a report. The chart is actually an ActiveX control—Access doesn't generate the chart. Access uses Microsoft Graph, which offers 20 chart formats, to generate the chart. The embedded chart lets you change its results by moving chart components to change the orientation. Or, you can modify the default calculations.

The following are two ways to add a chart to a report:

■ Base a report on a query that contains the data you want to chart.

■ Open an existing report and select Chart from the Insert menu to launch the Chart Wizard.

FIGURE 14.8
The wizard generated this label report.

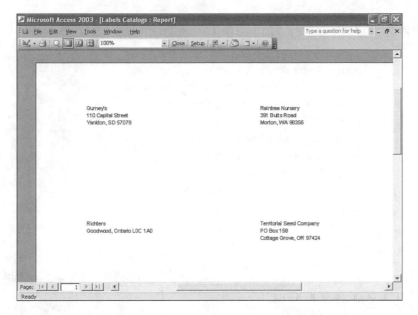

Now, let's create a simple pie chart that denotes the plants ordered from each catalog. Usually, you base a graph on a query because the wizard can't handle more than one data source or calculate the necessary values. Begin with a query that counts the number of plants ordered from each catalog by following these steps:

1. Click the **Tables** shortcut, select **Plants** in the Database window's list, choose **Query** from the New Object button's dropdown list, and then double-click **Design View**.

2. Add the **CatalogName** and **CommonName** fields to the grid, in that order.

3. Select **Totals** from the View menu on the Query Design toolbar.

4. Change the Group By aggregate in the CommonName column to `Count`, as shown in Figure 14.9. Save the query as `ChartQuery` and close it.

5. Click the **Queries** shortcut in the Database window and select **ChartQuery**.

6. Select **Report** from the Insert menu and double-click **Chart Wizard** in the New Report dialog box.

7. In the wizard's first pane, move both fields to the Selected Fields list and then click **Next**.

8. The next pane displays 20 chart formats. Select the **Pie Chart** (the first option on the last row) and click **Next**.

9. At this point, the wizard generates a sample chart based on the data, as shown in Figure 14.10. Don't be too concerned if the chart components don't display the correct proportions, but do check the axis controls to ensure the wizard is using the correct field(s). You want the pie chart to show the plants by catalog, so the wizard made the right choice by selecting the CountOfCommonName field. Don't change the wizard's choices; just click **Next**.

10. In the final pane, name the report **Chart** and click **Finish** without changing any other options. The results are shown in Figure 14.11. You can see with a quick glance that half the plants have come from Wildseed Farms.

You can click the Preview Chart button in the upper-left corner to get a more accurate look at the chart. In addition, you can change the default structure by rearranging the controls or double-clicking a control and choosing a different mathematical function.

FIGURE 14.9

Generating a chart from this query.

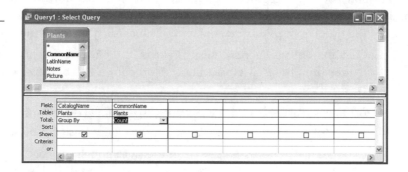

Double-click a control to summarize data

FIGURE 14.10

You can alter the wizard's charting choices.

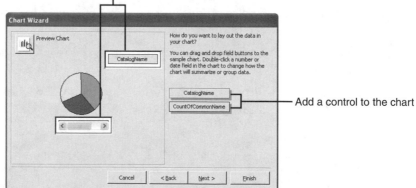

Add a control to the chart

FIGURE 14.11

The result chart shows the relationship, by count, of the plants from each catalog.

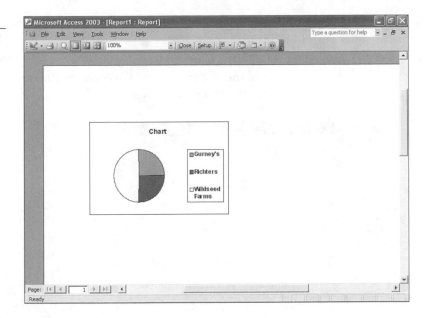

Now let's add a dynamic chart to a report. By *dynamic*, we mean the chart will reflect the values in each record. To create this report and chart, perform the following steps:

1. Use the AutoReport: Tabular Wizard to create a quick report on the Plantings table.

2. Click **View** on the Print Preview toolbar to open the new report in design view.

3. Select the **Photo** and Online Reference controls in the Detail section, and press **Delete** to remove it from the report. You'll use that spot to display the chart you're about to create.

4. Select **Chart** from the Insert menu.

5. Using the drag-and-drop method, insert a Chart control to fill the spot where the Photo control was. When you release the mouse, the wizard displays its first pane, which wants to know where the data for the chart is going to come from. Select the **Plantings** table and click **Next**.

6. In the next pane, identify the values you want to chart. In this case, move the **Bed** and **NumberPlanted** fields to the Fields for Chart list, and click **Next**.

7. Select the **Cylinder Column Chart**—the third option in the first row—and click **Next**.

8. Click **Next** without making any changes in the next pane. You don't need to alter any of the wizard's choices.

9. In the next pane, you can relate chart values to report values. The chart automatically relates the Bed fields. Add the **NumberPlanted** fields to the mix, as shown in Figure 14.12. Click **Next**.

FIGURE 14.12

Relate chart values to report values.

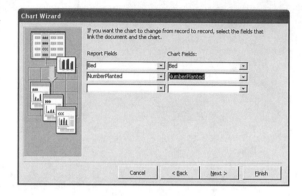

10. In the final pane, accept the default name of Plantings, and click **Finish**.

11. Click **View** on the Print Preview toolbar to see the results shown in Figure 14.13. As you can see, the axis values change from record to record. As is, this particular chart might not be effective, but you can see how easily you can chart individual values.

FIGURE 14.13

The axis values reflect each record.

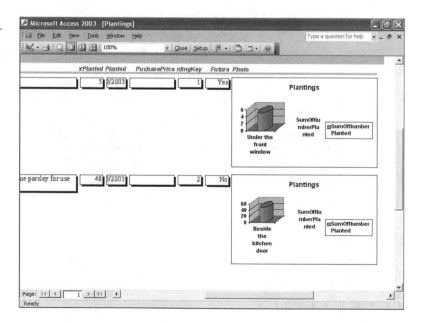

THE ABSOLUTE MINIMUM

We all use reports, and fortunately, Access has one of the best report generators on the market. Take advantage of it! In this chapter, you learned a number of ways to customize your reports, including

- Applying AutoFormat options or modifying individual report properties
- Generating label reports
- Adding charts to your reports

PART V

LETTING ACCESS DO YOUR WORK FOR YOU

IN THIS CHAPTER

- Using the Switchboard Wizard
- Setting startup options
- Working with macros

15

AUTOMATING YOUR DATABASE

Perhaps you've been wondering about that Macros shortcut in the Database window. Or, perhaps you've begun to tire of some of the repetitive actions in your database: opening and closing forms, picking which report to run, and so on. Either way, help is at hand. In this chapter, we'll introduce you to some of the ways to automate your work in Access. Yes, this does edge into programming, but don't worry—Access has made simple programming so easy that an absolute beginner can do it.

Using the Switchboard Wizard

By now, the Plants database contains dozens of objects: tables, queries, forms, and reports. Right now, you can find any of these objects by going to the Database window, selecting the proper shortcut, and then locating the object you want. But what if you're sharing the database with someone else? The Database window isn't the friendliest possible way to organize things. It's efficient, and it shows you everything, but it doesn't offer you any guidance for finding the important objects.

Over the years, Access developers have come up with several ways to tackle this problem. One of the most popular organizational devices for Access databases is the switchboard form. Figure 15.1 shows the switchboard form from the Northwind sample database.

note

You can download the `Chapter 15.mdb` sample file, which is inclusive of all the examples in this chapter, from `http://www.quepublishing.com/`. If you want to follow along with our examples, download `Chapter 14.mdb`.

FIGURE 15.1

The switchboard form in the Northwind sample database.

The Northwind sample database contains more than 100 objects. The switchboard form comes up automatically when you open the database and gives you buttons to open just the most important items. You can see that this is a much friendlier interface for new users than the Database window.

Building Your First Switchboard

Fortunately, adding a switchboard to your own database is easy because Microsoft includes a Switchboard Manager in Access. (A manager is similar to the wizards you've been using throughout this book.) You'll use this tool now to create a switch-board for the Plants database. Follow these steps:

1. Launch Access and load the Plants database.

2. Select **Tools, Database Utilities, Switchboard Manager**.

3. Because this is the first time you've loaded the Switchboard Manager in this database, Access asks whether you'd like to create a switchboard. Click **Yes**.

4. The Switchboard Manager opens, as shown in Figure 15.2. As you'll learn, you can actually have more than one switchboard in a database. When you start, the Switchboard Manager only creates the Main Switchboard (Default) for you. Click **Edit** to open the Edit Switchboard Page dialog box.

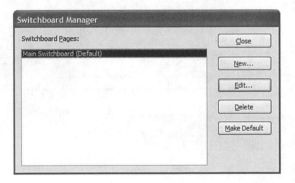

FIGURE 15.2

The Switchboard Manager creates a default switchboard the first time you run it.

5. The Edit Switchboard Page dialog box shows you all the items on a particular switchboard. The main switchboard doesn't have any items yet. Click **New** to open the Edit Switchboard Item dialog box.

6. Enter `Catalogs` for the text. Select **Open Form in Edit Mode** as the command; then select the **Catalogs** form. Figure 15.3 shows the filled in Edit Switchboard Item dialog box. Click **OK** to close the Edit Switchboard Item dialog box.

7. Click **Close** to close the Edit Switchboard Page dialog box.

8. Click **Close** to close the Switchboard Manager.

9. Click the **Forms** shortcut in the Database window.

10. Double-click the new **Switchboard** form to open it. Figure 15.4 shows the new switchboard.

FIGURE 15.3

Creating a
switchboard
item.

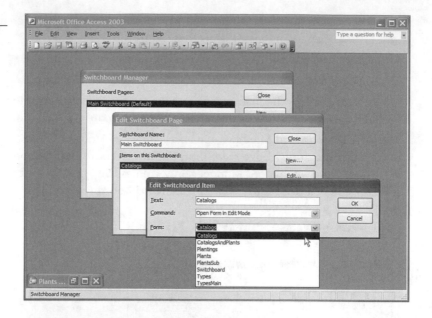

FIGURE 15.4

A new switch-
board with a
single button.

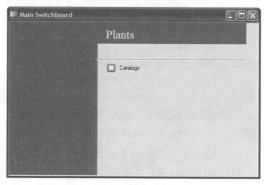

11. Click the **Catalogs** button, and the Catalogs form opens.

Congratulations! You've built your first switchboard. Table 15.1 lists the various commands you can select on the Edit Switchboard Item dialog box.

TABLE 15.1 Commands Available for Switchboard Items

Command	Meaning
Go to Switchboard	Opens another switchboard.
Open Form in Add Mode	Opens a form without showing existing records, so that you can add new data.
Open Form in Edit Mode	Opens a form showing existing records, so that you can edit data (you can also add data in this mode).
Open Report	Opens a report in preview mode.
Design Application	Opens the Switchboard Manager.
Exit Application	Closes the database.
Run Macro	Runs a macro. You'll learn more about macros later in this chapter.
Run Code	Runs Visual Basic for Applications (VBA) programming code. We don't cover VBA in this book.

> **note**
>
> You'll learn how to make the switchboard open automatically when you load the database later in the chapter, in the "Setting Startup Options" section.

Editing a Switchboard

One of the benefits of the Switchboard Manager is that it can be used repeatedly on the same switchboard. If you think of a change you'd like to make—adding a new item, editing an item, deleting an item— you can just open the Switchboard Manager again. You don't have to throw away your previous work. In this section, you'll make some changes to the main switchboard for the Plants database. Do the following:

1. Make sure the main switchboard (form) is closed.

2. Select **Tools, Database Utilities, Switchboard Manager**.

3. In the Switchboard Manager dialog box, select **Main Switchboard (Default)** and click **Edit**.

4. In the Edit Switchboard Page dialog box, click **New**.

5. In the Edit Switchboard Item dialog box, enter `View Plants` for the text. Select **Open Form in Edit Mode** as the command, and select the **Plants** form. Click **OK** to close the Edit Switchboard Item dialog box.

6. In the Edit Switchboard Page dialog box, click **New**.

7. In the Edit Switchboard Item dialog box, enter `View Plantings` for the text. Select **Open Form in Edit Mode** as the command, and then select the **Plantings** form. Click **OK** to close the Edit Switchboard Item dialog box.

8. In the Edit Switchboard Page dialog box, click **New**.

9. In the Edit Switchboard Item dialog box, enter `View Types` for the text. Select **Open Form in Edit Mode** as the command, and then select the **Types** form. Click **OK** to close the Edit Switchboard Item dialog box.

10. Select the **View Types** item on the Edit Switchboard Page dialog box. Click **Move Up** twice to relocate this item above the View Plants item. You can use the Move Up and Move Down buttons to arrange the switchboard any way you like.

11. Select the **Catalogs** item and click **Edit**. Change the Text to `View Catalogs`; then click **OK**.

12. Click **Close** to close the Edit Switchboard Page dialog box.

13. Click **Close** to close the Switchboard Manager.

14. Double-click the **Switchboard** form to open it. Figure 15.5 shows the edited switchboard.

FIGURE 15.5

The main switchboard after editing.

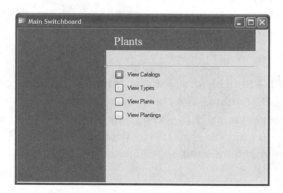

Besides adding new items to a switchboard and editing existing items, you can delete items that you no longer need. Just select the item on the Edit Switchboard Page dialog box and click **Delete**.

Adding a Second Switchboard

Switchboards are a good way to organize things, but they can be overdone. What happens when you go from four items on a switchboard to fourteen or forty? The switchboard can become just as overwhelming as the Database window. Access provides a way to handle this by letting you create nested switchboards. Follow these steps:

1. Make sure the main switchboard is closed.

2. Select **Tools**, **Database Utilities**, **Switchboard Manager**.

3. In the Switchboard Manager dialog box, click **New**.

4. Name the new switchboard Reports and click **OK**.

5. In the Switchboard Manager dialog box, select the **Reports** switchboard and click **Edit**.

6. In the Edit Switchboard Page dialog box, click **New**.

7. In the Edit Switchboard Item dialog box, enter Catalog Report for the text. Select **Open Report** as the command, and select the **CatalogsAuto** report. Click **OK** to close the Edit Switchboard Item dialog box.

8. In the Edit Switchboard Page dialog box, click **New**.

9. In the Edit Switchboard Item dialog box, enter Plant Report for the text. Select **Open Report** as the command, and select the **Plants** report. Click **OK** to close the Edit Switchboard Item dialog box.

10. In the Edit Switchboard Page dialog box, click **New**.

11. In the Edit Switchboard Item dialog box, enter Type Report for the text. Select **Open Report** as the command; then select the **Types** report. Click **OK** to close the Edit Switchboard Item dialog box.

12. Click **Close** to close the Edit Switchboard Page dialog box.

13. In the Switchboard Manager dialog box, select the **Main Switchboard (Default)** and click **Edit**.

14. In the Edit Switchboard Page dialog box, click **New**.

15. In the Edit Switchboard Item dialog box, enter Reports for the text. Select **Go to Switchboard** as the command; then select the **Reports** switchboard. Click **OK** to close the Edit Switchboard Item dialog box.

16. Click **Close** to close the Edit Switchboard Page dialog box.

17. Click **Close** to close the Switchboard Manager.

18. Double-click the **Switchboard** form to open it.

19. Click the **Reports** button, and the switchboard form changes to show the report items. Note that Access keeps only the most recent switchboard visible.

20. Click the **Plant Report** button to preview the Plants report, as shown in Figure 15.6.

> **tip**
>
> One good way to decide when to split off a second switchboard is to follow the "seven-plus-or-minus-two" rule. People can comfortably keep from five to nine things in mind. When you get up to seven switchboard items, consider splitting off a second switchboard.

FIGURE 15.6

Opening a report from a switchboard.

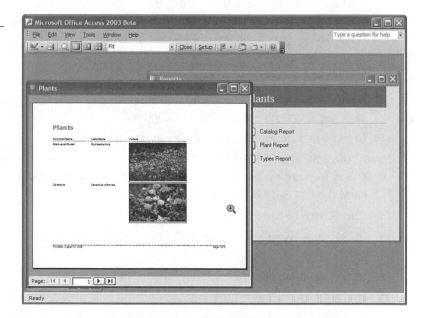

Customizing the Switchboard Form

As you probably already know, the switchboard is a form, just like any other form. In fact, the Switchboard Manager uses programming techniques to display all the switchboards using a single form, no matter how many you define. Because it's a form, this switchboard can be customized just like any other form. Here's an example of how you can personalize the switchboard form a bit:

1. Click the **Forms** shortcut in the Database window.

2. Select the **Switchboard** form. Then, click the **Design** button on the Database window toolbar.

3. Select **View, Properties** to display the Properties window if it's not already showing.

4. Select the **Label** control at the top of the switchboard. Change its Caption property to `My Garden Database`.

5. You may notice a second gray label behind the white label you just changed. Select **Label2** from the combo box at the top of the Properties window to select it. Change the Caption property of this label to `My Garden Database` as well.

6. Click in the empty area to the left of the switchboard buttons. In the Properties window, you'll see that this is an Image control named Picture. Click in the **Picture** property, and then click the builder button to browse for a picture. Select a picture file, such as `coneflower.bmp`, and click **OK**.

7. Select **File, Save** to save your changes.

8. Close the Switchboard form.

9. Double-click the form to open it in regular form view. Figure 15.7 shows the customized form.

FIGURE 15.7
A customized switchboard.

10. Click the **Reports** button. You'll see that your customizations remain visible even though the choices in the switchboard change.

Setting Startup Options

Using the Switchboard Manager, you can build an attractive and easy-to-use interface to your database. But how do you let users know that they should start with this form? Although you could ask them to read a manual or send them email, a better choice is to make Access automatically open the switchboard form when you launch the database. To do this, you can use startup options.

Startup options are a set of options that are applied when your database is opened. You can use these options to customize the user experience of your database. Here's how:

1. Select **Tools, Startup** to open the Startup dialog box, as shown in Figure 15.8.

FIGURE 15.8

Default startup options.

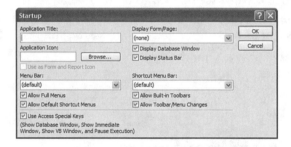

2. Type My Garden Database in the Application Title box.

3. Select the **Switchboard** form in the Display Form/Page combo box.

4. Uncheck the **Display Database Window** check box.

5. Click **OK**.

6. Select **File, Exit** to close Access.

7. Reopen your database. Notice that the title bar shows the database name you chose, the Switchboard form opens automatically, and the Database window is invisible (see Figure 15.9).

FIGURE 15.9

The database after setting startup options.

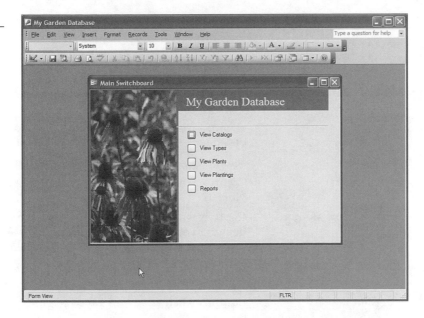

But what if you want to work with the Database window after making these changes? No problem! The following are three ways that you can still display the Database window, even if you turn it off in the startup options:

- Hold down the Shift key when you're opening the database. This prevents the startup options from being applied.

- Press the F11 key.

- Select Window, Unhide. Select the Database window in the Unhide Window dialog box and click OK.

Table 15.2 shows the complete set of startup options you can select for a database.

TABLE 15.2 Startup Options

Option	Meaning
Application Title	Specifies the text to appear in the Access title bar.
Display Form/Page	Specifies a form or data access page to be displayed when you first open the database.
Application Icon	Specifies an icon to use in place of the default Access key. You can choose any .ico or .cur file on your computer to use as an icon.

TABLE 15.2 (continued)

Option	Meaning
Use As Form and Report Icon	Controls whether to use a custom application icon for forms and reports also.
Display Database Window	Controls whether to display the Database window when you open the database.
Display Status Bar	Controls whether to display the status bar at the bottom of the screen.
Menu Bar	Selects the set of menus to use in this database.
Allow Built-In Toolbars	Controls whether the default Access toolbars can be displayed.
Allow Default Shortcut Menus	Controls whether the default Access shortcut menus can be displayed (those are the menus you see when you right-click an object).
Allow Toolbar/Menu Changes	Controls whether the user can customize menus and toolbars.
Use Access Special Keys	Controls whether special keys such as F11 are functional.

Writing Macros

Access actually comes with two built-in programming languages. Normally, professional Access developers work with a language called Visual Basic for Applications (VBA). Teaching you anything about VBA is far beyond the scope of this book. But the second language, called *macros*, is intended for beginning users. If you can select items from a combo box, you can write a macro.

If you've never done any programming, don't worry. Programming with macros is just writing down a list of instructions for the computer to follow. In the next few pages, we'll show you how easily you can write simple macros in Access.

note

One big difference between macros in Access and macros you might be familiar with in Word or Excel is that Access doesn't have a macro recorder.

Building a Macro

Your first macro will do something very simple: cause the computer to emit a beep from its speaker. To build your first macro, follow these steps:

1. Click the **Macros** shortcut in the Database window.

2. Click the **New** button on the Database Window toolbar to open a design grid for the new macro.

3. Click the drop-down list arrow in the first row of the Action column and select Beep from the list.

4. Select **File, Save**.

5. In the Save As dialog box, enter `Beep` as the macro name and click **OK**.

6. Close the macro window.

7. In the Database window, double-click the **Beep** macro. Your computer will beep.

A macro consists of one or more actions. In the case of the Beep macro, it consists of a single beep action, which instructs the computer to beep.

That's pretty simple, isn't it? Now we'll show you a more complex (and possibly more useful) example. This macro opens a form and then moves to a specific record within the form. Follow these steps:

1. Click the **Macros** shortcut in the Database window.

2. Click the **New** button on the Database Window toolbar, which opens a design grid for the new macro.

3. Select the **OpenForm** action in the first row of the Action column. When you do this, the lower pane of the macro designer shows the action arguments for the OpenForm action (see Figure 15.10). This is similar to what the table designer does when you add a new field to a table.

FIGURE 15.10

Setting action arguments for a macro.

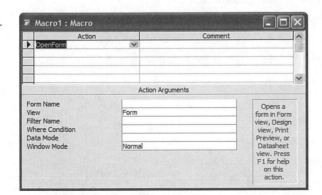

4. Select the **Plants** form in the Form Name action argument.

5. Click in the second row of the Action column (under the OpenForm action you just added), and select the **FindRecord** action.

6. Enter `Chamomile` in the Find What action argument.

7. Select **Any Part of Field** in the Match action argument.

8. Select **File, Save**.

9. In the Save As dialog box, enter `Chamomile` as the macro name and click **OK**.

10. Close the macro.

11. In the Database window, select the **Chamomile** macro. Click the **Run** toolbar button (in the Database window), and the Plants form opens and displays the record for German Chamomile.

When a macro contains more than one action, Access executes the actions in order from top to bottom. In this case, the first action opens a form and the second macro finds a record on the form (just as if you had opened the form yourself and then selected Edit, Find from the Access menu).

The macro programming language in Access consists of dozens of macro actions. Many of these perform advanced Access tasks beyond the scope of this book. Table 15.3 lists some of the macro actions you might want to experiment with.

TABLE 15.3 Some Macro Actions

Action	Meaning
ApplyFilter	Applies a filter to a form to limit the records shown
Beep	Causes the computer to beep
Close	Closes an open object, such as a form or report
FindNext	Repeats the previous Find operation
FindRecord	Finds a particular record on a form
Maximize	Maximizes the current window within Access
Minimize	Minimizes the current window within Access
MsgBox	Displays a message in a separate dialog box
OpenForm	Opens a form
OpenQuery	Opens a query
OpenReport	Opens a report
OpenTable	Opens a table
Quit	Quits Access
SendObject	Sends the current object via email

For a third macro example, you'll use the ApplyFilter action. You learned about filtering in Chapter 8, "Creating and Using Data Entry Forms." In this macro, we'll show you how to apply a filter automatically and combine multiple filters into a single macro. This example is fairly complex, but as you work through it, you'll see that it mainly involves putting together pieces you've already worked with. Here's how to do it:

1. Click the **Macros** shortcut in the Database window.

2. Click the **New** button on the Database Window toolbar. This opens a design grid for the new macro.

3. Select **View, Macro Names** to add another column to the macro design grid. With macro names, you can combine similar activities into a single macro for easier organization.

4. Type **Decorative** as the macro name in the first row of the Macro Name column.

5. Select the **ApplyFilter** action in the first row of the Action column.

6. Enter **[TypeID]=1** in the Where Condition action argument for this row. This tells Access that this particular filter will select only records in which the TypeID is equal to 1.

7. Type **Edible** as the macro name in the second row of the Macro Name column.

8. Select the **ApplyFilter** action in the second row of the Action column.

9. Enter **[TypeID]=2** in the Where Condition action argument for this row.

10. Type **Medicinal** as the macro name in the third row of the Macro Name column.

11. Select the **ApplyFilter** action in the third row of the Action column.

12. Enter **[TypeID]=3** in the Where Condition action argument for this row. Figure 15.11 shows the macro with all three rows entered.

13. Select **File**, **Save**.

14. In the Save As dialog box, enter **PlantFilters** as the macro name and click **OK**.

tip

If you don't want to use the mouse to click the properties fields in the different sections of the macro window, press F6 to toggle back and forth between the grid and the Action Arguments panel below the grid.

FIGURE 15.11

Creating a
macro to per-
form multiple
distinct activi-
ties.

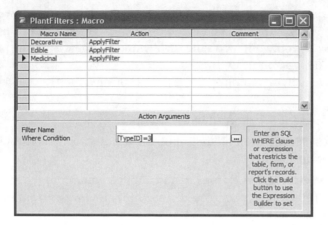

15. Close the macro.

16. In the Database window, click the **Forms** shortcut.

17. Select the **Plants** form and click the **Design** toolbar button.

18. Select **View, Toolbox** to show the Toolbox, if it is not already visible.

19. Select the **Command Button** tool in the Toolbox, and then click the form in an empty area to create a new button.

20. In the Command Button Wizard, select the **Miscellaneous** category. Then select the **Run Macro** action and click **Next**.

21. Select **PlantFilters.Decorative** as the macro to run. Click **Next**.

22. Select the **Text** choice and set the text of the button to Decorative. Click **Finish**.

23. Select the **Command Button** tool in the Toolbox; then click the form in an empty area to create a second new button.

24. In the Command Button Wizard, select the **Miscellaneous** category. Then select the **Run Macro** action and click **Next**.

25. Select **PlantFilters.Edible** as the macro to run; then click **Next**.

26. Select the **Text** choice and set the text of the button to Edible. Click **Finish**.

27. Select the **Command Button** tool in the Toolbox. Click the form in an empty area to create a third new button.

28. In the Command Button Wizard, select the **Miscellaneous** category. Then select the **Run Macro** action and click **Next**.

29. Select **PlantFilters.Medicinal** as the macro to run and click **Next**.

30. Select the **Text** choice and set the text of the button to Medicinal. Click **Finish**.

31. Select **File, Save**.

32. Select **View, Form View**.

33. Click the new buttons one at a time. You'll see that the form changes to display only the selected records. For example, Figure 15.12 shows the form with the Medicinal filter applied; you can see from the navigation bar that only three medicinal plants are visible.

FIGURE 15.12

The form filtered by applying a macro.

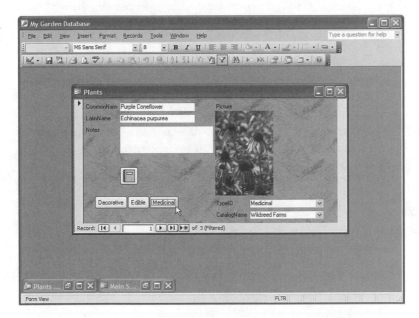

34. To view all the records in the table, click the **Remove Filter** button on the toolbar.

Whew! By now, you should have some hint of the automation that a few well-chosen macros can bring to your application. Next, we'll look at some ways to make working with macros easier.

Building Macros with Drag and Drop

Access includes shortcuts for some macro actions. For example, you can create a macro to open a form or a report without selecting any actions or action arguments. Here's how:

1. Click the **Macros** shortcut in the Database window.

2. Click the **New** button on the Database window toolbar to open a design grid for the new macro.

3. Arrange the windows in Access so that you can see both the macro window and the Database window at the same time.

4. Click the **Reports** shortcut in the Database window.

5. Drag the **CatalogsBySpecialty** report from the Database window and drop it on the first row of the macro. This creates an OpenReport action referring to the CatalogsBySpecialty report.

6. Change the View action argument to **Print Preview**.

7. Select **File, Save**.

8. In the Save As dialog box, enter `CatalogsReport` as the macro name and click **OK**.

9. Close the macro.

10. Click the **Macros** shortcut in the Database window.

11. In the Database window, double-click the **CatalogsReport** macro. The CatalogsBySpecialty report opens in print preview mode.

You can drag any object from the Database window—a table, query, form, report, or page—to a macro to create a macro that opens that object.

Creating Buttons from Macros

By creating buttons that run the macros, you can also use macros to make your forms more convenient. In fact, you can do this without writing any more code! Here's how to add the CatalogsReport macro to a form:

1. Click the **Forms** shortcut in the Database window.

2. Select the **Catalogs** form.

3. Click the **Design** toolbar button to open the form in design view.

4. Click the **Macros** shortcut in the Database window.

5. Drag the **CatalogsReport** macro from the Database window and drop it on the footer section of the form. This creates a new command button on the form.

6. Press **F4** to open the Properties window.

7. Change the Caption property of the command button by typing `Preview Report`.

8. Select **File, Save**.

9. Close the Properties window.

10. Select **View, Form View**; the form displays with the new Preview Report button in the footer.

11. Click the **Preview Report** button to open the CatalogsBySpecialty report in print preview mode, as shown in Figure 15.13.

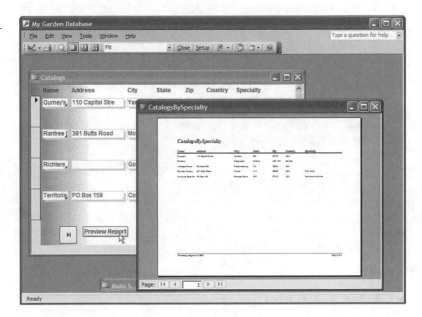

Any time you drag a macro to a form that's open in design view, Access creates a command button that runs that macro. This provides you with a powerful alternative to the Button Wizard for creating custom command buttons.

Pause for a moment and think about how all the pieces fit together in this example:

- The data is stored in the Catalogs table.
- The form is based on the Catalogs table.
- The CatalogsBySpecialty query is based on the Catalogs table as well.
- The CatalogsBySpecialty report is based on the CatalogsBySpecialty query.
- The macro was created by dragging the report to the macro designer.
- The button was created by dragging the macro to the form designer.

You've learned quite a bit about how all the pieces of Access fit together by now!

The Absolute Minimum

As you work with a database, you'll usually find that more and more objects accumulate in it and that you perform more and more repetitive tasks. That's when you should start thinking about automating the work. Access offers a number of ways to make things easier in a database:

- The Switchboard Manager lets you build and maintain switchboard forms to organize your objects into sensible groups.

- Startup options let you control some of the look and feel of your database, and they provide an easy starting point for yourself or other users.

- Macros can automate most common Access tasks, from opening forms to searching for records.

- You can turn macros into buttons by dragging them from the Database window and dropping them on forms.

IN THIS CHAPTER

- Export data to Excel and import Excel data into Access

- Export and import to text files

- Publish Access reports to Word

- Use Word's mail-merge with your Access names and addresses to create several letters at once

- Send Access data via email

16

SHARING DATA

Access is much more than just a database. It's part of the best suite of computer software on the market. Access, Word, and Excel all work well together, which means data that's entered in one application can be used in another.

Most of the time, you'll find Excel or Word just a button click away. The OfficeLinks button on the Database toolbar offers three options:

- Merge It with MS Word
- Publish It with MS Word
- Analyze It with MS Excel

But there's more. You can import data into Access, export data out of Access, or even link to data in other applications. In this chapter, we'll review the previously mentioned shortcuts and a few wizards that make sharing your Access data easy.

Exporting Data to Excel

Don't try to imitate Excel's powerful analysis functions in Access. Instead, export your data into Excel and run your analysis there. In short, don't ever work harder than you need to—let Office do its job!

note

You can download the Chapter 16.mdb sample file, which is inclusive of all the examples in this chapter, from http://www.quepublishing.com/. If you want to follow along with our examples, download Chapter 15.mdb.

Sending data to Excel is one of the easiest Office collaborations. You just select a table or query, select Analyze It with MS Excel from the OfficeLinks button, and you're done. After your data is in Excel, you can use any Excel feature—Excel doesn't care where the data came from.

Let's export the Plantings table from your gardening database to Excel. To do so, follow these steps:

1. Open the gardening database and display the Database window by pressing **F11**. (Just ignore the switchboard form for now.)

2. Click the **Tables** shortcut in the Database window and select the **Plantings** table.

3. Select **Export** from the File menu.

4. In the Export Table 'Plantings' To dialog box, select **Microsoft Excel 97-2002** from the Save As Type control. Access uses the table's name to also name the new spreadsheet, but you can enter another name if you want. You

can also specify a folder other than the default folder in which to store the new file. Don't change either of these default settings for this example. However, do check the **Save Formatted** option to the left of the Export button. Then, click **Export** to finish the job.

Figure 16.1 shows the new spreadsheet in Excel. As you can see, all your data retains its original formatting as a result of selecting the Save Formatted option. Notice also that Excel uses the field names as column headings.

FIGURE 16.1

Access easily exports data to Excel.

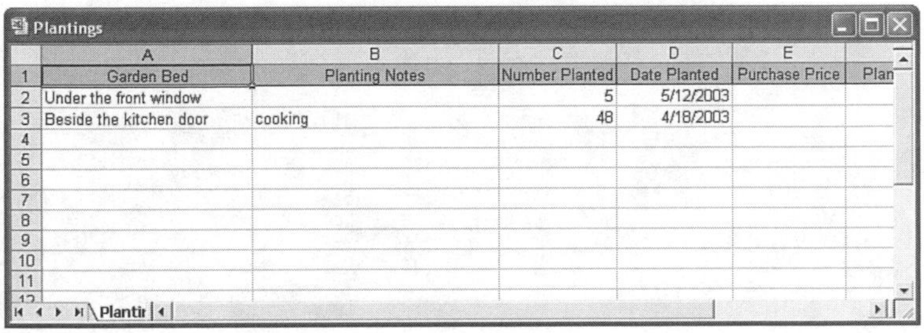

You can't see all the data onscreen, so just scroll to the right and you'll see that Excel even respects the hyperlink data in the More Info field. Only your pictures didn't make the trip. You're ready to start analyzing!

Now, let's export the Catalogs table and see how Excel handles it. Repeat steps 1—4 from the previous procedure. But this time, specify the Catalogs table and don't select the Save Formatted option. Open the new Excel spreadsheet based on the Catalogs table. This time, there's no formatting and Excel doesn't know how to interpret all the data. Can you see the small triangles in the upper-left corner of several of the ZIP entries?

Select one of those fields, and Excel displays an error icon. Click the drop-down arrow to see the possible types of errors shown in Figure 16.2. In this case, there really isn't a problem because ZIP codes don't need to be stored as numbers. If you want, you can select the fields and select Ignore Error, or you can do nothing. Save this file in Excel using the name `CatalogsInExcel.xls`; you'll use it in the next section.

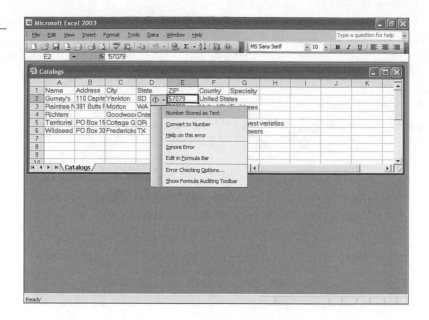

Using Excel Data in Access

Importing Excel data into Access can seem more complicated, but it really isn't. You just have more options. You can import data directly into an Access table, or you can link to an Excel spreadsheet. What's the difference? Imported data ends up in Access, whereas linked data stays in Excel—but you can still use it in Access. You'll see how this works in the next two sections.

Importing Excel Data into an Access Table

Importing is usually a simple process of transferring (copying) data from one file to another. Access doesn't change the data in any way. In this section, you'll see how easily you can copy Excel data into an Access table. After the data is in an Access table, changes made to the original data in Excel don't change the imported data in Access. Let's import CatalogsInExcel.xls by doing the following:

1. In Access, select **Get External Data** from the File menu, and then select **Import** from the resulting submenu.

2. In the Files of Type control, select **Microsoft Excel** Select **CatalogsInExcel.xls** from the list of files, and then click **Import**. Or, you could just double-click **CatalogsInExcel.xls**. You just launched the Import Spreadsheet Wizard.

3. The first thing the wizard wants to know is whether you're importing the entire spreadsheet or a named range. In Excel, a *named range* is a specific set of cells that you can refer to using a name you supply. This spreadsheet doesn't have any named ranges, so keep the Show Worksheets option. If you're curious, check the **Show Named Ranges** option, but you'll see that the list to the right doesn't change (because no named ranges exist). The bottom panel shows the data. Click **Next** to continue.

4. The next pane lets you determine whether to identify the Excel column headings as field names. We recommend that you check the **First Row Contains Column Headings** unless you have a specific reason not to. If you don't, Excel will assume the field names are normal entries. After selecting this option, click **Next**.

5. The wizard is flexible and lets you either append the incoming data into an existing table or create a new table. The default is the In a New Table option. Without making any changes in this pane, click **Next**.

6. This next pane lets you do a lot. First, you can rename any field by selecting the field in the bottom display and then entering a new name in the Field Name control. In addition, you can apply an index (you learned about indexes in Chapter 11, "Customizing Your Tables"). If Access isn't sure how to interpret the data, the wizard enables the Data Type control so you can specify the data type for the field. Checking the Do Not Import Field (Skip) option deletes the selected field from the import process. Don't make any changes to the wizard's choices—just click **Next**.

7. At this point, the wizard wants to help you define a primary key. By default, the wizard suggests that you add an AutoNumber data type field. Instead, select the **Choose My Own Primary Key** option, and select **Name** from the drop-down control to the right (it should be selected by default). Then, click **Next**. (Refer to Chapter 4, "Planning a Database" for information on primary keys.)

8. In the final pane, give the new table a name. You already have a table named Catalogs, so change the wizard's default name to `CatalogsFromExcel`; then click **Finish**. The wizard displays a message when the wizard has completed the import task. Click **OK** to clear that message.

9. Find the new table in the Database window and open it. Figure 16.3 shows the newly imported data. For the most part, this table is identical to the original Catalogs table—right down to the primary key field. All that traveling really hasn't changed anything.

FIGURE 16.3

The wizard has created a new table and copied the Excel data into it.

Linking to Excel Data

You don't have to import Excel data to use it in Access. Depending on your needs, you might choose to link to the spreadsheet. Linked data is *dynamic*, which means it reflects changes. If you change the data in Excel, the linked data reflects that change in Access, and vice versa. To illustrate this flexible and powerful feature, link to CatalogsInExcel.xls by performing the following steps:

1. In Access, select **Get External Data** from the File menu, and then select **Link Tables** from the resulting submenu.

2. In the Files of Type control, select **Microsoft Excel**, select **CatalogsInExcel.xls** in the list of files, and then click **Link**. Or, you can just double-click **CatalogsInExcel.xls**. (You can also use the Look In control to locate files in another folder, but we don't need to do this for our current example.) You just launched the Link Spreadsheet Wizard.

3. The first thing the wizard wants to know is whether you're linking to the entire spreadsheet or a named range. Keep the Show Worksheets option, and click **Next** to continue.

4. The next pane lets you determine whether to identify the Excel column headings as field names. We recommend that you check the **First Row Contains Column Headings** unless you have a specific reason not to. If you don't, Excel assumes the field names are normal entries. After selecting this option, click **Next**.

5. In the final pane, name the new linked table CatalogsFromExcelLinked, click **Finish**, and then click **OK** to clear the resulting confirmation message. The Database window displays the link along with the tables, as shown in Figure 16.4, but the icon to the left of the linked data clearly identifies it as a linked Excel table.

FIGURE 16.4
The Database window identifies the linked data source as an Excel file.

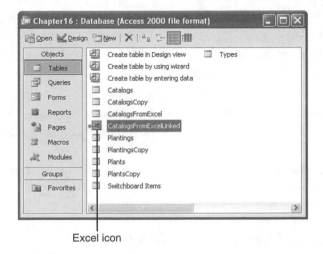

Excel icon

Feel free to open the linked spreadsheet in Access and change data. Then, open the spreadsheet in Excel and you'll see that the spreadsheet reflects the changes you made. Make a change in the spreadsheet, save it, and then close it. Open the linked spreadsheet in Access to view changes you made to the spreadsheet in Excel.

Copying Linked Data

At some point, you might decide that you want to have the data from a linked table stored directly in Access, instead of in its original application. No problem! Access 2003 lets you quickly copy a linked table to the local database. Follow these steps to see how this works:

1. Select the Tables shortcut in the database window.
2. Right-click the `CatalogsFromExcelLinked` linked table and select **Copy**.
3. Right-click in a blank area of the database window and select **Paste**.
4. In the Paste Table As dialog box, name the new table `CatalogsFromExcelPasted`. Select **Structure and Data (Local Table)** in the Paste Options section. Click **OK** to create the new table in Access.
5. Open the `CatalogsFromExcelPasted` table and you'll see that it contains all of the original data. You can verify from the table's icon in the database window that it's now a local table.

When you paste a linked table, the Paste Table As dialog box gives you four choices:

- **Linked Table**—Creates a new link to the original data, and shows the link in the database window.

- **Structure Only (Local Table)**—Creates a new empty table in Access, with the same fields as the linked table.

- **Structure and Data (Local Table)**—Creates a new table in Access with the same fields as the linked table, and imports the linked data to the new table.

- **Append Data to Existing Table**—Lets you add the data from the linked table to a table that already exists in your Access database.

Exporting Access Data to a Text File

Earlier in this chapter, you exported Access data to a specific type of file—an Excel spreadsheet. Access can export data directly to several software applications (see the "More Compatible Formats" section at the end of this chapter for a complete list).

Now, let's suppose you agree to share your list of catalogs with a gardening friend, but she has just bought her first computer and isn't familiar with the software she'll be using. You can't export the data to an Excel spreadsheet file if she's going to be using Word because these two software applications have incompatible formats. This means that you can't open an Excel (.xls) file in Word or open a Word document (.doc) in Excel. (We're just using Excel and Word as examples; this is true with almost all software applications.) In a situation such as this, you could export the catalog records to a text file because it's the most compatible format of all—most software can import a text file.

Exporting to a text file isn't quite as simple as the earlier export to Excel was because there are two types of text files: delimited and fixed-width. A *delimited* text file uses a character, such as a tab, space, or comma, to separate the fields of data. A record in a delimited text file might resemble the following: "red", "white", "blue".

A *fixed-width* text file assigns a specific number of characters to each field. That way, the fields of data line up in columns. Not every column in the file has to be the same width, but every entry in the same column must contain the same number of characters, even if some of those characters are spaces to fill in around the actual data. For instance, if the column width is eight characters and the entry is wagon, you must add three space characters (___wagon) so the entry equals eight characters. (The underscores just help you visualize the entire field, they're not really part of the data.)

Fortunately, Access has a wizard that can handle all the details. The following example demonstrates how to export Access data to a text file by exporting the catalog records to both a delimited and a fixed-width file. Begin with the delimited file by following these steps:

1. Click the **Tables** shortcut in the Database window and select **Catalogs**. (Don't try to export a form or report. You can export both, but we won't attempt to in this book.)

2. Right-click the table and select **Export**.

3. In the Save As Type control, select **Text Files**. You could rename the file at this point, but Access uses the table's name by default, so stick with that.

4. Click **Export** to launch the Export Text Wizard.

5. The first question the wizard asks is whether you're creating a delimited or fixed-width file. Access uses the comma character (,) as the default delimiter. You can click the Advanced button to change the default delimiter, the default language, or any number of settings. However, all are beyond the scope of this example, so don't worry about the advanced options. Just select the **Delimited** option, and click **Next** to continue.

6. The next pane lets you choose a delimiter other than the comma character, but just use the comma for this example. If you check the Include Field Names on First Row option, Access exports the field names along with the text. Whether you need the field names will really depend on how you're going to use the text file. Check it so you can see how the wizard responds in the display at the bottom of the dialog box. Click **Next**.

7. The last pane displays the full pathname for the new text file, which should include the default folder. Also notice that the filename itself contains the .txt extension because you're creating a text file. Click **Finish** to create the text file, and then click OK to clear the confirmation message.

8. Figure 16.5 shows Catalogs.txt in Word. The first line contains the Catalogs table field names, and each of the remaining lines represents a record for one catalog. You can see that sometimes a record wraps to the next line. That isn't a problem. Close Catalogs.txt and return to Access.

FIGURE 16.5

Open the text file in a Word processor.

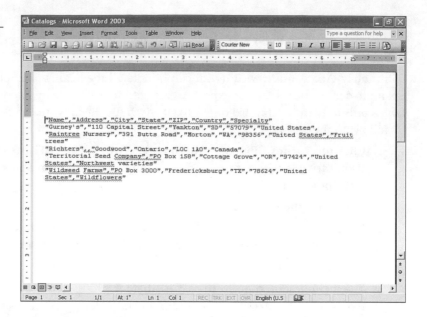

Don't worry if this file's format doesn't seem to make much sense to you right now. The truth is, you probably wouldn't use this file as is in Word. We're just using Word to show you the file's structure. If you really wanted to work with the catalog records in Word, you'd probably use the OfficeLinks button to publish the data to Word (you'll learn how to do that in the "Publishing to Word" section later in this chapter). Let's export the same Catalogs table as a fixed-width file. Here's how to do so:

1. Repeat steps 1–4 from the previous example. This time, however, name the file `CatalogsFixedWidth`. If you don't change the name, the wizard will write over the `Catalogs.txt` file you created in the previous exercise.

2. In the wizard's first pane, click the **Fixed Width** option, and click Next.

3. Things can get a bit complicated with a fixed-width file because the wizard uses a field's Field Size property as the width for each column. (You learned about field properties in Chapter 11.) In a table it doesn't matter if a field allows 225 spaces even though the field's largest entry contains only 15 characters. But those unnecessarily wide columns can be awkward to work with in a text file. So, click the **Advanced** button and you'll see a list of all the fields and their sizes. Some of them are way too large, and you should adjust these before you go any further. To do so, simply change the Start and Width values. Figure 16.6 shows our new values—take a minute to change yours. (The Start value equals the Start and Width value of the previous field.) When

you're done, click **OK** to return to the wizard's first pane. Then, click **Next** to continue.

FIGURE 16.6

Reduce the field widths.

4. The next pane lets you adjust the widths one more time. Look closely at the first column (the catalog name column), and you'll see that the column isn't wide enough to fully display Territorial Seed Company. Click the line that separates the name and address fields and drag it to the right a few spaces—to about 26 (there's a ruler just above the field display), as shown in Figure 16.7. Check each field the same way and adjust the width if necessary. We also stretched the State field to 84. When you're satisfied with the size of each field, click **Next**.

FIGURE 16.7

We made the name field wider.

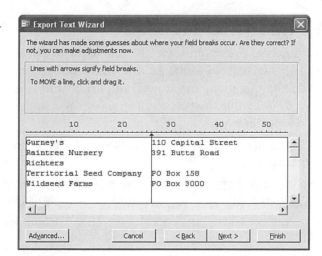

5. Click **Finish** in the final pane and then clear the confirmation message. Figure 16.8 shows `CatalogsFixedWidth.txt` in Word. Close `CatalogsFixedWidth.txt` and return to Access.

FIGURE 16.8

Open the text file in Word.

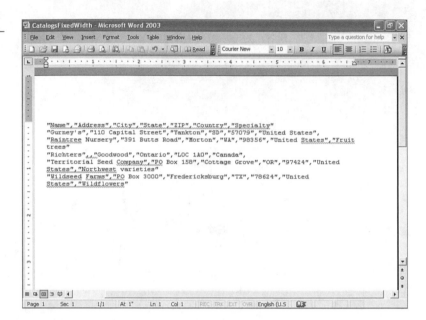

You probably won't actually work with a fixed-width text file in Word. As before, we're just using Word so you can see the file's structure. As you can see, each column comprises one of the original table's fields. It's okay if a record wraps to another line. Close both text files.

Importing Text Files into Access

To import text into Access, you might work with one of the two previously mentioned text files: delimited or fixed-width. As you learn more about other software applications, you'll find that many can export data to a text file. Let's demonstrate the import process by importing the two text files you created in the last section back into Access. Follow these steps:

1. In Access, right-click in the Database window, and then select **Import** from the shortcut menu.

2. In the Import dialog box, select **Text Files** from the Files of Type control.

3. Select **Catalogs.txt** and click **Import**. You could use the Look In control to find files in another folder, but `Catalogs.txt` is in the default folder.

4. The wizard tries to interpret the incoming data and select the appropriate file type: delimited or fixed-width. It won't always make the right choice, but this time, it does. The file is a delimited text file, so click **Next**.

5. In the next pane, check the **First Row Contains Field Names** option so the wizard will know what to do with the field names in the first row. (You might remember that you included the field names when you exported the data earlier.) When you do, the wizard removes the field names from the record display. The wizard also correctly identifies the delimiter, which in this case is a comma. Click **Next**.

6. You can import the data into an existing table or a new table. The default is to create a new table, and that's what you want to do, so click **Next**.

7. You can rename the fields, apply an index, or specify a data type in the next pane. Don't make any changes; just click **Next**.

8. Select the **Choose My Own Primary Key** option in the next window. The wizard defaults to the Name field, which is what you want, so after selecting the primary key option, click **Next**.

9. In the final pane, change the default name to `CatalogsDelimited`, click **Finish**, and then click **OK** to clear the confirmation message. You already have a table named Catalogs, which is why you need to change the name.

10. In the Database window, click the **Tables** shortcut and open **CatalogsDelimited**.

The new table looks just like the original, doesn't it (refer to Figure 16.3)? Exporting the data to a text file and then importing it back into Access hasn't changed any-thing—the data is no worse for the wear. Notice that Access used the names in that first row as field names for the new table.

To import the fixed-width text file, follow these steps:

1. Repeats steps 1 and 2 from the previous exercise.

2. In the Import dialog box, select **CatalogsFixedWidth.txt** and click **Import**.

3. The wizard correctly identifies the text file as a fixed-width file, so click **Next**.

4. There's an incorrect break in the first field, so double-click that first break line to delete it. Delete any other incorrect breaks you find. Then click **Next**.

5. You're importing the data into a new table, so retain the default option of **In a New Table**; then click **Next**.

6. Take a minute to review the wizard's choices in the next pane. You can change a field's name, change its data type, or apply an index. You don't need to modify anything at this point, though, so click **Next** when you're ready to continue.

7. In the next pane, select the **Choose My Own Primary Key** option, select the Name field (if the wizard doesn't), and then click **Next**.

8. In the last pane, click **Finish** and then click **OK** to clear the confirmation message.

9. Click the **Tables** shortcut in the Database window; then open the **CatalogsFixedWidth** table. It looks just like the original table (refer to Figure 16.3).

Importing a text file can require several settings, but the actual process is simple and the wizard usually does a good job of handling the data.

Publishing to Word

Despite Access's powerful reporting capabilities, you won't want to use it like a word processor. You might find that you occasionally need more formatting options than Access offers. When this happens, consider publishing your Access report (or data) to Word. By *publishing*, we simply mean copying the data and the existing format to a Word document.

During the publishing process, you'll probably lose some of the Access formats, but you'll likely be reformatting the data anyway. Now, let's publish the CatalogsAndPlants report to Word by doing the following:

1. In Access, click the **Reports** shortcut in the Database window and select **CatalogsAndPlants**.

2. Select **Publish It with Microsoft Office Word** from the OfficeLinks button on the Database toolbar. Figure 16.9 shows the report in Word.

After you have the data in Word, you can use all of Word's formatting capabilities. However, the published document doesn't start out as a Word file. Access publishes the data to a rich text file document. When you save the file, change the Save As Type setting to Word Document (*.doc). Otherwise, Word will save the file as an .rtf document.

FIGURE 16.9

Access copies
the selected
Access report to
a Word docu-
ment.

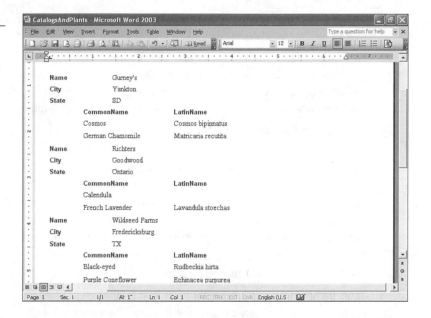

Merging Access Data with Word Documents

If all your names and addresses are stored in an Access database and you want to send the same letter to each person, you could compose the letter as an Access report. But it's often easier to merge the names and addresses with a Word document that contains the body of the letter instead. That way, you can use all of Word's advanced text-formatting features when you're writing your letter.

Assuming your names and addresses are already stored in an Access database, you'll also need a letter, which you create in Word as a special type of document—a mail-merge document. Within the body of the letter, you include special *field codes* that match the name and address field names in your Access database. Then, you merge your Access data with the mail-merge document, and Word inserts the Access data using the field codes as a guide.

Let's create a simple letter to send to all the catalog contacts in your gardening database asking for the most recent catalog. To do so, follow these steps:

1. In Access, click the **Tables** shortcut and then select the **Catalogs** table.

2. Select **Merge It with Microsoft Office Word** from the OfficeLinks button on the Database toolbar to launch the Mail Merge Wizard.

3. In the wizard's first pane, select the **Create a New Document and Then Link the Data to It** option because you need to create the letter. Click **OK** to continue.

4. The wizard launches Word and opens a new, blank document. The Mail Merge toolbar is also visible.

5. Enter the current date by selecting **Date and Time** from the Insert menu. In the Date and Time dialog box, select the third available format option. If you click the Update Automatically option, Word uses the current date the next time you use the document (if you decide to save it and reuse it). Click **OK**.

6. Press **Enter** four times to add four blank lines.

7. Now you need to enter your first field code, which is the catalog's name. To do so, click the **Insert Merge Field** button. In the Insert Merge Field dialog box, select **Name** and click **Insert**, and then click **Close**. Repeat this process until you've inserted all the address field codes (Address, City, State, ZIP, and Country). Be sure to include a comma and space between the City and State fields and a space between the State and ZIP fields. You can select all the fields at once and move them around later, instead of opening and closing the Insert Merge Field dialog box several times.

8. Press **Enter** twice and enter `To Whom It May Concern:`. Then press **Enter** twice more, and enter the body of the letter and the closing, as shown in Figure 16.10. (Feel free to close Word's task pane).

FIGURE 16.10

The mail-merge document contains both the letter and field codes for the merge.

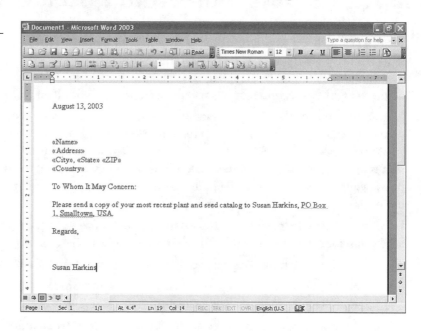

9. Format the letter, if you want.

10. When your letter is just the way you want it, you can either create a new document that contains all the letters or send the letters directly to your printer. In this example, you'll create a document to avoid the nuisance of actually printing these sample letters. To do so, click the **Merge to New Document** button on the Mail Merge toolbar.

11. In the Merge to New Document dialog box, you can limit the number of letters you print by specifying which Access records actually get merged. You want to send a letter to all your catalogs, so just retain the default option of **All**, and click **OK**.

12. Figure 16.11 shows the first page of your new document—it's a letter to Gurney's (including the correct address). Page through the new document, and you'll find that each page is actually a letter to a catalog. You can save the document and print your letters later, or you can print them now.

note

You created your mail-merge letter as part of the merge process. You can work with an existing document just as easily. In step 2, you would select the Link Your Data to an Existing Microsoft Word Document option. Most likely, the document already contains the necessary field codes, but the wizard enables you to change those settings before actually merging anything.

FIGURE 16.11

The new document contains all your letters.

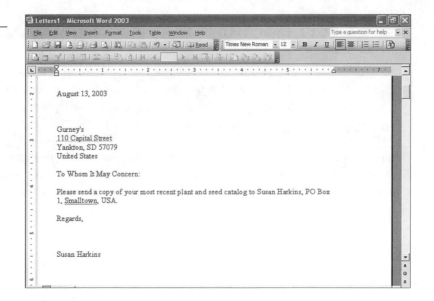

Although the merge process can take a while to set up, the process is simple and the wizard walks you through it.

Sending Access Objects in Email

Remember earlier when you wanted to share your catalogs with your gardening friend? Well, you could export that data to a disc or simply send the data to her via email. Certainly, if you both have email, that would be the easiest choice. Fortunately, Access 2003 makes sharing data via email extremely easy. In this next exercise, you send the catalog data to yourself using email. Follow these steps:

1. In the Database window, click the **Tables** shortcut and select **Catalogs**.

2. Select **Send To** from the File menu.

3. The resulting submenu offers two options, but only the **Mail Recipient (As Attachment)** is enabled, so select it.

4. In the Send dialog box, choose a format for the data you're sending. Table 16.1 explains the various options. For this example, select **Rich Text Format (*.rtf)**, and then click **OK**.

5. Access uses your default email software to display a new message that contains the Catalogs table as a text attachment (remember, you selected Text File in the previous step). Address the email to yourself.

6. Click **Send**.

> **note**
>
> In this section, you'll send email to yourself. That means you must have an Internet connection and an email account with a server (probably an Internet service provider or a service such as AOL). Without an email account, you can still go through the steps, but you can't actually send and then receive the email.

Download and open the email to view the attachment, shown in Figure 16.12. The .rtf file keeps most of the table's formatting, which makes the data easy to view. The text file isn't the greatest because it tries to maintain some of the table's properties.

FIGURE 16.12

Access was able to send the catalog data via your email account.

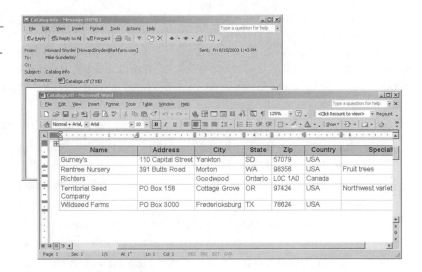

TABLE 16.1   Email Format Options

Send Option	Explanation
Rich Text Format	Sends the data as an .rtf file (a type of text file that retains some formatting).
Text	Sends the data as a text file (tabular).
Excel	Sends the data in Excel format (be sure to select the appropriate version).
HTML	Sends the data in a Web-ready file.
Snapshot	Sends the data as a Snapshot document.

Sharing Reports

Access reports contain a lot of formatting that can be lost when you share them outside your database. If you send a report via email as an .rtf file, it will retain some of its formatting. (The .rtf is the same format you used to send the Catalogs table in the previous section.)

A better choice is to use a special format known as a *snapshot* (*.snp*). This format produces a high-quality copy of each page in your Access report. Using this format, you can send a report and the receiver will have an exact copy of your Access report—both the data and the formatting, including graphics. Best of all, the recipient doesn't need Access to view the report as if it were in Access! The magic that makes this possible is a small program known as Snapshot Viewer that you install when you install Access. Users without Access can download the Snapshot Viewer separately from Microsoft's Web site.

Let's create a snapshot file of the Catalogs report by doing the following:

1. Click the **Reports** shortcut in the Database window and select **CatalogsAuto**.

2. Select **Send To** from the File menu, and then select **Mail Recipient (As Attachment)** from the submenu.

3. In the Send dialog box, select **Snapshot Format** and click **OK**. (The other options are basically the same as described earlier in Table 16.1.)

4. Enter your email address (so you can mail the report to yourself), and click **Send**.

5. After sending and retrieving the email, open the report attachment. Figure 16.13 shows the Catalogs report in the Snapshot Viewer window.

FIGURE 16.13

The report automatically opens in Snapshot Viewer.

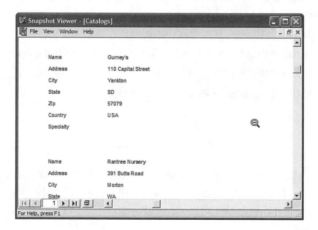

The report looks exactly like the Catalogs report in Access. Notice that the Snapshot Viewer window even has a menu of options so you can print or email the report to someone else.

More Compatible Formats

This chapter focuses on working with Office, but Access can also talk to non-Office applications. Access can import or link to all of the following formats:

- Any Access database files (.mdb, .adp, .mdw, .mda, .mde)
- Excel spreadsheet files (.xls)
- dBASE III, dBASE IV, and dBASE 5 database files (.dbf)
- Paradox 3.x, 4.x, 5.x, 7.x, and 8.x database files (.db)
- Lotus 1-2-3 spreadsheet files (.wk*, .wj*)
- Delimited text files
- Fixed-width text files
- Exchange and Outlook files
- HTML files (.html, .htm)
- ODBC database files
- XML documents (*.xml, *.xsd)
- Windows SharePoint Services
- Microsoft Active Server Pages (.asp)

THE ABSOLUTE MINIMUM

In this chapter, you learned about some of the ways to use your Access data in conjunction with other applications:

- Access can quickly and easily share data with Excel and Word.
- Access can import Excel data into an Access table.
- Access can link to an Excel spreadsheet and interact with its data from inside Access.
- How to export Access data to text and how to import text data into Access.
- How to take advantage of Word's impressive formatting capabilities to format your Access data.
- That it's sometimes easier to merge Access data with a Word document than it is to format an Access report just the way you want it.

IN THIS CHAPTER

- Begin Visual Basic from within Windows.

- Learn how to hire and fire the Office Assistant

- Use SpellCheck and AutoCorrect to prevent typos

- Use Help to find the answers to your questions

- Customize toolbars to suit your needs

17

USING COMMON OFFICE FEATURES

There are a number of features that the Office suite applications share. If you currently use Word, Excel, or even PowerPoint, you're probably familiar with a few of these features:

- SpellCheck

- AutoCorrect

- Help

In this chapter, we'll review these Office features, as they're used by Access.

The Helpful Assistant—Not!

Annoying co-workers are everywhere, and Access is no exception—we're referring to one of the more obnoxious Office features, the Office Assistant. Of course, you might end up liking the little guy, so give him a chance.

The Office Assistant is an interface that helps answer questions that crop up while you're using Access. The assistant's goal is to help you find the information you need so you can get your work done.

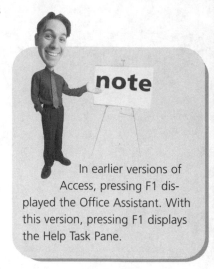

By default, the assistant is already hired and ready to go. If the assistant isn't available, choose **Show the Office Assistant** from the Help menu to display Clippit, the default Office Assistant. (Alternatively, you can choose **Hide the Office Assistant** to put Clippit temporarily out of work.) Double-click Clippit to display an area, called the balloon, where you can enter questions, as shown in Figure 17.1. After entering the question, click **Search**—that's all there is to it. Clippit displays a variety of possible Help items. Click one and Access deploys the appropriate Help text.

note

In earlier versions of Access, pressing F1 displayed the Office Assistant. With this version, pressing F1 displays the Help Task Pane.

Occasionally, Clippit won't find just the right answer. When that happens, check the Can't find it section at the bottom of the list of topics for more ideas.

Controlling Clippit

In Figure 17.1, Clippit displays both a Search and an Options choice. Clicking Search displays possible Help topics, as you've just learned. Clicking Options displays the Office Assistant dialog box shown in Figure 17.2.

You can select and deselect these options to suit your own tastes. For instance, you may not want to see alerts, but you may want help with wizards. In that case, you'd select the Help with wizards option and deselect the Display alerts option. It's really up to you.

You might be wondering about a few of these options. They're not all self-explanatory, so a quick explanation for each Office Assistant option follows:

- **Help with wizards:** When selected, the Office Assistant offers additional information when you run a wizard.
- **Display alerts:** When selected, the Office Assistant will display program or system messages as you work, even if you turn off the Office Assistant.

- **Search for both product and programming help when programming:** When working in the Visual Basic Editor (which we don't cover in this book), Help displays information on Visual Basic for Applications only, unless you select this item.

- **Move when in the way:** If selected, the Office Assistant will move if it blocks elements you're trying to work with or in, such as dialog boxes.

- **Make sounds:** When selected, this option allows your Office Assistant to make noises to get your attention.

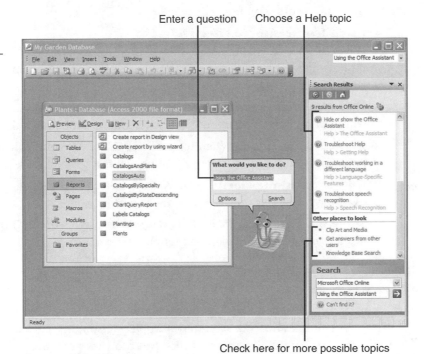

Enter a question   Choose a Help topic

FIGURE 17.1
Clippit is ready to go to work when you are.

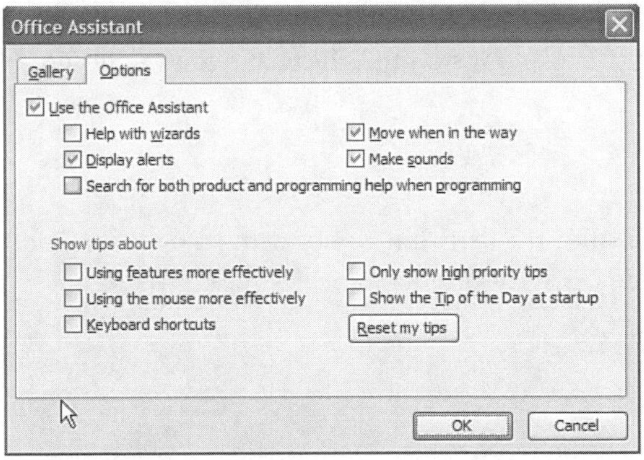

Check here for more possible topics

FIGURE 17.2
Change Clippit's default behavior to better match yours.

The assistant pays attention to what you're doing and has lots of helpful hints. When you see the light bulb appear next to the assistant, click it to read what might be a very helpful hint for your current task.

The bottom section allows you to determine whether or not the assistant displays helpful tips while you work. By default, the assistant displays only the Tip of the Day when you first launch Access. The other options are as follows:

- **Using features more effectively:** When selected, the Office Assistant will make suggestions about the tasks you're involved in, based on your keystrokes.

- **Using the mouse more effectively:** When selected, the Office Assistant will let you know about mouse shortcuts that might be helpful.

- **Keyboard shortcuts:** When selected, the Office Assistant will let you know about keyboard shortcuts that might be helpful.

- **Only show high priority tips:** When selected, the Office Assistant will display only those tips that it thinks are important.

- **Show the Tip of the Day at startup:** When selected, the Office Assistant displays a random tip when you launch Access.

Changing Assistants

If Clippit and you just don't click, you don't have to turn it off. Try one of the other assistant personalities instead. To change Clippit's personality, click the **Gallery** tab in the Office Assistant dialog box and click **Next** to view potential assistants.

Each pane will display a different assistant. When you find an assistant you'd like to try, click **OK**. At this point, Clippit may warn you that the character isn't installed. If this is the case, you'll need to install the character you've chosen. (You may need the Office 2003 CD.)

Firing the Assistant

You might not mind that the assistant comes with its own personality. On the other hand, if you find the assistant annoying, fire it. To do so:

1. Right-click Clippit (or the current assistant).

2. Select **Options** from the resulting submenu. Or, click **Options** in the Office Assistant balloon (refer to Figure 17.1).

3. Deselect the **Use the Office Assistant** option, and click **OK**.

You'll never hear from Clippit again—he won't even attempt to collect unemployment. If you decide to recall him, select **Show the Office Assistant** command from the Help menu.

Running SpellCheck

The Office SpellCheck feature checks your data for spelling errors. Office applications share a common dictionary file. That means that if you make a change from Access (for example, adding a word that's not in the default dictionary), your changes will be available in the other Office applications—and vice versa. When Access encounters a word it can't find in the dictionary, it alerts you and when available, provides a few alternate spellings for the word.

You can use SpellCheck in a table, query, or form by selecting Spelling from the Tools menu or pressing F7. If you find the option disabled, you can't use it in the current object.

Using SpellCheck

Chances are you're familiar with the SpellCheck feature. If not, work through the following example. First, open the Plants database:

1. Press **F11** to display the Database window.

2. Click the **Tables** shortcut and double-click **Catalogs** to open that table.

3. Choose **Spelling** from the Tools menu or press **F7**. SpellCheck begins the process of looking for words it can't match in its dictionary.

4. As you can see in Figure 17.3, SpellCheck stops at Raintree in the second record. At this point, you have several options. For now, click **Ignore** because you don't want to change the name of the catalog.

5. The next word highlighted is Richters. Again, you don't want to change the catalog's name, so click **Ignore**. In fact you won't want to change any of the words SpellCheck finds in this example, so continue to click **Ignore** until SpellCheck completes its check of the Name field.

6. Click **OK** when SpellCheck displays the informational message that the spelling check is complete.

Select an alternative spelling
and click Change

FIGURE 17.3

Run the
SpellCheck fea-
ture.

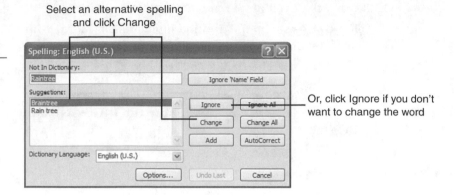

Or, click Ignore if you don't
want to change the word

You may have noticed that SpellCheck only considered the current field—the Name field. That's
because you're in a table, and SpellCheck only
considers one field at a time. Simply select a
field by clicking its heading cell and press F7 to
check the contents of that field.

In step 4 above, you found that SpellCheck
offered several options, which you didn't use.
Although the plants database doesn't contain
any misspelled words, it's easy enough to impro-
vise so you can experience a few of the other
options this feature has to offer. Are you ready to
try again?

tip

Selecting a field before
engaging the SpellCheck
feature forces SpellCheck to
check every entry in the field.
To check just one entry, select
that entry or click inside
that particular field and
press **F7**.

1. Open the **Plants** table, select the **LatinName** field and press **F7**. This time
   SpellCheck stops at Rubdeckia and suggests Rebecca, as shown in Figure 17.4.

FIGURE 17.4

SpellCheck stops
at the first word
it can't find in
the dictionary.

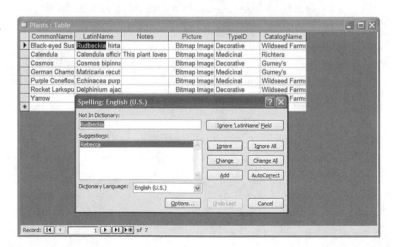

2. SpellCheck offers only one suggestion for replacing Rudbeckia—Rebecca. To make the switch, click **Change** or press **Alt+C**.

3. SpellCheck changes the encountered word to the suggested spelling and then highlights the next word it can't find in the dictionary, as shown in Figure 17.5

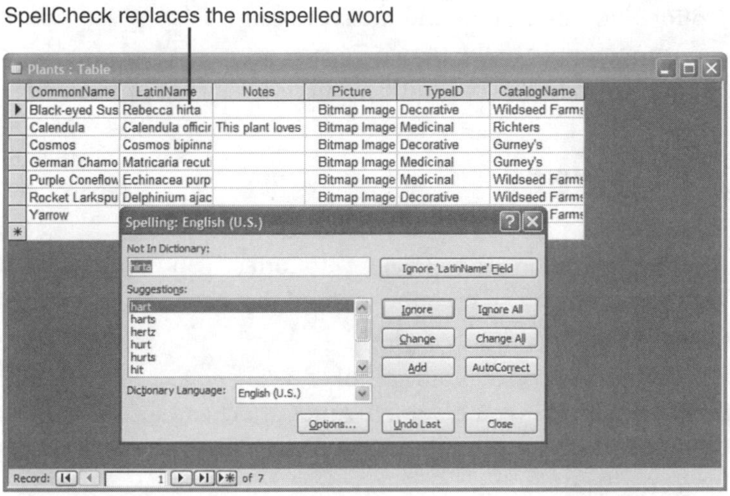

SpellCheck replaces the misspelled word

FIGURE 17.5

SpellCheck replaces the word with the alternate spelling and moves on.

4. You don't really want to replace Rudbeckia, so press **Escape** and then press **Ctrl+Z**.

There are a few other possibilities. Clicking the Add button will copy the word to the dictionary. That way, SpellCheck won't stop at the word again. This is a useful option when working with unusually spelled or uncommon names and terms. The word may be spelled correctly, but unless it's in the dictionary, there's no way for SpellCheck to know. That means SpellCheck will continue to stop every time it encounters the word, until you add the word to the dictionary.

If the word occurs several times, but you don't want to add it to the dictionary, Ignore All might be a better choice. The Ignore All option will bypass any other occurrences of the word within the current document, even though it isn't in the dictionary.

tip

If you happen to be reviewing data that's not in the current language (which will probably be U.S. English for most of you), you can select an alternate dictionary file. Simply select the appropriate dictionary from the Dictionary Language drop-down list.

Similarly, the Change All option will update all occurrences of a word in the current document. That way you don't have to individually change each one. You'll find information about the AutoCorrect option in the "About AutoCorrect" section later in this chapter.

The Options button displays another set of conditions you can apply to the search. These options are beyond the scope of this book.

About AutoCorrect

Have you noticed that when you enter data, Access sometimes changes it? That's AutoCorrect—an Office feature—at work. If you use Word or Excel, you've probably noticed that they also occasionally change the data you enter.

AutoCorrect tries to correct your mistakes before you store those mistakes permanently. For instance, if you enter *teh*, AutoCorrect changes it to *the*. That might or might not be what you want, but most of the time, AutoCorrect does a good job of catching your typos.

Let's take a closer look at the AutoCorrect feature to see just how hard it works for you. To do so, select **AutoCorrect Options** from the Tools menu to display the dialog box shown in Figure 17.6.

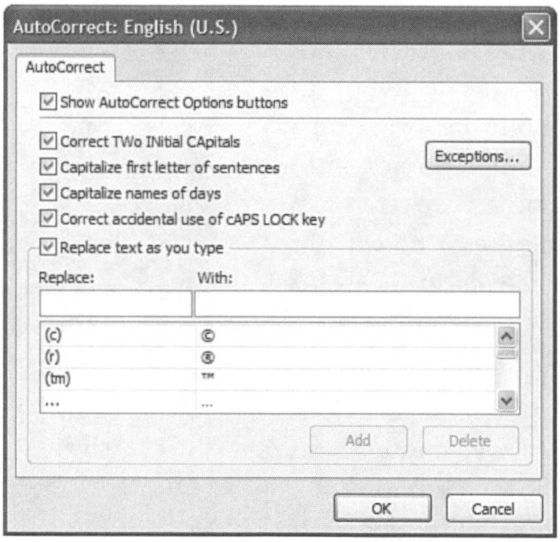

> **tip**
>
> SpellCheck will also check your grammar. Simply select the Check Grammar option (see Figure 17.5). It's selected by default. When this option is selected, SpellCheck will note broken grammar rules and make suggestions.

FIGURE 17.6

Open the AutoCorrect dialog box.

By default, all the options are set:

- If you enter two uppercase letters at the beginning of a word, AutoCorrect changes the second letter to lowercase.
- AutoCorrect always capitalizes the first letter in a sentence.
- AutoCorrect recognizes the names of the week and capitalizes each if you don't.
- If the first letter of a word is lowercase and the rest are uppercase, AutoCorrect automatically reverses the case and capitalizes only the first letter.
- AutoCorrect can automatically replace text as you type. This is where the teh/the example we used earlier comes from. Below the Replace Text As You Type option is a list of strings AutoCorrect watches for (in the Replace column). When AutoCorrect encounters one of the strings in the Replace column, it changes it to the corresponding string in the With column.

If you don't want AutoCorrect to change something, just uncheck the appropriate option.

Altering AutoCorrect to Fit Your Circumstances

The AutoCorrect feature can be annoying if it makes a change you don't like and you end up correcting AutoCorrect. Fortunately, most of the time, you can make AutoCorrect behave the way you want it to. Let's take a look at a couple of examples.

The first option in the Replace Text As You Type option is (c) and ©. Every time you type (c), AutoCorrect changes it to ©. If you enter (c) frequently, this can quickly become annoying. The simple solution to this problem is to delete that entry. To do so, display the AutoCorrect Options dialog box, select the **(c)**/© entry under the Replace Text As You Type option, as shown in Figure 17.7, and click the **Delete** button at the bottom-right corner of the dialog box.

> **tip**
>
> A quick way to undo an AutoCorrect correction without permanently changing an option is to press **Ctrl+Z** after AutoCorrect makes a change. Doing so returns the text you entered.

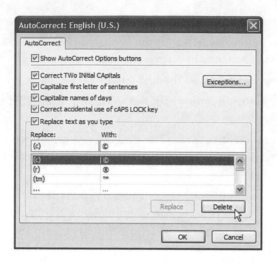

You can also add Replace Text As You Type entries of your own. Perhaps your best friend's last name is Gray and you often type it as Grey. AutoCorrect will fix the error for you. Display the AutoCorrect Options dialog box and enter Grey in the Replace box, enter Gray in the With box, and then click **Add**. The next time you type *Grey*, AutoCorrect will change it to *Gray*. The interesting thing about this particular entry is that AutoCorrect is case sensitive. So, if you enter *grey* instead of *Grey*, AutoCorrect won't change the spelling to *gray*. It only works if you capitalize the *g*, as in *Grey*.

When AutoCorrect goes to work and corrects a misspelled entry, it also displays a new smart tag. Specifically, it's called the AutoCorrect Options smart tag. From the list, you can choose one of the following:

- Change the corrected item to its original state
- Stop correcting the original entry altogether
- Display the AutoCorrect dialog box

You can see this new feature at work by deliberately entering a known AutoCorrect item into a table. Try that now:

1. Click the **Tables** shortcut in the Database window and double-click **Catalogs** to open that table.

2. In the new record (the blank line at the bottom of the table), enter Teh, and then press **Enter**. When you do, Access displays a smart tag icon close to the offending text.

3. Click the icon to open the list of options, shown in Figure 17.8.

FIGURE 17.8

View the
AutoCorrect
options.

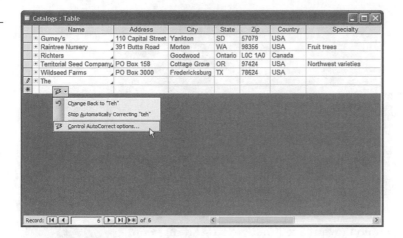

4. Select **Change Back to "teh"** to undo the AutoCorrect change. If you select
   Stop Automatically Correcting "teh" AutoCorrect will ignore teh entries while
   you're working with that particular table. Choosing that item permanently
   deletes the item from the AutoCorrect list. You must re-enter the item manually if you want AutoCorrect to react to it again.

Adding to AutoCorrect While Correcting Your Spelling

AutoCorrect is another shared Office feature you
probably use often. (I know I do!) If you encounter a
typo while performing a SpellCheck, you can add it
to the AutoCorrect list. That way, SpellCheck won't
complain about the word not being in the dictionary the next time you use it. Instead, AutoCorrect
will simply correct the typo when you enter it.
This capability is especially helpful when entering
words that aren't common, such as Latin names
for flowers.

To add a word to the dictionary, open the Plants
form and select **Spelling** from the Tools menu (or
press **F7**), with Yarrow as the current record. Right
away, the feature finds an entry that's not in the
dictionary—Achillea, as shown in Figure 17.9.

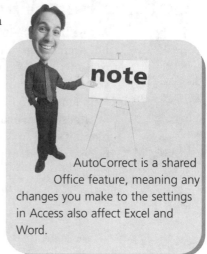

note

AutoCorrect is a shared
Office feature, meaning any
changes you make to the settings
in Access also affect Excel and
Word.

FIGURE 17.9

Part of the plant's Latin name isn't found in the AutoCorrect dictionary.

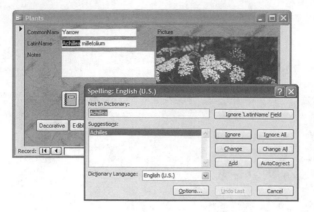

If you don't want SpellCheck to stop on this word again, click the **AutoCorrect** button at the bottom-right of the dialog box. When you're done, click **Close**.

Now, return to the first record by clicking the **First** button on the form's navigation bar. Then press **F7** to rerun the SpellCheck. This time, it ignores Yarrow's Latin name.

Getting Help When You Need It

Access tries to help you as much as possible, but not even a wizard can answer all your questions—it can only help you through the current task. When you have questions, the best place to look is the Help feature. To access this feature, simply press **F1** or choose **Microsoft Access Help** from the Help menu. Doing so will open the Microsoft Access Help pane (refer to Figure 1.1 at the beginning of this chapter).

note

You can turn off the AutoCorrect feature for individual form controls. Open the form in design view and double-click the control in question. Then, set the control's AllowAutoCorrect property to **No**. (To learn more about setting properties in a form, see Chapter 13, "Customizing Forms.")

There are several things you can do at this point:

- You can search the Help files for a particular word or phrase.
- View the Help feature's table of contents.
- Connect via the Internet to Microsoft online support sites for assistance, training, and downloading Office updates.

To close the Help pane, click the **Close** button (X) at the top right corner of the pane's title bar.

The Help feature is context sensitive. That means, it will open files that best relate to the selected object, item, property, or text. (When Help can't guess, it opens the generic pane you just saw.)

To see the difference between the generic Help Task Pane and the context-sensitive response, open the Catalogs table in design view. Select the **Country** field (any field will do really), and then select the **Input Mask** property in the lower pane.

Now, press **F1** and Access will display a Help topic that's specific to the Input Mask property, as shown in Figure 17.10. Close the Help window and return to the Catalogs table. Select a different property and press **F1** to see a Help topic that pertains to the selected property. That's context-sensitive Help.

note

If Help files aren't installed, Access will ask you if you want to install them. Be prepared to insert your Office 2003 CD if you decide to install those files.

FIGURE 17.10
Display context-sensitive Help topics.

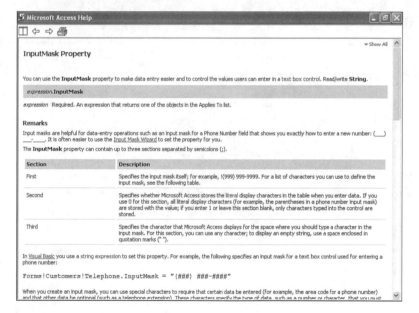

Finding Help Online

So far, the Help topics you've seen have been a part of Access' Help files that are available if you install them. There's more information online. To access these sites, click the Microsoft Access Help button on the Database toolbar to open the Help pane shown in Figure 17.11, and then click any choice in the Microsoft Office Online section. Or, **choose Microsoft Office Online** from the Help menu.

FIGURE 17.11
Find more information online.

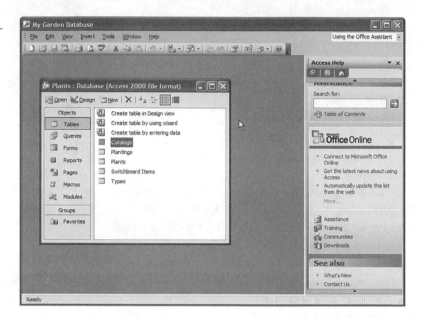

Customizing Access Toolbars

In Chapter 15, "Automating Your Database," you learned how to create macro buttons to open forms and reports. They work great, but they're not particularly intuitive. You must click the Macros shortcut and then click the right macro item, which means, you have to know the items are there to go looking for them.

There's an easier way—one that's just as easy to create, but more readily available. You can create a custom toolbar that grants easy access to the objects you use the most. Don't let the sound of that scare you—the process is simple:

1. You create a new toolbar.

2. You drag objects from the Database window and drop them on to the new toolbar.

It couldn't be simpler! Figure 17.12 shows a simple, custom toolbar that allows you to forego the Database window to open the objects you use the most.

FIGURE 17.12

Add this custom toolbar to your plants database.

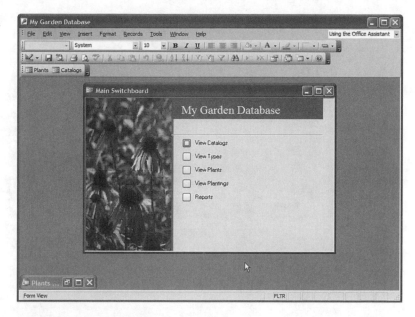

To create this toolbar:

1. Choose **Customize** from the Tools menu.

2. In the resulting Customize dialog box, click the **Toolbars** tab if necessary. Then, click the **New** button to the right of the Toolbars list.

3. Enter MyFavorites as the name of the toolbar in the New Toolbar dialog box, and click **OK**. Access will display the small empty toolbar shown in Figure 17.13.

4. Click **Close** to dismiss the Customize dialog box.

5. Press **F11** if necessary to display the Database window. Position the Database window so you can see the empty toolbar.

6. Click the **Forms** shortcut.

7. Drag the Plants form and drop it onto the new toolbar, as shown in Figure 17.14.

8. Drag and drop the Catalogs form to the custom toolbar.

9. Dock the toolbar just below the Database toolbar. To do so, simply drag the custom toolbar until it meets the existing toolbar. Access will take over for you and automatically dock the new toolbar below the existing ones.

FIGURE 17.13
Create a new,
empty toolbar.

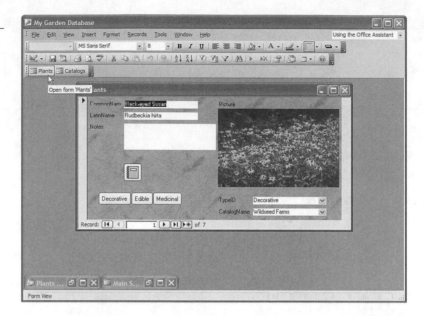

Drag the Plants form from here   Drop the Plants form here

FIGURE 17.14
Drag the Plants
form to the cus-
tom toolbar.

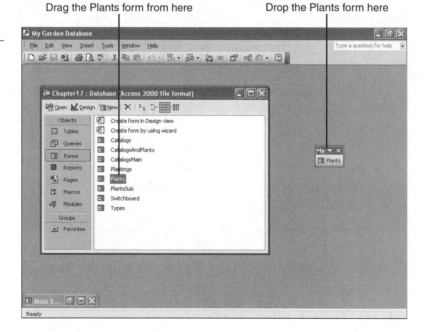

10. Right-click any of the toolbars and deselect the Formatting and Form View toolbars, so that only the new custom toolbar is available.

11. Click **Plants** to open the Plants form, as shown in Figure 17.15.

FIGURE 17.15
Click a button on the toolbar to open the corresponding object.

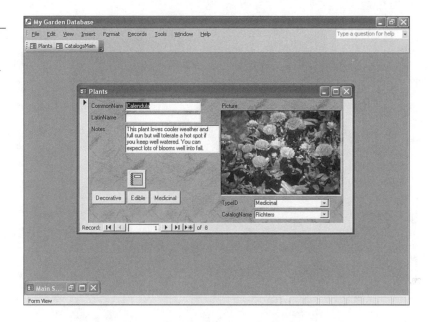

Of course, you're free to add as many buttons to the toolbar as you like, and you don't have to hide the Access toolbars. The choice is yours.

THE ABSOLUTE MINIMUM

Access is just one application in the best-selling suite of desktop software on the market. Many features are shared throughout the suite, which makes all of the applications easier to use and learn. In this chapter, you learned about several Office features that you can use in Access:

- Decide whether to use the Office Assistant.
- Use SpellCheck and AutoCorrect to correct misspelled entries.
- Display Help topics on the subjects you need, when you need it.

Index